I0131143

PEABODY
JOURNAL
OF EDUCATION

Volume 71, Number 3, 1996

Peace Education in a Postmodern World

(Continued)

PEABODY JOURNAL OF EDUCATION, 71(3), 1–11

Editor's Introduction

Ian M. Harris

During the 1980s, critics throughout the world advanced many reform proposals to address perceived failures of public education. Con-
servatives argued that the way to improve schools was to teach basic
skills and impose national standards. These reform efforts harkened
back to traditional notions of schooling, urging teachers to try harder
to teach basic academic curricula. Champions of this "back to basics"
effort blamed the failure of schools on problems within schooling
institutions themselves. Public debates about school policy ignored the
negative impact of violence on the lives of young people.

At the same time, in many countries of the world, educators were
arguing for a different approach to education reform, peace education,
which addresses problems of violence that distract students from the
cognitive lessons they are supposed to master. A peace education strategy for improving school productivity rests on three main assumptions: (a) Violence contributes to the poor performance of many
students; (b) for schools to improve, adults in school settings need to
address problems created by violence; and (c) anxieties that make it
hard for students to master traditional subject matter can best be ad-

IAN M. HARRIS *is Professor in the Department of Educational Policy and Community Studies,*
School of Education, University of Wisconsin–Milwaukee.

Requests for reprints should be sent to Ian M. Harris, Department of Educational
Policy and Community Studies, Enderis 529, School of Education, University of Wisconsin, P.O. Box 413, Milwaukee, WI 53201.

1

dressed by a comprehensive peace education strategy that makes school a safe place to learn and provides students with knowledge about nonviolent ways to resolve conflicts. Many children do not perform well in school because they are afraid or frightened, either by conflicts taking place outside school in their homes, communities, or in a wider global context, or they feel threatened and insecure in the school environment because of intimidations from other pupils and school personnel. Educational reforms that ignore these problems of violence are like rearranging the deck chairs on the Titanic. Students distraught by violence—whether it be homelessness, random killings, ethnic warfare, gang activities, or domestic abuse—have a hard time focusing on school lessons. The best intentions of educators will be undermined by icebergs of violence lurking directly under the surface of children's lives. The articles in this volume demonstrate that addressing the fears of youth trapped in violent circumstances can improve school productivity. Young people need to have a faith in the future in order to invest in their school work. When adults fail to address the concerns of young people terrified by violence, youth become alienated from school, often dropping out and refusing to complete assignments that ignore their deep worries about the future.

Peace education reforms have largely been ignored since the 19th century when they were heralded as a way to avoid the scourge of modern warfare. Initial attempts to teach about peace focused on war and concepts of national security. In this century, Maria Montessori argued that peace education was the best way to counteract the hatred of fascism. During the 1980s, a decade that saw considerable growth for peace education, teachers at all levels started to address the threat of a nuclear holocaust. More recently, feminist scholars have attacked patriarchal assumptions that support militaries and deny resources necessary to develop healthy children. Stimulated by fear of the destructive power of atomic weapons, modern peace education reformers assumed that children failed in schools because high levels of violence make school lessons seem absurd to frightened youth who despair about the future. In a postmodern world no longer divided along superpower axes, peace educators in unique cultural circumstances address many different concerns about violence—sexual assaults, ethnic and regional wars, human rights, domestic violence, refugees, street crime, handgun violence, problems of underdevelopment, ecology, and nuclear issues. School reforms based on principles of peace education have in common a belief in the power of nonviolence to create positive learning climates in schools and to address problems of violence in the broader culture. They help young people understand the sources of violence in their lives, stimulate a desire for peace, and provide skills needed to resolve conflicts nonviolently.

In a postmodern world, peace educators concerned about violent conditions outside school challenge popular uses of violence in the media and question the unflinching embrace of modernism at the core of schooling. Schools committed to modern paradigms of growth celebrate the Industrial Revolution with its material well-being and technological control over nature. Education becomes a path to enlightenment, which in most countries is tied to technological development, material standards of living, expansion of freedoms, and personal wealth. In the modern world, where educational systems produce human consumers tailored to fit an ever-expanding capitalist economic system, progress is seen as synonymous with the highest good. Textbooks praise inventions but ignore their unforeseen consequences to both the environment and social systems. This push for modernity has marginalized the contributions of women to social institutions, created nuclear weapons, stimulated human population growth, depleted resources, devastated the environment, and polarized the haves and have nots. At the same time that the forces of modernity have created great comfort for millions of people on this planet, other segments of society live in communities with such high levels of violence that back to basic lessons on traditional school subjects seem absurd.

Postmodern thinking calls into question a commitment to rapid-scale technological changes that contributes to a culture of violence. It underscores the negative impact of scientific advances on ecosystems and human communities. Peace educators in the postmodern world grapple with problems of violence that seem so overwhelming, arguing that education must be life-centered. They point out how the world view adopted by modernity is spiritually, environmentally, and socially destructive. In the past decade, over 2 million children have been killed in wars and millions more were physically disabled or psychologically traumatized. To help youth counteract the negative effects of modernity, promoters of peace education reforms in schools celebrate the diverse forms of life on this planet and motivate students to enhance living systems. They teach that a person's relationship to the environment ought to involve moral judgments and not just economic considerations about profit. They give voice to women and people of color who have been excluded from policy discussions carried out in Western capitals. Postmodern peace educators are skeptical about the ability of science and technology to provide solutions for the ecological crisis, but believe that educators at all levels can change cultural values away from the use of force to advance human interests toward following the various tenets of nonviolence.

One postmodern form of peace education based on the work of the Brazilian educator, Paulo Friere, helps adults name forms of violence in their lives and identify ways to respond to the problems of structural violence, where citizens are denied human rights, live in violent neighborhoods, and lack such basic essentials as health care, housing, food, or shelter. Peace educators do not ignore the impact of social inequalities on the way children learn. Supporters of peace education reforms understand that children may not successfully complete their academic assignments until their security needs are met.

In a postmodern world, educational reformers adopting the goals of peace education study all different forms of violence, both international and domestic. Violence, in its broadest sense, includes physical, psychological, and structural violence and can be caused by thoughts, words, and deeds—any dehumanizing behavior that intentionally harms another. Physical violence includes direct harm to others—juvenile crime, gang attacks, sexual assault, random killings, and physical forms of punishment. Psychological forms of violence occur often in schools and homes, diminishing a child's sense of worth. Structural violence comes from social institutions that deny certain basic rights and freedoms, when citizens can't get jobs that pay decent wages, health care, social security, safe housing, or civil rights. Many problems of violence come from a commitment to militarism to solve problems. Environmental violence caused by destruction of natural habitats threatens people's security and creates fear about the future. Violence at home, in the form of domestic abuse, sexual assault, and child neglect causes students to have low self-esteem and to distrust adults.

At the end of the 20th century, students in peace education classes study many different aspects of the complex nature of violence in the modern world. At the international level, peace educators provide insights about why countries go to war and how nations can resolve disputes without using force. At the national level, they teach about defense and the effects of militarism. How do countries provide for the security of their citizens? What military arrangements contribute to peace and security? In a postmodern world, peace educators attempt to build a culture of peace by supplementing concepts of national security based on high-tech weaponry with concepts of ecological security based on reverential relationships to the natural environment. At the cultural level, peace educators teach about social norms, like sexism and racism, that promote violence. At an interpersonal level, they teach nonviolent conflict resolution skills. At the psychic level, they help students understand what patterns exist in their own minds that contribute to violence. Peace educators go right to the core of a person's values—teaching respect for others, open mindedness, empathy, cooperation, concern for justice, willingness to become involved, commitment to human rights, and environmental sensitivity. A student in a peace education course acquires both theoretical concepts about the dangers of violence and the possibilities for peace, as well as practical skills about how to live nonviolently.

At the end of the 20th century, peace education takes many different forms. Historically, peace studies have focused on interstate rivalries and war—how to prevent hostilities between nations and build security systems that reduce tensions between nation states. In a postmodern world, peace educators are more concerned with how to reduce conflicts between individuals in families, communities, and ethnic groups, and how to live on this planet in sustainable ways. They want to use their professional skills to stop the many forms of violence inundating the lives of the children they are trying to teach.

As violence from home and community creeps into elementary, middle, and high schools, school personnel throughout the world are on their own using three different levels of peace education strategies. At the peacemaking level, they employ violence prevention strategies to respond to dangerous threats in schools. At the peacekeeping level, they teach skills to youth so they can resolve their conflicts without using force, and at the peacebuilding level, they fill the minds of young people with such a strong belief in alternatives to violence that they will make choices that promote peace.

Violence prevention programs attempt to make schools safe by deterring youth from committing acts of violence. These peacemaking strategies are often punitive, based on a negative approach to peace, that is, stopping the violence. Many school personnel approach problems of violence with a law and order mentality threatening disorderly children with suspension and expulsion. Frightened school personnel in communities with gang-related violence and high incidence of juvenile crimes are responding to increased levels of violence with a variety of peacemaking strategies that attempt to create an orderly school climate. These violence prevention strategies include weapons sweeps, locker searches, and even metal detectors. In some schools, surveillance cameras create a prison-like atmosphere, enhanced when policemen in uniforms patrol the halls. Additional staff are added to monitor student activities and halt criminal behavior. These strategies enhance the power of adults to control deviant youth behavior.

In reaction to violent behavior of youth, school personnel utilize peacekeeping strategies in schools to point out the dangers of violent interpersonal relations, to teach anger management strategies, and to challenge prejudices. These approaches to the problems of violence in the postmodern world attempt to empower young people to resolve their own conflicts peacefully. They teach children and adults that mediation resolves conflicts better than the use of force. Instead of punishing youth, teachers pursuing peacekeeping strategies teach about alternatives to violence, using a proactive strategy that empowers young people to deal with increasing levels of violence in the postmodern world.

Peacebuilding reforms go beyond responding to immediate forms of violence that may be overwhelming students and teachers to promote positive images of peace through the study of nonviolence. To prepare young people to contribute to building a peace culture, peace educators promote ethics and moral relationships of care, a commitment to truth, the interdependence of life, and the power of love to build what Martin Luther King Jr. called *beloved communities.* They draw on standards of justice encouraging students to build a multicultural democratic world by advocating human rights, peace through justice, and critical thinking. In a postmodern world, peace educators counteract the effects of militarism, nuclearism, and ecological devastation with a worldview based on the power of healing and personal transformation. Peace education reformers use the insights of a nonviolent approach to life that reflect the teachings of Jesus Christ, Buddha, Martin Luther King, Jr., Tolstoy, Thoreau, and Gandhi. Another postmodern aspect of peace education is the attempt by feminists to introduce into school curricula the concepts of care, compassion, and connectedness. Peace education reforms include, but also transcend, earlier efforts to introduce international concepts as a way of teaching young people ways to avoid war. They involve global education, awareness about the environment, skills for interpersonal peace, and strategies for building social cohesion.

Peace educators use these three different levels of peace strategies to establish in schools a safe haven where young people can learn about alternative dispute-resolution techniques. These different levels are not mutually exclusive. In fact, they complement each other. Adults use peacemaking strategies in school to establish an orderly learning environment so that students can learn the skills of peacekeeping and the higher order learnings involved in peacebuilding. Children in inner-city areas throughout the industrialized world who suffer from stress disorders similar to what children in Lebanon, El Salvador, Bosnia, Angola, or Northern Ireland experience need sensitive adults to respond to their security needs before they can master the traditional lessons they are supposed to learn in school. Peace educators have added a fourth "R" (resolution) to the standard canon of "the three Rs" (reading, writing, and arithmetic) that are considered basic to all learning endeavors. Although schools often seem powerless to counteract the influence of media, parents, and peers who promote violence, teachers who embrace peace education are trying to nurture in children the seeds of compassion rather than hatred and revenge. In a postmodern world, learning how to successfully resolve conflicts has become a necessary condition for progress. Without these skills youth are in danger of becoming thoughtless adults who contribute to further deterioration of both the social system and the natural order.

Although these reforms have not been covered very widely in the popular press and academic journals, this collection of articles will indicate how educators have been applying insights from peace theory at many different levels of schooling enterprises. At the macrolevel, administrators use peace education strategies to create a cooperative school climate. Thus, at a peaceful school, teachers have a high level of trust with each other and meet on a regular basis to discuss school problems. The administrative style would be inclusive, supportive of a democratic community in which the contributions of all members are valued. At the microlevel, peace education sets guidelines for teacher–student classroom relationships based on the principles of love and caring. Peace educators use a peaceful pedagogy to deemphasize competition and to encourage cooperative learning. Peace education also has a curricular component that provides important but often neglected knowledge about struggles to achieve peace. All these different forms of peace education have at their core a commitment to nonviolence.

This issue of the *Peabody Journal of Education*, "Peace Education in a Postmodern World," provides a comprehensive overview of the latest developments in peace education reform. The articles in this issue were collected at the Peace Education Commission sessions during the International Peace Research Association conference held in Malta during the fall of 1994. These articles by established experts in the field of peace education from six different countries provide a unique overview of the current concepts and practices of peace education, discussing how educators in trouble spots like South Africa and Israel use conflict resolution teaching strategies to help build a new social order and to address long periods of violence and war. Not only does this collection of articles represent a wide variety of peace education practices from different corners of the globe but it also represents different academic perspectives. Several authors of these articles are psychologists; others are philosophers; one is a curriculum developer; one is a community activist, promoting conflict resolution in South Africa; and another is a social worker. This diversity of disciplines provides fascinating insights into the practice of peace education in a postmodern world.

This issue has been divided in two sections—the Overview, which provides some general background about the principles and practices of peace education, and Peace Education in Different Cultures, which provides specific case studies of how educators are struggling to implement peace education projects in different parts of the world.

The first article in the overview section, "Conflict-Resolution Skills Can Be Taught," by Benyamin Chetkow-Yanoov of Israel, suggests what education and social work might contribute to the field of conflict resolution. It assumes that peacemaking attitudes and skills can be taught and should be part of the curriculum of all public schools and universities. This article describes a diversity of available conflict resolution curricula geared for nursery, grade school, junior high school, high school, university, and adult learners. Implications are explored toward the conclusion.

The second article, "Developing Concepts of Peace and War: Aspects of Gender and Culture," by Solveig Hägglund of Sweden, discusses various assumptions about peace education and child development. Hägglund raises interesting questions about the long-term impact of peace education and ties peace education goals into cooperative education, gender studies, and environmental concerns. What role can peace education play in socializing children away from violence and involve them in contributing to a peace culture?

The final article in the overview section, "Educating for the 21st Century: Beyond Racist, Sexist, and Ecologically Violent Futures," by Francis P. Hutchinson of Australia, explores some resources of hope in preparing students for the next century. It argues the importance of actively listening to children's voices about the future and of resisting fatalistic fallacies that violent social trends are destiny. This discussion emphasizes the importance of educational innovations such as peace education, multicultural education, nonsexist education, and environmental education. A discourse is invited in schools to move beyond disabling or destructive fears by encouraging alternatives to violence.

The first article in the section on peace education in different cultures, "Peace Education in an Urban School District in the United States," by Ian M. Harris (author of *Peace Education*, 1988), reports on the efforts of one school district in Milwaukee, Wisconsin to respond to escalating violence in students' lives by teaching peace education. Peer mediation, courses on nonviolence, environmental awareness, curricula based on teaching respect, anger management, and violence prevention have been initiated to help students deal with the problems of violence in their lives.

"Australian Aboriginal Constructions of Humans, Society, and Nature in Relation to Peace Education," by John Synott of Australia, states that many conflicts around the world today come from clashes between advanced technological cultures and indigenous cultures. Synott argues that to resolve these conflicts attempts have to be made to understand what indigenous people are trying to defend. He describes salient features from the belief systems of Australian Aborigines who embrace an interdependency between all forms of life. A recognition of kinship and a holistic relationship between humans and other forms of nature will provide peace educators important insights into how to deal with global conflict.

"Early Tendencies of Peace Education in Sweden," by Bengt Thelin of Sweden, traces the development of peace education from the second part of the 19th century and ties it to the growth of peace movements in Europe and in the United States. Many peace associations during this period were headed by women who argued that education can help break down the barriers that promote hatred, war, and violence. This article discusses the contribution of many outstanding Swedish educators concerned with disarmament and development. Efforts to promote peace education have been cyclical, rising and falling with the two world wars and other regional conflicts.

"Nonviolent Conflict Resolution in Children," by Diane Bretherton of Australia, presents an evaluation of a conflict resolution program conducted in Australia. Young children exposed to a videotape were asked to find solutions to conflicts and encouraged to seek nonviolent ways to resolve conflicts presented to them. Bretherton provides suggestions for how to best engage children in peacemaking while they are being pulled toward violence by their broader culture. She argues that adults need training in nonviolence and that gender is a central issue in how children respond to peace education activities.

"Exploring Peace Education in South African Settings," by Valerie Dovey of South Africa, one of the most violent places in the world, explains that young people experiencing high levels of violence want to learn conflict resolution skills. Teachers are responding to demand from the community for peace education programs. This article discusses how staff at the Center for Conflict Resolution at the University of Capetown and the Quaker Peace Center have been pioneers in promoting peace education among South African youth.

"Educational Violence and Education for Peace in Africa," by Clive Harber, a professor at the University of Natal in South Africa, describes various forms of violence in Subsaharan Africa and argues that part of the reason that there has been so much conflict since African countries have gained independence is that these countries have not spent the time or resources to promote democracy and peace concepts in schools. Deep ethnic divisions and a shallow sense of nationhood have lead to authoritarian regimes and an authoritative approach to schooling. In their rush to modernize, schools have excluded the teaching of democratic values. Tolerance promoted in school settings and a multicultural approach to education are seen to be a crucial part of the efforts to build more democratic and peaceful cultures in African countries.

"Peace Education in Postcolonial Africa," by Birgit Brock-Utne of Norway (author of *Feminist Perspectives on Peace*, 1989), discusses three points raised at the Jomtien, Thailand, World Conference on Education for All: the effects of structural adjustments policies on the education sector, the effects on higher education of a concentration of resources on basic education, and the possibilities of education to strengthen indigenous cultures. Examples from Tanzania and Zimbabwe show that economic policies are making it impossible for African countries to print their own textbooks and hence promote their unique cultural values.

Postmodernism raises a crucial question, "What is progress?" These articles hint at how educators can use the insights of peace education reform to help students prepare for life in the 21st century. Confronted with teen pregnancies, drug and street violence, and growing numbers of students sinking below the poverty line, educators at all levels are challenged to contribute to the transformation of a consumer society based on patriarchal values. They can no longer hope to improve school performance while ignoring social problems that leave children hungry, without positive parental guidance, and fearful of violence. Articles in this issue point out promising practices of peace education to help youth confront the problems of violence so prevalent in the postmodern world.

These articles demonstrate that educators can play a key role in helping human societies progress toward more sustainable ways of living on this Earth. They explain how conflict resolution techniques in the Middle East and South Africa have helped overcome enemy images and moved warring camps toward reconciliation, how throughout the modern world peace educators have been trying to warn people about the threats of war, how providing children with skills can help them deal with violence, how tribal traditions of interdependence can provide important models for so-called "civilized societies," how environmental awareness is crucial to help children construct positive images of the future, how democratic educational practices can promote self-esteem in post colonial societies, how alternative dispute resolution mechanisms can positively resolve conflicts, and how peace education efforts create positive learning climates in inner-city areas beset by high levels of violence. These peace education reforms point to a new way of thinking about schools that uses insights from nonviolent theory to build a peace culture concerned about the plight of animals, humans, and ecological systems throughout planet Earth.

References

Brock-Utne, B. (1989). *Feminist perspectives on peace education*. London: Pergamon.
Harris, I. (1988). *Peace education*. Jefferson, NC: McFarland.

PEABODY JOURNAL OF EDUCATION, 71(3), 12–28

Conflict-Resolution Skills Can Be Taught

Benyamin Chetkow-Yanoov

After I became an Israeli citizen, I experienced a growing urgency to put my social science and social work knowledge into a framework suitable for use with schoolchildren. Because it takes a long time to achieve personal maturity, or to learn the skills of intergroup cooperation, I wanted to start teaching conflict resolution in a systematic way as early in the life cycle as possible (Chetkow-Yanoov, 1991; Sullivan, 1993).

Furthermore, most human attitudes and behaviors seem to be learned. For example, in my years as a summer camp director, I found that children's fear of water (in the swimming program) was always learned from one of their parents—actually, babies can learn to swim before they can walk. Children learn to be wary of snakes around the age of 2. Disrespect for unusual skin color, shape of eyes, or differing religious practices comes later. In the catchy words of a song from the musical "South Pacific": "You've got to be taught to be afraid/ of people whose eyes are oddly made/ and people whose skin is a different shade/ you've got to be carefully taught." Similarly, years of formal and informal socialization teach us to respond aggressively to real or

BENYAMIN CHETKOW-YANOOV *is Professor in the School of Social Work, Bar-Ilan University, Ramat Gan, Israel.*

Requests for reprints should be sent to Benyamin Chetkow-Yanoov, School of Social Work, Bar-Ilan University, Ramat Gan, IL-52900, Israel.

imagined attacks, and to fight when faced with demands or threats. These various considerations motivated me to participate in the development of three different curricula for teaching conflict resolution in the Israeli public schools.

Contribution of Education to Conflict Resolution

Contemporary social science contends that human nature is not intrinsically violent or warlike (Avruch & Black, 1990; Clark, 1990; Smoker, 1990). If we have to be taught to be wary of strangers, anti-Semitic, racist, sexist, or disrespectful of the elderly, we can also be socialized to trust, appreciate others unlike ourselves, cooperate, and respect the law. We can also learn how to negotiate, mediate, share, compromise, and to bargain in conflict situations.

Because the public schools have long helped socialize young persons into roles and attitudes considered essential for adult citizenship, formal education efforts must now prepare pupils, adults, and retired seniors for a nonviolent lifestyle within a framework of pluralism. For this, the incremental processes of education are central (Chetkow-Yanoov, 1988; Harris, 1988). It is also important that peace education be initiated in stable settings like universities, and that such efforts receive a level of prestige commensurate with that of our national military academies.

At the fourth conference of the World Council for Curriculum and Instruction (which took place in Edmonton, Canada in 1984), a keynote speech suggested that although education attempts to be nonpartisan, it cannot stay neutral when dealing with issues of justice and injustice, cooperation and domination, or peace and violence. Education that does not emphasize the importance of international understanding and peace is merely training and instruction. In education, we must choose whether to socialize into the existing order, or to teach that every social order can be changed. If teachers and pupils learn to conquer situations of domination, oppression, and negative forms of dependence, we may learn to coexist with other people (regardless of sex, nation, race, or culture) who act similarly.

Curriculum Goals

Peace education enterprises call for content and techniques that contribute to the learners' cognitive enrichment, practical skills, and attitude formation. Specific learning goals might include the following:

1. Increasing the learner's objective knowledge about the actual diversity of people, viewpoints, and ideologies in his or her own country, and of the tensions between them.

2. Helping learners understand the influence of attitudes and feelings on human behavior in situations of tension, of enmity, and of cooperation.

3. Equipping learners to analyze the concept of *peace* as both a state of being and an active process, as well as to enquire into the major obstacles to peacemaking.

4. Showing learners how power is used to make conflicts escalate (in a variety of family, intergroup, organizational, and community settings), as well as how to utilize nonviolent ways to deescalate and resolve them.

5. Helping learners take part in simulations and other participatory learning situations, in order to master some skills and techniques in conflict resolution.

6. Bringing about constructive encounter meetings (and other forms of communication) between members of opposing political parties, religions, ethnic/racial/language groups, and social movements in order to develop trust relationships, expand self-awareness, and search for projects of mutual benefit.

Eight Examples of Available Teaching Technologies

So many diverse curricula exist today that it may be difficult to choose among them. For the purposes of this article, examples of available teaching materials have been selected on the basis of the age level of their intended learners—from nursery children to adults. A summary of the basic characteristics of these materials is presented at the conclusion of the article.

Resolving Conflicts in Nursery School

In February 1991, when I gave a workshop in South Africa, a local (White) teacher told about a kind of conflict resolution that she initiated in her nursery school. At the beginning of each school year, she introduces her little ones to a special corner that contains an "ear-chair," a "mouth-chair," and a "friend-chair."

When any two children get into a fight, they sit alternatively in the mouth and ear chairs for 2 min. During this time, the mouth person tells his or her side of the problem and the ear person listens silently. After 2 min, they switch chairs, and the former talker now listens to the former listener. If matters have been sufficiently clarified by this process, the two children shake hands and go back to their former activities. If they still feel tense or unhappy, they may invite any other third person (e.g., another pupil, the teacher, the janitor, a parent) to fill the friend-chair, and they all talk together until they resolve the conflict.

Our informant explained that this system is generally effective at its basic level, seldom requiring the help of a third person (in the friend-chair) to settle the dispute. She was pleased to tell us how comfortably nursery children internalize the idea that listening to each other works better than hitting or screaming. Although she had not checked personally, she was convinced that the format could be equally effective in Black, colored, or integrated nursery schools in any part of the world.

Language Learning As a Vehicle to Peacemaking

Concerned citizens in every country might lobby for a national policy that all children be taught two or three languages—their own (local) one and two others. In Israel, for example, all pupils learn Hebrew. Arabic has become compulsory in all the Hebrew-speaking Jewish schools, and all pupils must learn English as a third language. A norm of trilinguality is also found in countries like Holland and Switzerland. Such a practice, worldwide, would give all children access to another worldview, as well as help them internalize the reality that their group, unique as it is, is not the only worthwhile one on the planet.

Freudenstein (1992) took the idea one step further. Teaching English as a second language can go beyond merely acquiring linguistic skills and communication competence. The curriculum might also guide pupils toward living peacefully with speakers of other languages. Documents, class activities, exercises, and so forth can be used to link learning any foreign language with peace-education content.

In this connection, activist parents might insist that all schoolchildren be exposed—from the prenursery level—to objective information about, as well as to the language of, other ethnic groups living in their region. These groups of language learners should also encounter each other in structured educational situations throughout the grade school and high school years. Parallel sophisticated programs should be set up for their parents, who often have to cope with the ignorance, anger, and fear that they have accumulated over a lifetime (Chetkow-Yanoov, 1985; Wein, 1984).

Furthermore, we must ensure that existing texts and films—whether in language, history, or any other curricula—have been cleansed of bigoted stereotypes. Sensitive training programs (often funded by voluntary contributions from abroad) must be arranged each year for training classroom personnel who are to teach innovative curriculum content (Crane, 1986; Freudenstein, 1992).

Fourth-Grade Pupils Learn Peer Mediation

Based on developments in San Francisco (see *Training Elementary School Conflict Managers*, 1985), a team on Canada's west coast developed a set of lessons for fourth-grade pupils (Davis, 1983; Kalmakoff, Hargraves, Cynamon, & Witheford, 1986). This curriculum was the joint product of the teaching staff of a grade school in Burnaby, British Columbia; the Public Education for Peace Society of New Westminster, British Columbia; and the Faculty of Education of Simon Fraser University, also of Burnaby, British Columbia. Geared to 10-year-old children, this curriculum includes such content areas as:

- Lesson 1. *Conflict:* Definition of conflict, examples of personal conflict situations, analysis of causes of personal conflict.
- Lesson 2. *Conflict Resolution:* Analysis of personal conflict—point of view, alternative resolutions to personal conflict situations, "win/win" resolutions.
- Lesson 3. *Handling Anger:* Definitions of anger, examples of anger-producing situations, usual angry responses, hurtful and nonhurtful responses.
- Lesson 6. *Images of the Enemy:* Analysis of hate—how it affects behavior, video "Neighbors", transition from conflict on the personal level to conflict on the international level, analysis of causes of international conflict.
- Lesson 13. *"I Can Do ... ":* Identification of concrete actions for peace, prioritizing actions, cooperative planning of steps toward taking action.

In a stimulating article on "Peaceful Playgrounds," Cheatham (1988) reviewed various efforts to engage schoolchildren in mediating classroom and playground disputes. One charming picture shows a grade school girl, wearing a "Conflict Manager" T-shirt, listening intently while mediating between two of her angry male peers. Cheatham approves Roderick's (1987) assertion that resolution of conflicts should become the fourth "R"—along with reading, (w)riting, and (a)rithmetic—in the curricula of grade and high schools all over the United States.

Children who have learned this kind of grassroots peacemaking are expected, later in life, to be able to make connections between their personal conflict management experiences and peacemaking requirements on national and global levels (Brager, 1968; Fisher & Ury, 1983).

Computerizing the Junior High School Curriculum
"Neighbors"

A voluntary association of Jewish and Arab teachers, psychologists, and social workers devoted 8 years to producing educational materials on coexistence for Israel's Jewish and Arab junior high schools. Some of the organization's accomplishments include the following:

1. Developing a curriculum of lessons, both in Hebrew and Arabic, for teaching coexistence knowledge, attitudes, and skills in Israel's junior high schools. Both the Hebrew and the Arabic texts have been officially approved as a program of choice by the Ministry of Education.

2. Holding intensive teacher-training workshops each summer, along with some follow-up workshops during the school year.

3. Pioneering parallel local community workshops for parents of the children in the program (Whiteman, 1987).

4. Between 1984 and 1990, exposing an average of 10,000 Jewish and Arab junior high school pupils to the curriculum each year.

Although the organization has worked for years to create and improve its "Neighbors" curriculum, the idea of teaching parts of it by means of computers is recent. Social science researchers have demonstrated that if the computer is used creatively in educational settings, it can serve as a powerful tool for widening students' cognitive processes, as well as for improving their interpersonal relationships (Fisk & Taylor, 1984; Hamilton, 1981). Interaction with the computer and with classmates can stimulate such collaborative activities as constructive controversy or sharing of resources. Because learning in such an environment is interactive but at the same time independent of time and distance, it offers educational opportunities that are different from the typical face-to-face classroom.

"Neighbors" started using computers to enhance both the cognitive development and intergroup (or intercultural) perceptions of pupils in one Jewish and one Arab junior high school within Israel. A joint team of teachers, "Neighbors" staff, and computer experts met during the summer of 1990 and worked out a basic action-plan for the two schools—with mutual hosting and visiting set up for the end of the school year. During the 1990–1991 school year, volunteer experts prepared a computerized curriculum based on the "Neighbors" program, trained some teachers to use it, and launched it. It was still operating during the 1993–1994 school year.

A High School Curriculum—"The Pursuit of Peace"

On the assumption that distrust, prejudice, and racism are learned behaviors, I prepared a series of lessons to enable the teaching of trust, tolerance, and peaceful ways to resolve conflicts (Chetkow-Yanoov, 1985). The principles and skill exercises in each chapter of this book were derived from social work practice, as well as from my personal experience in the field of Arab–Jewish reconciliation in Israel during the early 1980s. Many of these lessons later proved relevant in other pluralistic sociocultural settings characterized by intergroup conflict. The text contains such chapters as: "Various Ways to Introduce the Topic in a Classroom," "Simulation of the Cost of Competition Vs. Cooperation," "Typical Dilemmas in Majority–Minority Relations," "Defining the Concept 'Peace'," "Victims, Victimizers, and Archetype Behaviors," "Meet and Know Your Neighbor," "Cooperative Games and Classroom Activities," "Conflict and Conflict Management," "How are Peace Treaties Made?" "What the Ordinary Citizen Can Do to Enhance Peace," "Findings From the Field: Peace Studies in Practice," and "Going Beyond Education."

I am convinced that this sort of curriculum, taught by properly trained personnel and backed by school administrators, could equip teenagers with facts, attitudes, and beginning skills for making coexistence work.

Parts and combinations of the previously mentioned curriculum were tried in the school systems of four Jewish and two Arab municipalities. Some of the basic ideas soon appeared in other educational efforts in Israel and in a week-long workshop for immigration workers in Sweden. Gradually, I became convinced that the field of peace education can be enhanced by what the social sciences and the helping professions know about human motivation and behavior (Burton & Sandole, 1986; C. R. Rogers, 1965).

Adults Settle Disputes at the Grassroots Level

San Francisco is credited with the first training of local residents to function as volunteer mediators of grassroots-level conflicts (Shonholz, 1984). This program developed a formal curriculum for training local volunteers to function in conflict resolution panels. A 1984 manual lists such curriculum units as communication skills, outreach, case development, getting cases to hearings, managing the panel during hearings, and advanced conflict-resolution work. Such topics are taught to equip neighborhood volunteers with the capacity to (a) intervene early in local disputes, (b) create a safe place for describing and analyzing such conflicts, (c) reduce the potential of violence, and (d) enhance the quality of daily life at the neighborhood level.

This model spread rapidly within the criminal justice system. By the end of the 1980s, S. J. Rogers, Kanrich, and Steinhouser (1990) reported that 1,500 citizen volunteers were active in community dispute resolution throughout New York State alone. They were donating their time, energy, and experience to conciliating, mediating, and arbitrating thousands of criminal and civil disputes a year!

As described earlier, this San Francisco initiative also gave birth to a curriculum for teaching conflict resolution to fourth-grade children in the public schools (Davis, 1983).

Peace Courses at the University Level

Over the last decade, a number of universities in North America, England, and Europe have begun to offer fully accredited academic courses in peacemaking, conflict resolution, or both (Harris, 1988; Wein, 1984). One, George Mason University of Fairfax, Virginia, offers a master's degree and a doctorate in this field. In my opinion, such courses should be offered at all schools of social work in all countries. The curriculum should include lessons in theory, information gathering or research, examples of conflict resolution interventions, supervised field practice, the reading of recommended texts, written assignments, feedback procedures that increase self-awareness, and examinations. All the usual standards of good scholarship are to be maintained. During the first years of any such conflict-resolution program, seminars and courses might be offered in the following areas.

Courses in theory. In "Introduction to Conflict Resolution," after learning basic concepts and definitions from the behavioral sciences, students look into causes and types of conflict, stages of escalation, some strategies for resolving conflicts, and some ways to rehabilitate conflict victims (Burton, 1991; Chetkow-Yanoov, 1987, 1991; Deutsch, 1973; Eisler, 1987; Purnell, 1988). This course serves as prerequisite for all other studies in this field.

In "Theories of Human Violence and Potential," to examine if human beings are inherently violent, the concepts "aggression" and "assertiveness" are reviewed in biological, theological, and anthropological sources. Definitions of human nature are examined according to the values embedded in religion, psychology, Shakespeare, and a contemporary philosopher. This course looks at the nature of "trust" and "cooperation," as well as the impact of culture on archetypal behaviors within diverse population groups.

In "Victimization and Persisting Conflicts," theories of crisis and victimization suggest that rage and fear are at the core of continuing conflicts. This course examines these ideas, and suggests a range of therapeutic interventions that could help individuals, small groups, and ethnic populations to achieve release from victim behaviors. This is seen as a necessary prelude to their being able to function effectively as parties in any conflict-resolution negotiations.

In the "Philosophy and Methods of Conflict Research" course, research literature is surveyed to apply relevant technologies to gathering data about conflict situations, monitoring interventions systematically, and evaluating the effectiveness of efforts made to resolve conflicts. Research sophistication is also required to test a number of hypotheses about conflict dynamics and escalation.

The "Special Colloquium" forum would be used to introduce students to experts in the field from other universities, or visitors from abroad. They could, for example, listen to the experiences of persons who have been engaged in the Middle East peace talks, or to United Nations personnel who negotiated the cease fire in Namibia. Students also investigate modern applications of traditional conflict-resolution practices like the Jewish *Din Torah*, the Arab *Sulcha*, or the Hawaiian *Ho'oponopono* ceremonies.

Courses in practice. "Skills and Techniques for Resolving Conflicts" parallels the introductory theory course. Students first explore the principles of conflict deescalation, basing their efforts in a number of conflict models. Basic principles of mediation, arbitration, negotiation, and treaty making are taught as applied skills through games, simulations, and field-work experiences in a variety of life settings (Bickmore, 1984; Lingas, 1988; Shook, 1985; Weingarten & Leas, 1987). This course serves as a prerequisite for all other practice studies in the field.

The "Alternative Dispute Resolution (ADR)" seminar examines a number of dispute-resolution formats that can serve as alternatives for the traditional court trial (or civic litigation). Students take a beginning look at such alternative methods as facilitation, negotiation, mediation, arbitration, and trial by peers. The seminar includes lectures, simulation exercises, videotaping, and presentations from expert practitioners of ADR.

The "Small Group Processes in Negotiation and Mediation" seminar demonstrates the relevance of small-group process to conflict resolution technologies—especially to basic processes of mediation (Chandler, 1985; Kelman, 1991; Northen, 1969) and working with multiracial audiences (Davis, Galinsky, & Schopler, 1995). The seminar includes some of the theoretic and skill essentials for persuading parties to negotiate in diverse small-group settings.

Based on the work done in Israel, the "Computer-Assisted Intercultural Meetings" course examines a curriculum of lessons that teaches coexistence facts, attitudes, and skills in pairs of computer-linked schools, and concludes with a hosting and visiting experience at the end of the school year. Students examine various applications of this format, and are encouraged to develop similar computer-based pedagogic programs.

Courses in special topics.   Israel, for example, situated as it is among the traditional societies of the Middle East, is changing into a modern posturban society. In the "Women and Men in a Changing Society" course, students will examine the changing roles of women and men in the family, the professions, politics/government, and in society generally (Hayes, 1989; Lambert, 1994). Developments like the feminist movement will be studied and evaluated.

As in any modern country, ways will have to be found to serve the needs of both traditional orthodox and modern secular citizens. The "Religious–Secular Dialogue" course will look at reasons for the continuation of religious–secular tension in the country. A number of suggested interventions, including encounter dialogue meetings, will be studied and evaluated. New ways will be explored for loving our neighbor as ourselves.

As countries become more and more pluralistic, the "Intergroup Relations" course will introduce students to ethnically different groups and cultures in specific neighborhoods, cities, the nation, or the region. A review of intergroup relations over the past decades will be included. This course includes experiencing an encounter with representatives of another group, and discussions of how all parts of society might start to practice the basics of coexistence.

The "Labor Relations" course provides broad knowledge about labor-management relations locally and abroad, both in the public and private sectors. It focuses on labor organizing, negotiating collective bargaining agreements, grievance procedures, minority rights, and managing the problems of retrenchment or technological change. Lectures are supplemented with in-class role plays and small-group simulation sessions.

The "Teaching Conflict Resolution in the Public Schools" course focuses on utilizing social-science knowledge in grade and high school curricula of peace studies. Basic principles of social change, unlearning and relearning habits, human nature, and trust-building will be tailored to the needs of teachers, pupils, and parents. Participants will also explore how to make the administration of specific schools more democratic and supportive of student-parental initiatives.

After the first full year of courses, and in accordance with an evaluation of results, courses should be adjusted to make them more effective. Assuming that the evaluation proves basically positive, the following 3 years can be devoted to developing such additional interdisciplinary offerings as "Theological Traditions and Peace-Making," "Limits of the Earth: Applying Conflict-Resolution Technologies to Physical Environment and Human Ecology Issues," "Democracy in a Pluralistic or Multicultural Society," "Images of Peace in Utopian Communities, Literature, and the Performing Arts," "The Communications Media in Conflict and Peacemaking," "Alternative Futures and Citizen Action," and "Directed Reading and Research."

Certainly, enough options are possible to offer a major in conflict resolution (Lundy, 1987; Walton, 1969).

Communicating Creatively in the Midst of Conflict

Human beings of all ages, when caught up in conflict situations, can learn a way of communicating that should help them deescalate the conflict. This process can be used by families in conflict, in labor-management disputes, by motorists in a collision, children from rival schools, secular humanists who clash with deeply religious believers, leftists who scream at rightists, neighborhood citizens who fight with city hall bureaucrats, street gangs, rival ethnic groups, and feuding neighbors—if they are ready to change old habits and learn new skills.

In many countries today, groups and individuals are learning a process evolved by Marshall Rosenberg, an American psychologist. He developed what he calls a *Giraffe* or compassionate way of responding to anger and violence. When attacked by upset persons either physically or verbally, instead of reacting with anger, blaming, or counterviolence, we can learn to give silent respect to our own emotions and then try to understand the feelings and unmet needs of our opponent (i.e., empathize with whatever might be causing them to explode at us). This process breaks the vicious circle of escalating conflict, and releases energies to get our own needs met in a way that also meets the need of our opponent. It is equally helpful when we want to initiate a nonviolent confrontation with someone else.

People who have learned Giraffe are able to respond compassionately to one another. Responding in this way requires a high level of self-awareness, and a willingness to learn how to be empathic. Empathy means deliberately projecting our consciousness (by means of imagination and fantasy) into the situation and feelings of another person to understand what pain or passion might be making him or her behave as they do. We can empathize without losing our own identity, without becoming overidentified with the other person, but also without approving the other person's behavior.

For upset people who generate conflict because of their own vulnerability or frustration, receiving compassion and empathy often enables them to feel safe enough to deal with difficult issues nonviolently. Clearly, the offering of empathy is unconditional, is not judgmental, does not limit the other's range of choices, and does not include arguments about who has "the facts" right.

The basic framework for such (compassionate) communication involves four steps we can take as a Giraffe person:

1. Describe the behavior we are observing in objective rather than judgmental language ("My father keeps saying that I can't buy a motorcycle").

2. Express the feelings that we experience in relation to what we have just observed ("I feel sad and disappointed").

3. Describe the needs and desires out of which our feelings have emerged. In other words, our feelings are based both in what we have observed and in our desires relating to such events ("I want to be independent regarding my transportation needs").

4. Request the specific action(s) that would be a first step toward getting our needs met. If people sometimes contribute to our discomfort (or prevent our needs from being fulfilled), we can request a change in their behavior. These requests should express what we want, rather than what we do not want, and also be stated in nonjudgmental terms ("I'd like him to tell me what I could do to show that I am responsible enough to own a motorcycle").

To put the Giraffe process into effect, several preconditions are usually necessary. First, we need training and opportunities to practice the newly learned skills in our daily lives. We need to feel secure, and know that other important people in our lives support us. Workbooks and audiovisual aids are available for learning the basics, but these are best practiced in small-group settings with an experienced leader. Such a guided group experience seems essential for playing Giraffe roles, as well as for giving and receiving feedback (Green, 1990; Rosenberg, 1983).

Implications

The previously mentioned curriculum models are based on social science principles relevant to motivation, human nature, social change, unlearning and relearning habits, and trustbuilding. They are meant to enable learners to develop simultaneously at the intellectual, the emotional-attitudinal, and the action-skills levels. Also, the program is meant to be applicable to events and values indigenous to the country in which they are taught (see the Appendix).

Participants are expected to learn to take responsibility for their own behavior, define strength in both physical and nonphysical terms, and apply these in their own lives—not in the abstract or at some distant international level (Bickmore, 1984; Kalmakoff & Shaw, 1987; Kreidler, 1984). Similarly, teachers who have learned to speak in the Giraffe way might serve as role models for the pupils in their classrooms, in the school yard, and in the neighborhood around the school.

Actually, the teachings described in this article are based on an assumption: It is possible to educate all age groups toward greater psychological and political maturity. In the United Nations Educational, Scientific, and Cultural Organization bulletin called "Features" (Derksen, 1982), such maturity is operationalized to mean that we become human beings who can (a) stop analyzing problematic situations in terms of who is right or wrong (i.e., innocent or guilty); (b) learn to recognize the relativity of our own viewpoint; (c) become aware of the difference between facts and opinions, as well as show sensitivity to the norms and opinions of others; (d) analyze the causes of a conflict, and what might be making it escalate; (e) recognize, and become capable of coping with, our own aggressiveness—especially when we are under tension or pressure; (f) learn to handle personal conflicts in nonviolent ways (e.g., by listening, expressing empathy, or bargaining); (g) act as an informal facilitator or mediator among our friends and peers; and (h) overcome the tendency to resist change, especially if it means I have to change my habits or reexamine my beliefs. In an increasingly pluralist world, we should be trying to produce more flexible human beings who are happy with their own identity, and capable of appreciating others for their unique qualities.

Peace learning can also be reinforced by a positive educational climate. Well-organized schools, increasingly open to democratic patterns of educating and cooperation with other agencies, are essential for the success of education for peaceful living. Peacemaking knowledge, attitudes, and skills like reading or mathematics should be taught and retaught several times during a person's learning career.

The continuum of conflict resolution might start in nursery, with the three chairs format, as well as with songs and folk dances of other peoples. Learning to speak and read several languages follow. Fourth-grade pupils should experience being a "conflict manager." In junior and senior high schools, peacemaking courses can include formal academic content, and be supplemented by educationally focused encounter meetings with members of another group or culture. Courses taught at universities would strengthen the thrust with audiences of adults and might be supplemented by continuing education programs for retirees.

The aforementioned teachings should be reinforced by programs and articles in the mass media, in popular music, in the theater, and in both fiction and nonfictional literature. In fact, the time has come for us to merchandise our accumulated experiences, insights, and generalizations about conflict resolution in "packages" that can be learned by normal people in all walks of life in all countries.

We must also make sophisticated efforts to press beyond the status quo, make plans to influence social policy, and strive for the emergence of well-informed public opinion. The implementing of peace education cannot be left to others.

References

Avruch, K., & Black, P. W. (1990). Ideas of human nature in contemporary conflict resolution theory. *Negotiation Journal, 6*, 221–228.

Bickmore, K. (1984). *Alternatives to violence: A manual for teaching peacemaking to youth and adults.* Cleveland, OH: Friends Meeting.

Brager, G. A. (1968). Advocacy and political behavior. *Social Work, 13*, 5–15.

Burton, J. W. (1991). Conflict resolution as a political system. In V. D. Volkan, D. A. Julius, & J. V. Montville (Eds.), *The psychodynamics of international relations* (Vol. 2, pp. 71–92). Lexington, MA: Lexington.

Burton, J. W., & Sandole, D. J. D. (1986). Generic theory: The basis of conflict resolution. *Negotiation Journal, 2*, 333–344.

Chandler, S. M. (1985). Mediation: Conjoint problem solving. *Social Work, 30*, 346–349.

Cheatham, A. (1988, September). Peaceful playgrounds. *Fellowship, 54*, 12–15.

Chetkow-Yanoov, B. (1985). *The pursuit of peace—A curriculum manual for teachers.* Haifa, Israel: Partnership.

Chetkow-Yanoov, B. (1987). *Dealing with conflict and extremism.* Jerusalem: Joint (JDC) Israel.

Chetkow-Yanoov, B. (1988). Teaching peace to adults: Dare we practice what we preach with leaders and officials? In T. R. Carson (Ed.), *Toward a renaissance of humanity* (pp. 254–265). Edmonton, Canada: World Council for Curriculum and Instruction.

Chetkow-Yanoov, B. (1991). Teaching conflict resolution at schools of social work: A proposal. *International Social Work, 34*, 57–68.

Clark, M. E. (1990). Meaningful social bonding as a universal human need. In J. Burton (Ed.), *Conflict: Human needs theory* (pp. 32–59). London: Macmillan.

Crane, J. (1986). Potential contributions of social work education to peace studies. *The (Canadian) Social Worker, 54*, 102–106.

Davis, H. (1983, July). *The conflict managers' program: Teacher's manual* [Mimeograph]. San Francisco: Community Boards, Center for Policy Training.

Davis, L. E., Galinsky, M. J., & Schopler, J. H. (1995). RAP: A framework for leadership of multiracial groups. *Social Work, 40*, 155–165.

Derksen, S. C. (1982). Education for survival [Mimeograph]. *Features: UNESCO Bulletin of the News Media, 48*, 2–6.

Deutsch, M. (1973). *The resolution of conflict: Constructive and destructive processes.* New Haven, CT: Yale University Press.

Eisler, R. (1987). *The chalice and the blade.* San Francisco: Harper & Row.

Fisher, R., & Ury, W. (1983). *Getting to yes: Negotiating agreement without giving in.* New York: Penguin.

Fisk, S. T., & Taylor, M. S. (1984). *Social cognition.* New York: Random House.

Freudenstein, R. (1992). Communicative peace. *English Today, 31*, 3–8.

Green, N. S. (1990). *The giraffe classroom.* Cleveland Heights, OH: Center for Nonviolent Communication.

Hamilton, D. L. (Ed.). (1981). *Cognitive processes in stereotyping and intergroup behavior.* Hillsdale, NJ: Lawrence Erlbaum Associates, Inc.

Harris, I. M. (1988). *Peace education.* London: McFarland.

Hayes, K. (1989). *Women managers in human services.* New York: Springer.

Kalmakoff, S., Hargraves, S., Cynamon, H., & Witheford, J. (1986). *Conflict and change—A peace education curriculum.* New Westminster, Canada: Public Education for Peace Society (PEPS).

Kalmakoff, S., & Shaw, J. (1987). *Peer conflict resolution through creative negotiation: A curriculum for grades 4 to 6.* New Westminster, Canada: Public Education for Peace Society (PEPS).

Kelman, H. (1991). Interactive problem solving: The uses and limits of a therapeutic model for the resolution of international conflicts. In V. D. Volkan, D. A. Julius, & J. V. Montville (Eds.), *Psychodynamics of international relationships* (Vol. 2, pp. 145–160). Lexington, MA: Lexington.

Kreidler, W. J. (1984). *Creative conflict resolution: More than 200 activities for keeping peace in the classroom.* Glenview, IL: Scott, Foresman.

Lambert, S. J. (1994). Persistent gender differences amid changing requirements for organizational advancement. *Journal of Applied Social Sciences, 18*, 89–108.

Lingas, L. G. (1988). Conflict resolution within family and community networks. *Nordic Journal of Social Work, 8,* 48–58.

Lundy, C. (1987). The role of social work in the peace movement. *The (Canadian) Social Worker, 55,* 61–65.

Northen, H. (1969). *Social work with groups.* New York: Columbia University Press.

Purnell, D. (1988). Creative conflict. *WCCI Forum, 2,* 30–52.

Roderick, T. (1987). Johnny can learn to negotiate. *Educational Leadership, 45,* 87–90.

Rogers, C. R. (1965). Dealing with psychological tensions. *Journal of Applied Behavioral Science, 1,* 6–24.

Rogers, S. J., Kanrich, S., & Steinhouser, I. (1990). *Understanding our criminal justice volunteers: A study of community mediators in New York State.* New York: Brooklyn Mediation Center.

Rosenberg, M. B. (1983). *A model for nonviolent communication.* Philadelphia: New Society.

Shonholz, R. (1984). Neighborhood justice system. *Mediation Quarterly, 5,* 3–30.

Shook, E. V. (1985). *Ho oponopono: A Hawaiian problem-solving process.* Honolulu: University of Hawaii Press.

Smoker, P., Davies, R., & Muske, B. (Eds.). (1990). Appendix: The Seville Statement on Violence. *Reader in peace studies* (pp. 221–223). New York: Pergamon.

Sullivan, M. (1993). Social work's legacy of peace: Echoes from the early 20th century. *Social Work, 38,* 513–520.

Training elementary school conflict managers. (1985). San Francisco: The Community Boards Program.

Walton, R. E. (1969). *Interpersonal peace making: Confrontations and third party consultations.* Reading, MA: Addison-Wesley.

Wein, B. J. (Ed.). (1984). *Peace and world order studies: A curriculum guide.* New York: World Policy Institute.

Weingarten, H., & Leas, S. (1987). Levels of marital conflict: A guide to assessment and intervention in troubled marriages. *American Journal of Orthopsychiatry, 57,* 407–417.

Whiteman, M. (1987). Cognitive-behavioral interventions aimed at anger of parents. *Social Work, 32,* 469–474.

Appendix
Example Classroom Exercises

1. *Learning to break old habits.* What specific curriculum content would you plan if you had to teach a group of parents:

  a. How to stop judging and blaming others.

  b. How to behave when others judge or blame them.

Please support your viewpoint with theoretic ideas and examples.

2. *Designing a minicurriculum.* Set up a 5-hr session for a group of colleagues who currently suffer from a long-lasting interpersonal or interdepartmental conflict. Try to focus on one or two specific topics that you think must be covered (such as listening skills, meeting needs, overcoming victimization, and so on).

3. *Evaluating the effectiveness of educational efforts.* With help from your research staff, what would you want to know to be convinced that a curriculum of lessons has accomplished either of the following:

    a. Changed (from negative to positive) the attitudes of those who participated in the seminar.
    b. Taught the participants one or two specific new conflict-resolution skills that they feel ready to try out in their continuing work or personal lives.

PEABODY JOURNAL OF EDUCATION, 71(3), 29–41

Developing Concepts of Peace and War: Aspects of Gender and Culture

Solveig Hägglund

How do we know that peace education will obtain the expected impact on children's learning and development? And, provided that a particular peace education program is successful at an individual level, how can we be certain that the learned skills and attitudes will contribute to a peaceful world, today and tomorrow?

Questions like these are important to anyone dealing with peace education, be it as a teacher, politician, or researcher. Unfortunately, there is no universal theory for peace learning—its conditions, processes, and potential effects—and we lack conceptual tools to guide us in describing and evaluating peace education practice. However, as peace education involves elements that are essential in the child's development of "social theories,"—that is, the understanding of society, its norms, rules, values, and structure—theories on child development and socialization can offer useful models when initiating systematic and critical research approaches to peace education.

From a developmental perspective, peace education in school constitutes a part of the child's total context for peace learning, competing

SOLVEIG HÄGGLUND *is Associate Professor in the Department of Education and Educational Research, University of Göteborg, Göteborg, Sweden.*

Requests for reprints should be sent to Solveig Hägglund, Department of Education and Educational Research, University of Göteborg, Box 1010, S-43126, Mölndal, Sweden. E-mail: s.hagglund@ped.gu.se

29

with and adding to other information and experiences from various sources. When interpreting and selecting information in the environment, the child is guided by the wish to make sense of the world. To make sense of the world, from the perspective of a child, involves knowing where one belongs and perceiving a social identity. Important mediating mechanisms in this process are cultural norms and social conventions and rules, including those that emphasize the social meaning of gender.

With this general introduction to the relation between peace education and theories on child development as a background, some assumptions in peace education will be discussed from a developmental perspective. Gender and culture, representing two key concepts in children's social and sociocognitive development, will be particularly focused on.

This article is a product of ideas and thoughts from the perspective of a researcher in child development and socialization. Peace and peace education are looked on as desirable environmental conditions in children's socialization, but will not be elaborated on conceptually or epistemologically. Peace education primarily refers to activities in formal schooling, and the "learner" is assumed to be a child of school age. This article is a broad and explorative discussion, suggesting some themes as a common ground for an integrating dialogue between peace education and child development. They should be interpreted as a first draft in trying to sketch one step toward a comprehensive theory of peace learning.

Peace Education and Assumptions About Child Development

Peace education as defined and described in local and national programs is a difficult and complex educational enterprise (Bjerstedt, 1993; Haavelsrud, 1983). More or less explicitly expressed, three general assumptions concerning the impact of peace education efforts are distinguished in several programs: (a) peace education has an impact on tomorrow's world through the children and the knowledge, skills, and attitudes they learn; (b) if peace education has an impact on individual children, an impact at a collective level is anticipated as well; and (c) successful peace education efforts have a long-lasting impact on children's knowledge, skills, and attitudes.

The first assumption has to do with the fact that peace education programs explicitly define educational goals in terms of societal and global change (a peaceful world, a human society, respect for the environment, democratic societal structures, nonviolent societies, etc.). Because this kind of educational goal in its deepest sense is political, the introduction of peace education into formal schooling is subject to controversy and suspicion. The assumption that peace education in school can be a step toward a better society implies that attitudes and skills learned by the child in school will, through the child, influence social structures and enable societal and global change. A developmental comment to this assumption would focus on the interaction between the child, the close (micro) environment and the distant (macro) environment. Furthermore, a discussion concerning factors of mutuality and significant entities in the micro–macro interaction would be relevant.

The second assumption concerns the relationship between the individual and the group. Peace education programs rarely differentiate between teaching individual children and teaching groups of children. In research on teaching and instruction in, for example, mathematics, language, or art, it is a well-known fact that individual children need different amounts of guiding and attention in their learning process. Teaching peace-related issues probably faces the same need of differentiating instructional style. A second problem has to do with the fact that peace education directs the children's attention to social and societal knowledge, strongly connected with sociomoral values and attitudes. By this it follows that learning processes are initiated that are likely to be tested and confirmed in a social situation like the classroom. The learning situation in the classroom, its social atmosphere, and patterns of interaction between individual children and subgroups thus become a critical part of the educational setting. The developmental comment in relation to this would focus on those characteristics in the school setting that set up conditions for the interaction between the child and the various social groups to which he or she belongs. Furthermore, a search for mechanisms in child–group interactions that are likely to support the development of shared attitudes, norms, and beliefs would be very relevant.

The final and third assumption anticipates that what the child learns about peace in school will last; the child learns for life and not just for school. At least as important as stability over time, however, is stability over different settings. A relevant developmental issue would be to define factors that have an impact on the stability of peace-related knowledge and values and to explore the relation between universal and contextual peace learning over time and space.

The Child as the Creator of a Better World

A general outlook on the conditions for peace education in formal schooling to promote competence and skills for peacebuilding and peacekeeping cannot ignore the fact that peace learning is taking place within a social institution—the school. What does it mean that messages about peace are given within an institution with a powerful reproducing societal function where the social climate is signified by individualism, competition, and achievement? Brock-Utne (1989) stated, "It is a thought provoking fact that the same countries responsible for the main threats facing human-kind today, ecocide and genocide, are also the ones having the populations with the highest formal education or schooling" (p. 155). Thus, educational level per se, with or without peace education, does not correlate very highly with successful peace strivings. In her discussion of schools as societal institutions, Brock-Utne argued that Western schools are good examples of subcultures where structural violence operates. The dominating competitive norm encourages oppression of children who do not fulfill the demands of individual achievement, thereby excluding them from power and social positions. Thus, from the child's perspective school offers a social reality not very different from the rest of society; competitive norms may even be more prevalent inside than outside of school. If this is true, the content in peace education messages may contradict not only the social reality in general but also the specific social reality in the school setting in which it is transmitted.

Given the fact that peace education fundamentally directs its goals and activities against the existing society, including schools, what are the possibilities of initiating activities at a microlevel that may change conditions at a macrolevel? Is any child a potential peacemaker? Haavelsrud (1983) took a stand that implies a differentiated agenda for peace education when he argued that as "the purpose of peace education is to change oppressive attitudes, practices and structures, it would be in the interest of those who are the victims of oppression" (pp. 278–279). Haavelsrud referred to Freire's (1970) *Pedagogy of the Oppressed* and argued that education for change in oppressive societies is most effective among the oppressed individuals and groups, that is "the victims of oppression who have the most significant role to play in the elimination of that oppression" (p. 279). Haavelsrud thus suggested an emancipating peace education directed primarily toward the oppressed children, as they are more likely to internalize attitudes and motives for change than nonoppressed children.

Brock-Utne and Haavelsrud discussed conditions for peace education in essentially sociological terms. Following their arguments, we would conclude that formal schooling may offer a subculture contradicting peace education messages and that the impact of peace education is most likely to occur among socially oppressed children. A developmentally oriented conclusion would be that it matters where peace education is taking place and that it matters who the children are. Social institutions and social power structure are important elements in mapping the conditions for peace education and peace learning, but this is not enough if we want to uncover the complex and dynamic interactions between the macro- and the microsystem, including the developing child, that are significant in the peace learning process.

A transfer of attitudes, values, and norms between individuals and society demands interaction. Peace education, like all education, depends on interaction between individuals (teacher–child, parent–child, parent–teacher, child–child) and between groups (boys–girls, classmates–friends outside of school, home team–visiting team, immigrants–nonimmigrants). It is in the verbal and nonverbal communication that individuals and groups confirm and support shared or nonshared views and knowledge of the social world. Appropriate contributions from developmental psychology to formulate critical elements in these interaction processes may be the sociohistorical (Vygotsky, 1978) and the socioecological (Bronfenbrenner, 1979) approaches. Although considerable differences exist between the two—for example, Vygotsky emphasized language and symbols as cultural tools for the interaction processes between individual and society (Wertsch, 1991), whereas Bronfenbrenner focused on supportive characteristics of the socioecological environment—they both assume that development and learning take place through social interaction.

Vygotsky, as well as Bronfenbrenner, regard the child as taking an active part in his or her development. Furthermore, they assume that social relationships are of vital importance for development and learning to take place. Both stress the link between the child and a continuously changing society.

Applying a Vygotskian frame of reference to peace education in formal schooling would direct the attention to patterns of social language used by the children and encourage "non instructional experience statements" (Wertsch, 1991, p. 128). This refers to a teaching strategy allowing and encouraging children to talk about events and experiences from outside of the classroom, to talk about and explore phenomena where the child is the expert, and to talk about things unasked for by the teacher. This implies a peace pedagogy allowing differentiation, flexibility, and openness in every respect. Language as a tool for social growth and understanding is essential not only in terms of what is actually said, but also in the way language is being used in a social context. More specifically, attention should be paid, for example, to what ideas about peace and war are expressed by whom in what social position. The familiar Vygotskian concept the *zone of proximal development*, defined as the potential for achievement and learning, deserves particular notion. Although frequently studied within the academic field, it rarely has been applied in the social domain such as development of prosocial competence and cooperation skill. It would be a challenging task for researchers in peace education to define the proximal zone of development in peace learning.

Vygotsky's theory is based on the idea that conditions for learning and development are closely related to the specific sociocultural environment surrounding the child; the individual and the culture are regarded as inseparable entities. Symbols and language serve as instruments for interaction and transfer of cultural messages between the two. The focus in the socioecological theory (Bronfenbrenner, 1979) is on the interaction between the child and elements of the environment. According to Bronfenbrenner, four interrelated socioecological systems constitute the developmental ecology for a child. Apart from the macro (culture) and micro (close-to-the child environment) systems, two additional systems are operating, labeled *meso-systems* and *exo-systems*. It is not necessary to detail the ecological model for human development here, but a quick look at what it implies concerning interaction between micro- and macrolevels would be relevant. The definition of development in this paradigm states that parallel with a growing understanding of the world, the individual acquires skills not only to support the existing society but also to change it:

> Human development is the process through which the growing person acquires a more extended differentiated and valid conception of the ecological environment and becomes motivated and able to engage in activities that reveal the properties, sustain or restructure that environment at levels of similar or greater complexity in form and content. (Bronfenbrenner, 1979, p. 27)

According to the socioecological view, peace learning takes place in activities, roles, and relations in the child's everyday life. Processes of learning in the classroom setting are regarded as nonseparable from those at home, with friends, or elsewhere. By this it follows that the impact of what is taught at school necessarily is related to what is learned in other settings. Peace learning is no exception.

The ecological paradigm fits well into Galtung's (1983) and others' statement that peace education has to include the element of action (Haavelsrud, 1993; Thelin, 1993). According to Galtung, peace education has to be

> concerned with what to do about it, which means that there has to be not only a theory of how to avoid war and build peace, but a "do-able" theory, linked to some kind of practice for those who study this field, not only for others. (p. 283)

So far my reasoning has centered around the idea that peace education is a part of children's total context for learning and development and that elements in the interaction between micro- and macroaspects of the environment need to be described and identified to gain the whole picture. The fundamental assumption that macrofactors such as cultural values, traditions, ideologies, and norms are present in microsettings and influence learning conditions is widely accepted in social science, as is the idea that societal characteristics influence its members. But even though it may be true that peaceful cultures produce peaceful individuals and violent cultures produce violent members (Mead, 1935), it is not necessarily true that peaceful individuals produce peaceful societies. The mutuality in the micro–macro dynamics is more complex than that. Thus, although it has been shown empirically that macroconditions influence microconditions and individuals (Elder, 1974; Leavitt & Fox, 1993; Luria, 1976; Staub, 1991), it does not imperatively imply that the opposite is true. The implication for research in peace education should be to systematically identify those mechanisms in the micro–macro interaction that support and strengthen influential links from the individual to society.

The Child and the Group

Certainly one such mechanism has to do with the interaction between the child and those groups to which he or she belongs. The target group for peace education is normally a group of children sharing the same classroom. Even if this group means different things and is of different social importance for different children, the way in which social interaction styles and patterns operate are important factors for learning processes at an individual as well as a collective level. Worth noting is that childhood itself is not a homogenous entity but presents the same richness of social stratification and subcultures as adulthood (Qvartrup, 1991). A key task for the child is to find out where he or she belongs in this diversity. Those groups defined as the "own" will have a significant meaning for the development of social identity and thereby for the development of social knowledge. Few studies in peace education and its impact on children seem to focus on these aspects of the classroom as a specific context for peace learning.

Relevant research approaches in studies of the influence of peer groups on children's peace learning might be based on a cognitive constructivistic theoretical perspective (Piaget, 1953), according to which social knowledge is assumed to be a result of generally the same process of gradually increasing conceptualization of the world as is the case for nonsocial phenomena. In this tradition, the peer group is important as it presents to the child social events and social problems to be interpreted and understood.

Another theoretical perspective on the importance of the social group in children's understanding of the social world is offered by a sociogenetic approach. The theory of social representations, as presented by Moscovici (1984), anticipates that the formation of meanings of social events is created collectively through social interaction. According to this theory, group members develop a common "theory" for interpreting and explaining social events. This implies that social knowledge may be "distributed" differently over different groups in society; different groups of people "know" different things as a result of their gender, class, race, age, social position, profession, and so on.

The theory of social representations would be a relevant tool when discussing the role of social groups in children's peace learning. From the perspective of educational practice, it implies that teaching efforts consciously should be directed toward groups as well as toward individual children. From a research perspective, the theory particularly contributes to an understanding of how social mechanisms serve as barriers for changing attitudes and behavior among groups of children and adolescents. It also implies a methodology in research on children and peace in which assessments of individual children's knowledge, attitudes, values, and behavior should be accompanied by systematic definitions of groups and their shared "social theories."

Peace Education for Life

What about the long-term impact of peace education? Is it possible to teach children about peace in such a way that knowledge, attitudes, and skills will last? From what has been said so far, it is obvious that development and learning go hand in hand, and that the learning context is far broader than the classroom. It should also be rather obvious that from my perspective, the question of long-term impact of peace education is strongly connected with the link between the child and the sociocultural environment.

An illustration of peace education practice based on goals expressed in terms of children's psychological growth is presented by Wahlström (1991). In her study, psychological objects (socioemotional, cognitive, and behavioral) were generated from UNESCO's goals for environmental education. Cooperative learning was used as a mean to improve the children's cooperative skills and attitudes. The results showed an immediate effect on the children's responses to the instruction and the teacher.

The critical question in relation to studies like this is whether the increasing skill in cooperation is restricted to the classroom situation or whether it is observed in other settings as well. Unfortunately, other studies report that short-term programs are not very effective in the sense of stable, long-term impact (Bjerstedt, 1993; Cairns & Toner, 1993). Assumptions about the long-term impact of peace education need to be anchored in a description of the potential supportive links between the specific peace learning situation and other settings significant for the child's learning and development—the family, the peer group, future classes in school, and so forth. Without such a contextual map over competing or supportive learning settings, peace education runs the risk of becoming an isolated endeavor with limited impact on the child's learning and development.

Gender and Culture

From the perspective of the child, the social world is a complex and difficult phenomena to grasp. In striving to understand sometimes contradictory messages, cultural norms and values function as guides for selection and interpretation. In learning and developmental processes, such clusters of social rules mediate the social information internalized by the child (Cole, 1995). Gender may be regarded as a "special case" of culture in this sense (Haste & Baddeley, 1991).

Culture and gender are particularly crucial in a discussion of peace and peace education. Several of those behaviors and attitudes that are expressed as goals in peace education (e.g., social responsibility, nonviolence, prosocial skills, egalitarian attitudes, and awareness of principles for justice) have been reported to be distributed in gender-differentiated ways among individuals and groups. According to Brock-Utne (1989), peace education lacks analyses from a gender perspective and "the fact that boys and girls are educated differently is normally a nonissue in peace education. ... The whole field of peace education has ... been lacking an analysis of patriarchy" (p. 82). When describing the typical peace-oriented school student, Brock-Utne referred to a Swedish survey based on more than 1,000 adolescents (Lindholm, 1986). In this study, the most peace-oriented student is a girl who

> considers the risk of nuclear war to be very great, but at the same time she believes that she herself can help to prevent it and that this can be better done through the peace movement than through national defence. (cited in Brock-Utne, 1989, pp. 161–162)

Numerous studies in differential psychology show gender differences in achievement, abilities, personality, and behavior. An increasing amount of feminist research in recent decades has shifted the focus of interest from the static and individualistic "sex variable" to the concept of gender as a sociocultural category. This allows for analyses of the diverse ways in which the dimension of gender operates across the societal system and the micro–macro spectrum. Hirdman (1988) suggested a conceptualization of what signifies the cultural gender relations in the Western countries as organized by a social gender order, operating through two logics—the logic of gender segregation and the logic of male superiority. These principles are anticipated to exist not only between individuals but also between professions, interests, and activities.

In an earlier study (Hägglund, 1993), it was shown that microsettings (i.e., school and preschool) differ in ways of interpreting cultural gender norms into organizational and pedagogical practice. The principles of segregation and dominance were displayed differently in the two educational settings. When boys' "rough and tumble" play was not accepted by the teachers in the preschools, the boys were not told to stop, but to go away. The boys were obviously disturbing order, but instead of trying to keep them inside the setting, adjusting to its demands and rules, they were offered another "boys'" space where they could continue their activities. They were segregated from the girls, but their social position was not threatened. In the school setting, segregation in the classroom was observed in the different roles assigned to girls and boys. In observations as well as in child interviews and teacher ratings, the girls were assumed to be responsible for attaining order in the classroom, whereas the boys were regarded as "troublemakers." A common way of interpreting these frequently reported results is that "boys will be boys," that is, their behavior is explained in terms of individual characteristics and rarely in terms of underlying gender structures. An alternative interpretation of the empirical examples would be to regard the observed gender patterns as expressions for operating cultural gender structures within children's microsettings, thereby supporting the segregation and patriarchal principles.

In studies of children's concepts of peace and war, girls are more frequently reported to define both concepts in terms of relationships between human beings (e.g., peace is to be friends, war is to quarrel with friends), whereas boys tend to talk about peace as a result of disarmament and about war in terms of war activities. Furthermore, girls tend to relate their associations with peace to their own social environment and relations, whereas boys more frequently refer to peace as something distant (e.g., peace is when war has stopped; Hakvoort, 1989; Hakvoort & Oppenheimer, 1993). In Hakvoort's research, girls refer to peace more frequently in terms of positive peace (Galtung, 1985), whereas boys refer to negative peace. In line with these findings is the model of male and female orientation in moral reasoning presented by Gilligan (1982), in which it is suggested that women develop a caring and interpersonal orientation in moral issues, whereas men stress rules of justice and fairness (Gilligan, Ward, & Taylor, 1988).

The aforementioned examples indicate that peace education faces a problem related to gender, namely that culture and society tend to segregate issues of peace and war into male and female domains and to label the male-marked areas with a higher value than the female areas. War activities with technologically advanced resources receive higher cultural priority than peace activities with socially advanced resources. Gender in terms of social identity in the individual child, as well as in terms of societal power structure, is highly relevant in the proceeded work on peace education. In any setting in which peace is taught, children will encounter the red and blue gender markings, guiding their ways of understanding what values, knowledge, and behavior are appropriate to learn, including those related to peace and war.

Conclusion

Peace education is a part of the child's socialization experience and, as such, it will have an impact on the development of his or her understanding of the world and his or her position and responsibility in the same. The outcome of the experience from the peace lesson depends on hundreds of factors and their interaction, among which gender and culture are of particular importance. The agenda for future research on peace education and peace learning needs an interdiscipli-

S. Hägglund

nary approach, allowing for designs and analyses that broaden the perspective on the possibilities and barriers of peace education. Our knowledge about children's learning and development stresses contextually related factors as the fundamental and most important contributors to content and direction of the development. The challenge for peace education in a postmodern world is to systematically conceptualize such contexts and their significant elements.

References

Bjerstedt, Å. (1993). Peace education in schools around the world in the beginning of the 1990s. In Å. Bjerstedt (Ed.), *Peace education: Global perspectives* (pp. 149–169). Stockholm: Almqvist & Wiksell.

Brock-Utne, B. (1989). *Feminist perspectives on peace and peace education*. New York: Pergamon.

Bronfenbrenner, U. (1979). *The ecology of human development. Experiments by nature and design*. Cambridge, MA: Harvard University Press.

Cairns, E., & Toner, I. (1993). Children and political violence in Northern Ireland: From riots to reconciliation. In L. A. Leavitt & N. A. Fox (Eds.), *The psychological effects of war and violence on children* (pp. 215–230). Hillsdale, NJ: Lawrence Erlbaum Associates, Inc.

Cole, M. (1995). Culture and cognitive development: From cross-cultural research to creating systems of cultural mediation. *Culture & Psychology, 1,* 25–54.

Elder, G. H. (1974). *Children of the great depression*. Chicago: University of Chicago Press.

Freire, P. (1970). *Pedagogy of the oppressed*. New York: Herder & Herder.

Galtung, J. (1983). Learning to hate war, love peace and to do something about it. *International Review of Education, 29,* 281–282.

Galtung, J. (1985). Twenty-five years of peace research: Ten challenges and some responses. *Journal of Peace Research, 22,* 141–157.

Gilligan, C. (1982). *In a different voice*. Cambridge, MA: Harvard University Press.

Gilligan, C., Ward, J. V., & Taylor, J. M. (Eds.). (1988). *Mapping the moral domain*. Cambridge, MA: Harvard University Press.

Haavelsrud, M. (1983). An introduction to the debate on peace education. *International Review of Education, 29,* 275–280.

Haavelsrud, M. (Ed.). (1993). *Disarming: Discourse on violence and peace*. Tromsø, Norway: Arena.

Hägglund, S. (1993). The gender dimension in children's learning of prosocial competence in early educational settings. *European Early Childhood Education Research Journal, 1,* 67–79.

Hakvoort, I. (1989). *Children and adolescents about peace and war*. Unpublished master's thesis, University of Amsterdam, Department of Developmental Psychology.

Hakvoort, I., & Oppenheimer, L. (1993). Children's and adolescents' conceptions of peace, war and strategies to attain peace: A Dutch case study. *Journal of Peace Research, 30,* 65–77.

Haste, H., & Baddeley, J. (1991). Moral theory and culture: The case of gender. In M. W. Kurtines & J. L. Gewirtz (Eds.), *Handbook of moral behavior and development: Vol 1. Theory* (pp. 223–250). Hillsdale, NJ: Lawrence Erlbaum Associates, Inc.

Hirdman, Y. (1988). Genussystemet: Reflexioner kring kvinnors soicala underordning [The gender system: Reflections on women's social subordination]. *Kvinnovetenskaplig Tidskrift, 3*, 51–64.

Leavitt, L. A., & Fox, N. A. (Eds.). (1993). *The psychological effects of war and violence on children.* Hillsdale, NJ: Lawrence Erlbaum Associates, Inc.

Lindholm, S. (1986, April). *A thousand students on war, peace and peace education.* Paper presented at the meeting of the International Peace Research Association, University of Sussex, England.

Luria, A. R. (1976). *Cognitive development: Its cultural and social foundations.* Cambridge, MA: Harvard University Press.

Mead, M. (1935). *Sex and temperament in three primitive societies.* New York: Morrow.

Moscovici, S. (1984). The phenomenon of social representations. In F. R. Farr & S. Moscovici (Eds.), *Social representations* (pp. 3–70). Cambridge, MA: Cambridge University Press.

Piaget, J. (1953). *The origins of intelligence in the child.* London: Routledge & Kegan Paul.

Qvartrup, J. (1991). Childhood as a social phenomenon. *Eurosocial Report, 36*, 11–42.

Staub, E. (1991). Psychological and cultural origins of extreme destructiveness and extreme altruism. In W. M. Kurtines & J. L. Gewirtz (Eds.), *Handbook of moral behaviour and development: Vol. 1. Theory* (pp. 425–446). Hillsdale, NJ: Lawrence Erlbaum Associates, Inc.

Thelin, B. (1993). Education for global survival. In Å. Bjerstedt (Ed.), *Peace education: Global perspectives* (pp. 94–110). Stockholm: Almqvist & Wiksell.

Vygotsky, L. S. (1978). *Mind in society. The development of higher psychological processes.* Cambridge, MA: Harvard University Press.

Wahlström, R. (1991). Growth towards peace and environmental responsibility. *Theory Into Practice, 67*, 1–78.

Wertsch, J. (1991). *Voices of the mind.* Hertfordshire, England: Harvester.

PEABODY JOURNAL OF EDUCATION, 71(3), 42–62

Educating for the 21st Century: Beyond Racist, Sexist, and Ecologically Violent Futures

Francis P. Hutchinson

This article explores some "resources of hope" in educating for the 21st century. It argues the importance of active listening to our children's voices on the future, and of choice and engagement in resisting fatalistic fallacies that negative trends are destiny. The latter discussion draws on a significant principle from critical futurism and contemporary movements of educational innovation, such as peace education, multicultural education, nonsexist education, and environmental education. According to this principle, although we cannot go everywhere from here, we are not constrained to unilinear necessity. "Casualties of change," or victimological accounts of young people, are questioned for their stereotyping and perpetuation of fatalistic assumptions. A discourse is invited on our schools as being among contemporary sites

FRANCIS P. HUTCHINSON *currently teaches at the Faculty of Health, Humanities, and Social Ecology, School of Social Ecology, University of Western Sydney, Richmond, Australia.*

An earlier version of this article was presented at the 15th General Conference of the International Peace Research Association, conducted at the Mediterranean Conference Centre and the University of Malta, October 29 to November 4, 1994.

Requests for reprints should be sent to Francis P. Hutchinson, Faculty of Health, Humanities, and Social Ecology, Locked Bag 1, School of Social Ecology, University of Western Sydney, Hawkesbury, Richmond, New South Wales 2753, Australia.

of possibility in moving beyond disabling or destructive fears and in encouraging alternatives to violence.

Challenge and Opportunity

The post-Cold War world is a contradictory one. It is a time of challenge and opportunity. Our children and their children will spend most or all of their lives in the 21st century. What kind of world will they inherit? In the aftermath of the Cold War, already there have been important opportunities lost in terms of a substantial peace dividend. This lack of proactive responses, in the context of the breakup of the Soviet empire, has meant a fertile ground for ethnic chauvinisms and other fundamentalisms that revive or reconstruct old hatreds and project new ones. Yet, are these trends or other negatives ones—such as those relating to environmental degradation—a unilinear necessity? Must we resign ourselves to colonizing assumptions about the future whether in terms of ethnic relations, gender relations, North–South relations, or our relations with the natural environment? Beyond both the fatalism of assumed inevitabilities and the easy temptation in such circumstances to seek escapist release are there alternative paths for would-be journeyers into the 21st century (Hutchinson, 1996; United Nations Educational, Scientific, and Cultural Organization, 1994)?

Resources for Journeys of Hope

What resources exist, especially in school contexts, for lessening the risks of a journey in which hope becomes an escapist crutch, or is even abandoned in fatalistic despair? Through combining the languages of critique and possibility, this article does not seek to come up with a detailed route map listing "essential" recommendations for educating for the 21st century. Rather, the intention is to invite discovery, choice, and engagement in the present by teachers, students, parents, and schools in negotiating futures. In this, an important dialogical principle of attempting to refrain from dogmatic closure in our ways of knowing is affirmed.

The power-over notion of expert, objectively derived knowledge has been axiomatic in Western modernization theory, with its assumptions of trickle-down development and technological transfer. Technofixes are proffered as easy "answers" for complex human and environmental needs and crises. Both humility and a good sense of humor are important in offering insights for would-be travelers into the 21st century. There is the Taoist saying, "the further one travels, the less one knows," that contains ironic comment on the easy temptation to be persuaded by narrowly specialized "expert" knowledge and dogmatic closure about one-true-world of reality and potential reality. A Western educational critic has similarly used humor to deflate pretensions: "Any PhD who thinks s/he has nothing to learn from a five year old should go back to school" (Curle, 1990, p. 166).

Reflexive Cartography on Futures

All our maps of world geography, despite the best efforts of cartographers, are lacking in some ways. It is difficult to project something three-dimensional, such as our planet, in two-dimensional terms. Yet, arguably some projections are likely to be less Western-centric in their cultural lens than others, as illustrated by the difference between the conventional Mercator's projection and the newer Peters' projection. How much more difficult is it, then, if it comes to questioning taken-for-granted "mind maps" or images of "the future." Figure 1 offers a simplified conceptual map of several possible paths rather than one set route forward.

This kind of reflexive cartography recognizes the importance of critical consciousness about empirical trends and of societal, institutional, and ecological limits at different periods of human history. Yet, it also strongly questions the fatalism that trend is destiny. It challenges dehumanizing epistemological frames of reference that propagate assumptions of necessary monocultural "progress" and invariance in Western technology's evolutionary path. Such assumptions, if left unchallenged, devalue human consciousness and human agency in shaping in nonviolent ways a better world. It raises key questions about moral choices, more holistic forms of literacy, broader democratic participation, and new ethical considerations about intergenerational equity. It affirms that teachers and students, as would-be journeyers into the 21st century, can make some difference. Individually the contributions are likely to be quite small, but collectively they may be quite significant even if the negotiations are protracted and the pathways ahead are difficult. Indebted to both the narratives of the peace and environmental movements, there is a saying that raises profound political and ethical questions for our choice and engagement: "The world was not left to us by our parents: It was lent to us by our children."

Exploring present contextualities for beginning journeys of active hope in schools

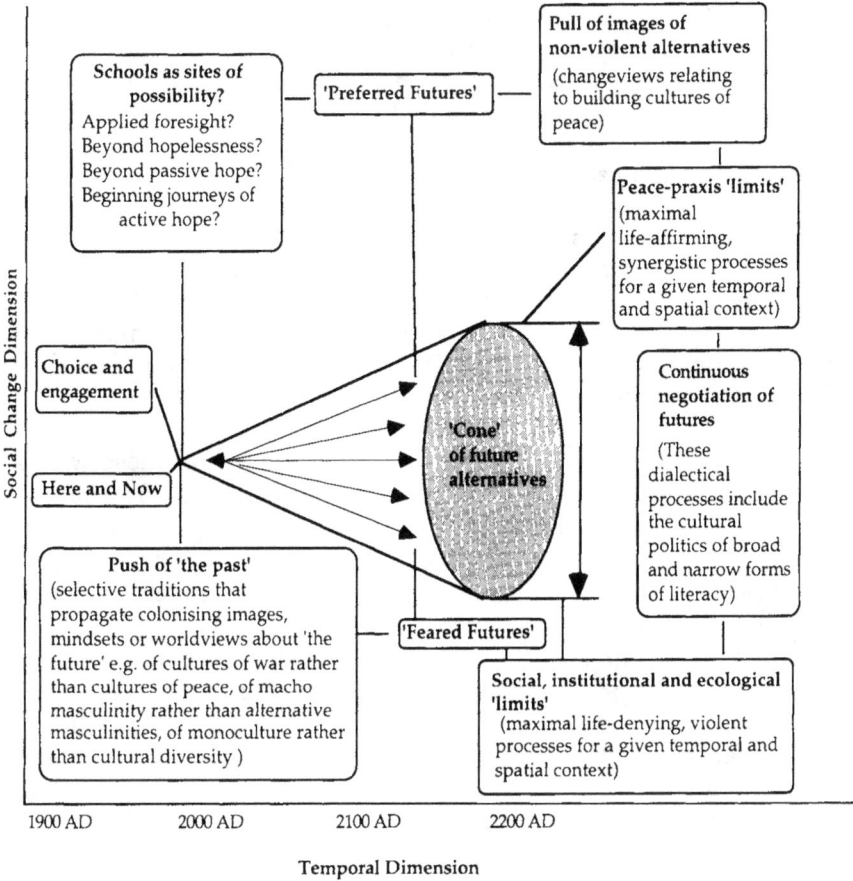

Figure 1. Exploring present contextualities for beginning journeys of active hope in schools.

Synergistic Relationships

There are, moreover, possible significant synergistic relationships. The negotiation of futures in schools is not so much isolated from as dialectically related to developments in nonformal education such as the creative work of many nongovernmental organizations (NGOs) and international nongovernmental organizations (INGOs). Over the past century, there has been a major growth of INGOs such as the Red Cross, YWCA and YMCA, Amnesty International, Greenpeace, and the

45

World Wide Fund for Nature. On the eve of World War I, there were less than 200 such organizations. There are now around 18,000 of these organizations. They may be interpreted as aspects of an emergent, albeit still strongly provisional, global civic culture in which sectional nation-state interests are beginning to be transcended by new images and loyalties of global interdependence, ecologically sustainable development, and peace praxis (Boulding, 1988).

Throughout this article, the argument is advanced that the way is dialectical and provisional rather than linear and strictly determined for would-be journeyers in schools, other institutions, and transnational networks into the 21st century. Although it is rational to be alerted by negative trends in empirical reality, it is a fallacy of restricted alternatives to simply extrapolate such trends. As Boomer and Torr (1987) commented,

> The inertia of schools sometimes creates despair in those who see them as constrained by decades of habit, behaviourist learning theory, and inviolable rules. ... It is almost as if the memory traces of certain behaviours have become impersonally embedded in the very fabric of the school, so that it operates on an implacable kind of automatic pilot. The agency is invisible. ...
>
> But, infinitesimal as it may be, each individual action does change the balance of power. Each resistance or contrary impulse is a force, even if it is but a new thought, because imminent in every thought is an action. Each rethinking, each piece of new theorising creates a new tendency, a potential change of direction. Each thought shared and confirmed begins to multiply the potential.
>
> Here lies much hope. (pp. 2–3)

Possible Compass Bearings: Applied Ethics

It is important, therefore, to reflect on not only how aspects of cultural violence mediate restricted meanings of reality and potential reality in schools but how, in site-specific contexts, nonviolent resistances may emerge. In the remainder of this article, some insights gained so far are reviewed briefly. To use the metaphor of a stopping point on a much longer journey, several exploratory principles are suggested as to possible ethical and procedural compass bearings at these crossroads in human history (see Table 1).

These principles help to illuminate some resources for open-ended journeys of active hope. They are intended to encourage discussion in

Table 1. Negotiating Futures in Education: Some Possible Compass Bearings for Would-Be Journeyers Into the 21st Century

P	E	A	C	E
Proactive Skills	Eco-Relational Ways of Thinking	Alternatives	Civics for an Interdependent World	Ends and Means
Learning to actively listen to young people's anticipations about the future. Encouragement of empathy and other proactive skills in conflict resolution, nonviolent social change, and applied foresight.	Learning to question dogmatic closure in ways of knowing worm's eye and bird's eye views.	Learning about alternatives to violence and how to challenge self-fulfilling prophesies, learning about other cultural lifeways and alternative knowledge traditions, learning skills of imagination.	Learning broad rather than narrow literacies that help to integrate the personal, the political, and the planetary—"thinking globally, acting locally."	Learning about peace, in and for peaceful, equitable, and ecologically sustainable futures, peace praxis, peaceful pedagogies. Developing peer mediation programs in schools, cooperative learning, gender equity, and nonracist programs.

both formal and nonformal educational sectors of possible, probable, and preferable futures in education. They seek to elucidate how schools might become less institutions of cultural reproduction, in which perpetual trends in gendered and other forms of violence are taken for granted, and more sites of possibility as agencies of applied foresight, creative imagination, and creative endeavor.

Proactive Skills

In both Taoist and Buddhist epistemologies, the way is not linear. It is provisional and dialectical, combining theory and various attempts at peaceful praxis. The Chinese character for Tao or "the way" combines a head, representing foresight and wisdom, with the symbol for journeying. Lao Tzu (c. 600 BC), a legendary Chinese philosopher regarded as the founder of Taoism, advised foresight for would-be journeyers:

Begin difficult things while they are easy,
do great things when they are small.
The difficult things of the world must have been easy;
the great things must once have been small ...
A thousand mile journey begins with one step. (Yutang, 1995, p. 616)

Arguably, it is crucial to such foresight that young people's needs and fears about "the future" are actively listened to by parents, teachers, fellow students, and politicians. Otherwise, there are unlikely to be quality responses on a variety of scales and levels. At the school level, such active listening offers an important futures-oriented peace research technique.

In Buddhist knowledge traditions, there is the metaphor of the noble eight-fold path. For would-be travelers, utter determinism is rejected, while affirming the wisdom of such ethical principles as *samma ajiva* or "right livelihood." Whether the eight-fold path or some other path is taken entails our making some choice. "You yourself must make the effort" (*Dhammapada*, canto xx in Kaviratna, 1980, p. 109).

Active listening to young people's fears and anxieties about the future implies compassionate listening. This kind of dialogical approach neither denies an ethical dimension nor succumbs to fatalistic fallacies. Galtung (1990) put this succinctly as follows:

Compassion is the point of departure [for beginning journeys of active hope]. ... Start with data alone, theory alone or praxis alone, and the chances are that you will go astray. Granted, the person staying on the safe side, running up and down the data-theory [route] may become a professor. But is that the ultimate goal of peace research? (p. 281)

For proactive, compassionate responses to occur, it is an important action research step to acknowledge that a major problem may actually exist, as expressed in young people's voices on the future, and is likely to worsen if nothing practical is done about it. There is, perhaps, a legitimate complaint that we often fail to listen properly. It has been said that we need to become "less illiterate in [these] signs of the times" (Berrigan, 1981).

A kind of diagnostic signaling is involved with active listening to young people's anticipations. Such signaling, however, should not be confused with forms of prediction so beloved in the empiricist futurological tradition of epistemology. It avoids the empiricist futurological fallacy of law-like invariance in patterns of development. It questions the fatalism of self-fulfilling prophecies. It invites proactive skills in schools. In other words, a major resource for a journey of active hope is the compassionate application of foresight. The wisdom of Western and non-Western proverbs, such as "prevention is better than cure" and "begin difficult things while they are easy, do great things when they are small," is affirmed (Beare & Slaughter, 1993).

There are crucial challenges to be considered in terms of quality responses by teachers, parents, and schools to the fears expressed by many young people about physical violence, environmental degradation, and economic insecurity in the 21st century. Yet, to categories young people as undifferentiated "victims of future shock," "casualties of the disease of change," or as "children of the apocalypse" is particularly short-sighted and stereotypic. It is a brake on applied foresight. Active listening to what many young people are actually saying about the condition of the world suggests that although negative images of the future are widespread, there is also the positive suggestion by many that much more needs to be learned about ways of constructively dealing with feared futures (Hutchinson, 1994a; Page, 1996). In educating for the 21st century, active listening to such young people's voices questions the appropriateness of narrow educational agendas and narrow conceptualizations of literacy:

In a world in which local, national and global conflict is a daily fact of life, it is all too easy for children to become fearful, to lack hope and to believe that they are powerless in the face of forces larger than themselves. Few things are more empowering to young people than the opportunity to acquire the knowledge, skills and attitudes which enable them to resolve conflicts peacefully, and to work creatively for changes. (Fountain, 1990, p. 7)

Eco-Relational Ways of Thinking

Tightly specialized, atomistic, and often strongly Western and male-centric ways of knowing may offer "a worm's eye" view, but they arguably fail to offer the adequate foresight that may come from a combination of "a worm's eye" view and "a bird's eye" view. One is reminded of the comment by Laszlo (1972): "The demand for 'seeing things whole' and seeing the world as an interconnected interdependent field ... is in itself a healthy reaction to the loss of meaning entailed by overcompartmentalised research" (p. 6). It is salutary to hear the words of an insightful 11-year-old from a late industrial society on the need for more eco-relational ways of knowing:

We've seen the age of enlightenment
And the age of discovery
And enjoyed the benefits of the age of technology
We've been like children who love taking apart
We've almost perfected the specialist's craft
Now we view our world in many compartments
and listen to very specialized views
Which often offer opposing advice
In many ways we're lost in looking at the parts,
We're children who have mastered the art of taking apart
But forgotten the reassembly task. (Wilson-Fuller, 1990, p. 91)

Alternatives

Evidence has been presented elsewhere about the major traces of selective traditions in young people's media artifacts (Hutchinson, 1994b). Among these traces are cultural assumptions relating to "peace-through-strength," the rich–poor divide, gender differences, the commodification of nature, and a machine at the heart of reality and potential reality. It is not concluded, however, that simply because such data illuminate aspects of the processes of legitimization or normalization of direct, structural violence and ecological violence, that a reflectionist or copy-cat hypothesis about media portrayal of violence and young people's behavior is valid. The processes of childhood and adolescent socialization are more complicated, uneven, and dialectical.

Influential narratives on "the disease of change" and of young people as "future shock victims" may be problematized rather than taken for granted. If there are to be a greater number of quality responses by teachers and students themselves as beings of praxis, it is important to enhance the opportunities for creative futures work in the classroom and school environment. Both within the formal and informal curriculum, too often there are missed opportunities in terms of facilitating critical and creative readings of school textbooks and newer media.

Arguably, much more needs to be done in our schools to develop programs of multimedia literacy and for preservice and postservice education for teachers on related issues. The development of the school textbook and other print media literacy remains important, but increasingly, electronic media literacy is likely to be vital for an informed citizenry. Some example teaching techniques are suggested in Hutchinson (1992a) for analyzing sexist, racist, militarist, and other cultural biases in the print and electronic media.

To posit the importance of such a broadening of predominantly cognitive- or analytical-oriented literacies is not to suggest allowing a further rusting of affective- or imaginative-oriented literacies. A more holistic approach to teaching and learning is implied. It is equally important that we broaden and deepen our skills for imaging a better world. Contemporary print and electronic media often propagate foreclosed, violent images of the future. "To rescue imagination," as argued in Freire and Shor (1987), our ways of teaching and learning need "to stimulate alternative thinking. This can offer some distance from the enveloping message and images of mass culture" (p. 185).

What we do or do not do in the present or "extended present" as teachers, parents, or students is strongly influenced by our past histories and our readings of the past. There is a push of the past involved in our decisions. However, there is also the pull of what we anticipate about the future. Such a dialectical situation raises crucial questions for choice and engagement by teachers and schools. In making such choices, it is pertinent to recall the observation by Jacob von Uexkull, Founder and Chairman of the Right Livelihood Award:

Today it is easy to be a pessimist. ... But being a possibilist ... means rejecting the self-fulfilling pessimism of those who tell us that we must of necessity pollute our environment, poison ourselves and consume the future for the sake of short-term greed and comfort, because such is human nature. (cited in Ekins, 1992, pp. vii–viii)

Despite many young people's feared futures, it is feasible to encourage imaginative thought about alternative social futures (Hutchinson, 1994a). Even if such capacities have been allowed to go rusty in conventional pedagogy, the evidence suggests that much still may be done by teachers using "right brain" and "left brain" learning techniques in more holistic ways. This is not to imply, however, that the very act of imaging a better world is sufficient. It may be translated as an "impossible dream." The Brazilian archbishop Helder Camara has commented on the inadequacies of dreaming about a better world that is uninvolved with dialogue among others on their dreams and with action-planning: "When you dream alone, it is just Utopia—But when you dream together, reality begins" (cited in Hutchinson, 1992a, p. 290).

There exists, in other words, an important pedagogical challenge to facilitate dialogue among students about how their feared futures may become less likely and their preferable futures more likely. In such dialogue, past follies and present mistakes should be addressed. They should be learned from and not be normalized as an ad infinitum part of "human nature":

> Given the complexity and seriousness of the present situation, and the danger of shallow fantasies [or passive hope], it ... is high time to ground would-be journeyers into the 21st century in the history of the twin human capacities for folly and utopia building. ... [It is also important to ground] them in a sensitivity to the aspirations that come out of other cultural lifeways [or alternative knowledge traditions].
>
> It is finding the way past destruction that makes the imaging so important. Clarity about those ever-present twin capacities, and recognition of an undreamed-of human diversity, can save us from shallow optimism. We do not have to abandon the methods to image that better world, only broaden and deepen them. ... [As] long as we can imagine a better world with minds adequately equipped for the complexities of the 21st century, we will be able to work for it. (Boulding, 1991, p. 532)

Civics for an Interdependent World

In a complexly interdependent world, there are arguably important implications for curriculum design and practice in preparing for the

21st century. For teachers and schools, there are important choices to be made about whether to broaden imaginative horizons and to infuse a global perspective by learning from other cultural lifeways. Needham (1969), the noted Asianist, made the point some years ago:

> We have good reason to think that the problems of the world will never be solved as long as they are considered only from a [Western] point of view Many people in Western Europe and European America suffer from what may be called spiritual pride. They are firmly convinced that their own form of civilization is the only universal form. We need a real conviction that all racialism, all self-satisfied beliefs of cultural superiority, are a denial of the world community. (pp. 11, 29–30)

Similarly, there are major considerations about encouraging a "dialectical consciousness." What has been regarded as normal, inevitable, or immalleable in past times (e.g., an absolute monarchy, slavery, or the Soviet empire) are no longer considered to be so. Studies of the latter historical isomorphisms may help, for example, to challenge fatalistic assumptions. They may help to revise contemporary assumptions about the inevitability or immalleability of "the greenhouse effect," patriarchy, and the institution of war.

In this, there is no suggestion that a series of historical examples about the fallacy of restricted alternatives will do. It remains a very sound pedagogical principle to start from where students are "at" in their own lives. There needs to be grounded imaging and actions grounded in the situations that young people actually experience in present times. Creative futures work with young people in small-group dialogues brings this point home. One is reminded of the comment by Peavey (1986) in *Heart Politics:*

> As listener, I try to give people a chance to explore an issue openly; I focus on the aspects that are unresolved or painful to them, and on their hopes and visions of how the situation could be different. This allows ideas to emerge that can become the seeds of strategy. (pp. 73–91)

Various forms of experiential learning, such as student action-research projects in cooperation with NGOs and INGOs, are one positive approach to encouraging pro-social skills (see the Appendix). They are likely to encourage active hope and a sense of global interconnectedness and civic responsibility. For our teachers and schools, this implies important questions about "the world in the classroom" and ways of futures teaching:

> One way to give a more empowering experience to young people is not to ignore problems, certainly not, but to focus on: Where do we want to go? What sort of world do we want? This means to develop young people's and teachers' capacities to dream and have visions, but also having done that, to come back very much to the here and now and say: What does that mean about what I'm going to be doing in my community, in my school, at home, in relation to my local world and the wider world? (Hicks, 1990, p. 39)

Some practical possibilities for futures teaching are offered in Waddell and Hutchinson (1988), Hutchinson (1992a), Hutchinson, Talbot, and Brown (1992), and Hutchinson (1996).

Ends and Means

Another important insight for starting journeys of active hope in school education relates to achieving greater compatibility between means and ends in the formal and informal curriculum. It is a contradiction in terms, for example, to proclaim a peaceful end but to attempt to reach this end by culturally violent means in the classroom. To educate for a peaceful future implies doing it in peaceful, friendly, and dialogical ways, not authoritarian, unfriendly, and monological ways. To educate for an equitable and democratic future implies doing it in nonsexist, nonracist, and participatory ways. To educate for an interdependent and ecologically sustainable future implies doing it through cooperative group work rather than individualistically competitive learning environments. To take as one's avowed objectives in the formal curriculum a partnership model with, for instance, gender equity as a major policy goal, while leaving essentially intact a dominator model in the hidden curriculum with a blind eye turned to "boys will be boys" and playground bullying, is to fail to address crucial questions of ends and means (Eisler, 1990, 1991; Hutchinson, 1992b; Woolf, 1938).

The principle expressed here draws much of its inspiration from Gandhian, feminist, and other alternative knowledge traditions on nonviolence. In terms of choice and engagement in classroom pedagogies, it is worth recalling Huxley's (1937) observation:

> You cannot reach a given historical objective by walking in the opposite direction. If your goal is liberty and democracy, then you must teach people the arts of being free and of governing themselves. If you teach them ... the arts of bullying and passive obedience, then you will not achieve the liberty and democracy at which you are aiming. Good ends cannot be achieved by inappropriate means. That is why we find ourselves in our present predicament. (pp. 184–185)

A practical example at the school level of an attempt to address this predicament may be given. As part of the flow-on from a total school staff in-service held in the early 1990s on the theme "Educating for the 21st century," in which I was invited to participate as a critical friend, a number of initiatives have been taken. This 2-day in-service, which occurred at a nonmetropolitan, Catholic systemic high school, provided creative opportunities for teachers to imagine a better school for the early 21st century and to begin the processes of action planning. It also provided a forum to present dialogical research on student opinions at the school on probable and preferable futures both locally and globally.

In the ongoing processes of negotiating futures, several initiatives have been taken so far at this particular school. They have included initiatives relating to student government, an action-research project on cooperative learning that involves both science and humanities teachers, and another action-research project that seeks to lessen gender discrimination in the science classroom. In addition, there has been collaborative research on a "streamwatch" environmental project; practical work on infusing a Koori (Australian Aboriginal) perspective across the curriculum, including the introduction of a two-unit Aboriginal Studies course at the senior secondary level; and staff in-servicing on specific futures techniques in the classroom. There are other planned initiatives to link the formal and informal curriculum in more compatible ways. These include proposals for staff and student training in conflict resolution, the introduction of a peer mediation program and participation in a "global thinking" project that links schoolchildren internationally through computer networking. Many of the staff acknowledge that there is a long way to go but are positive, at least, that a start has been made on active journeys of hope (Hutchinson, 1992a).

Sites of Possibility

Major emphasis has been placed in this article on the importance of active listening to what young people have to say about the future, and on crucial questions of applied foresight that address young people's concerns, fears, and needs. In this, it is argued that schools may become less institutions of cultural reproduction, in which selective traditions propagate foreclosed images of what is "real" and what is "potential," and more sites of possibility. With the latter, applied foresight, skills of imagination and pro-social skills in areas such as conflict resolution and environmental literacy are cultivated.

For would-be journeyers into the 21st century, it is important to challenge fatalistic assumptions that trend is destiny and to resist counsels of "realism" that new ideas and imaginative approaches in education are "well meaning but unworkable." Undifferentiated or homogenous images of teachers as "structural dopes" and school students as "casualties of future shock" are far too superficial and stereotypic. Reality and potential reality in our schools and other formal and informal educational institutions are significantly more complex and negotiable than hard determinist narratives imply.

Possible "compass bearings" for enhancing nonviolent resistances in the formal and informal curriculum to colonization of the future have been suggested. They are by no means exhaustive. These "resources of hope" raise crucial questions about teacher education and curriculum design and practice in preparing for the 21st century. In this, there is an invitation for choice and engagement by teachers, parents, students, and schools. Both individually and collectively, some practical contributions may be made in our schools to negotiating a better world by taking, at least, the first tentative steps of journeys of active hope (see Table 2). As Mumford (1955) commented,

> When ... awakened personalties begin to multiply, the load of anxiety that hangs over ... our present-day culture will perhaps begin to lift. Instead of gnawing dread, there will be a healthy sense of expectancy, of hope without self-deception, based upon the ability to formulate new plans and purposes: Purposes which, because they grow out of a personal reorientation and renewal, will in time lead to a general replenishment of life. (p. 310)

Dogmatics about what is and what might be not only risk limiting our diagnostics but also our prognostics (Polak, 1971). Forms of medicine, like forms of literacy, that aspire to be authentically holistic do not take

Table 2. Hope, Literacy, and a Dialogue on Futures

Anticipations About the 21st Century	Related Motivational States
Hopelessness	Low self-esteem, feelings of worthlessness, impoverished creative imagination about social alternatives, flight, violence turned against self or others.
Passive hope	Bland optimism, technological cargo-cultism, reductionist literacies for accommodation to "future shock."
Active hope	Foresight, prosocial skills, appropriate assertiveness, enriched social imagination, optimal literacies for facilitating integration of the personal, the political, and the planetary.

as axiomatic only one true path of development (Eisler, 1990; Jones, 1993; Teixeira, 1992). They seek to learn from warning signs of negative trends, but also to transcend fatalistic assumptions of invariance or monocultural development on a dominator model. They take into account what Peavey (1986) aptly described as a "niche theory" of nonviolent resistances and social change. In so doing, they place emphasis on eco-relational thinking, on active listening to young people's voices on the future, and on an increased openness to possible insights and constructive ideas from various cultural lifeways and alternative knowledge traditions in starting open-ended journeys for well-being, peace, and active citizenship on planet Earth. They acknowledge, as commented by Tough (1991), that through the moral choices we make, to a greater or lesser extent, "each person shares in the destiny of all humankind" (p. 121). They recall the observation by Gandhi that whatever we choose to do or not do in the present as teachers, parents, and students cannot be without implications. "The future depends on what we do in the present" (cited in Larson & Micheels-Cyrus, 1986, p. 228).

References

Beare, H., & Slaughter, K. (1993). *Education for the 21st century.* London: Routledge.
Berrigan, D. (1981). *Ten commandments for the long haul.* Nashville, TN: Abington.
Bickmore, K., & Alternatives to Violence Committee. (1984). *Alternative to violence: A manual for teaching peacemaking to youth and adults.* Cleveland, OH: Alternatives to Violence Committee of the Cleveland Friends Meeting.
Boomer, C., & Torr, H. (1987). Becoming a powerful teacher. In D. Comber & J. Hancock (Eds.), *Developing teachers: A celebration of teachers learning in Australia.* North Ryde, Australia: Methuen.

F. P. Hutchinson

Boulding, E. (1988). *Building a global civic culture: Education for an interdependent world.* New York: Teachers College Press.

Boulding, E. (1991). The challenge of imaging peace in wartime. *Futures, 23,* 528–533.

Cooney, R., & Michalowski, H. (Eds.). (1987). *The power of the people.* Boston: New Society.

Curle, A. (1990). *Tools for transformation.* Stroud, United Kingdom: Hawthorn Press.

Eisler, R. (1990). *The chalice and the blade: Our history, our future.* Mandala, England: Unwin.

Eisler, R. (1991). Cultural evolution: Social shifts and phase changes. In E. Laszlo (Ed.), *The new evolutionary paradigm* (pp. 179–200). New York: Gordon & Breach.

Ekins, P. (1992). *A new world order: Grassroots movements for social change.* London: Routledge.

Flood, M., & Lawrence, A. (1987). *The community action book.* Sydney, Australia: Council of Social Service.

Fountain, S. (1990). Getting off to an early start in global education. *World Studies Journal, 8,* 1–2.

Freire, P., & Shor, I. (1987). *A pedagogy for liberation: Dialogues on transforming education.* London: Macmillan.

Galtung, J. (1990). *60 speeches on war and peace.* Oslo, Norway: International Peace Research Institute.

Hicks, D. (Interviewer). (1990). In Å. Bjerstedt, Peace education in school. *Peace, Environment and Education, 1*(2), 38–47.

Hicks, D. (1994). *Educating for the future: A practical classroom guide.* Godalming, England: World Wide Fund for Nature.

Hill, S., & Hill, T. (1990). *The collaborative classroom: A guide to cooperative learning.* Melbourne, Australia: Elanor Curtain.

Hutchinson, F. (1992a). *Futures consciousness and the school.* Unpublished doctoral dissertation, University of New England, Armidale, Australia.

Hutchinson, F. (1992b). Making peace with people and planet: Some important lessons from the Gandhian tradition in educating for the 21st century. *Peace, Environment and Education, 3*(3), 3–14.

Hutchinson, F. (1994a). Educating beyond fatalism and impoverished social imagination. In Å. Bjerstedt (Ed.), *Education beyond fatalism and hate* (pp. 24–45). Malmö, Sweden: School of Education.

Hutchinson, F. (1994b). Education beyond violent futures in children's media. *Futures, 26,* 5–23.

Hutchinson, F. (1996). *Educating beyond violent futures.* London: Routledge.

Hutchinson, F., Talbot, C., & Brown, L. (1992). *Our planet and its people.* Melbourne, Australia: Macmillan.

Hutchinson, F., & Waddell, L. (1986). *People, problems, and planet Earth.* Melbourne, Australia: Macmillan.

Huxley, A. (1937). *Ends and means.* London: Chatto & Windus.

Johnson, D. W., & Johnson, F. P. (1994). *Joining together: Group theory and group skills.* Boston: Allyn & Bacon.

Jones, K. (1993). *Beyond optimism: A Buddhist political ecology.* Oxford, England: Jon Carpenter.

Kagan, S. (1991). *Cooperative learning.* San Juan Capistrano, CA: Resources for Teachers.

Kaviratna, H. (Trans.). (1980). *Dhammapada.* Pasedena, CA: Theosophical University Press.

Kennedy, T., & Kelly, C. O. (1991). *All in: Cooperative education.* Melbourne, Australia: Curriculum Corporation and Ministry of Education.

Larson, J., & Micheels-Cyrus, M. (Eds). (1986). *Seeds of peace.* Philadelphia: New Society.

Laszlo, E. (1972). *Introduction to systems philosophy: Towards a new paradigm of contemporary thought.* New York: Gordon & Breach.

Mumford, L. (1955). *The human prospect.* Boston: Beacon.

Needham, J. (1969). *Within the four seas: The dialogue of East and West.* London: Allen & Unwin.

Page, J. (1996). Education systems as agents of change: An overview of futures education. In R. Slaughter (Ed.), *New thinking for a new millenium* (pp. 126–136). London: Routledge.

Peavey, F. (1986). *Heart politics.* Philadelphia: New Society.

Polak, F. L. (1971). *Prognostics.* Amsterdam: Elsevier.

Sharp, G. (1973). *The politics of non-violent action.* Boston: Porter Sargent.

Shields, K. (1991). *In the tiger's mouth: An empowerment guide for social action.* Sydney, Australia: Millennium.

Teixeira, B. (1992). *A Gandhian futurology.* Madurai, India: Valliammal Institution, Gandhian Museum.

Tough, A. (1991). *Crucial questions about the future.* Lanham, MD: University Press of America.

United Nations Educational, Scientific, and Cultural Organization. (1994). *Tolerance: The threshold of peace.* Paris: Author.

Waddell, L., & Hutchinson, F. (1988). *Learning for a fairer future.* Sydney, Australia: Geography Teachers Association and World Development Tea Cooperative.

Wilson-Fuller, J. (1990). *Will you please listen.* Sydney: Australian Broadcasting Commission.

Woolf, V. (1938). *Three guineas.* London: Hogarth.

Yutang, L. (Ed.). (1995). *The wisdom of China and India.* New York: Modern Library.

Appendix: Sample Futures Workshop

Active Citizenship and Nonviolent Social Change: Ideas Into Action

Purpose

To encourage students to do basic social research on techniques of nonviolent social change used by international nongovernmental organizations (INGOs) and nongovernmental organizations (NGOs). This is a good way to heighten awareness of participatory and democratic skills, skills employed by various groups in resisting their feared futures and working toward their preferred futures.

Preparation

• Gather case-study materials, both past and present, of ordinary people involved in social change. Consideration will need to be given here to age levels and to particular student interests or concerns.

• Arrange for school visits by various community groups involved in nonviolent social change (e.g., the Wilderness Society, Community Aid Abroad, World Development Tea Co-operative, Action for World Development, Greenpeace, Friends of the Earth, Amnesty International, Australian Conservation Foundation, United Nations Association). Many further useful suggestions are contained in Hutchinson and Waddell (1986), Flood and Lawrence (1987), Peavey (1986), and Shields (1991). Useful background works include Bickmore and Alternatives to Violence Committee (1984), Sharp (1973), and Cooney and Michalowski (1987). Hicks (1994) is an excellent source for practical ideas.

• Where possible, organize field research by students to study specific examples of groups involved in nonviolent social change (e.g., the Total Environment Centre, the Australian Consumers' Association, Community Aid Abroad, the Wilderness Society Shops). The lists of resource centers and contacts in Waddell and Hutchinson (1988) and Hutchinson, Talbot, and Brown (1992) are likely to assist your preparation.

Procedure

• Divide class into cooperative learning teams. For practical ideas, see Hill (1990), Kennedy and Kelly (1991), Kagan (1991), and Johnson and Johnson (1994).

• Distribute to each learning team a guide to strategic questioning (see Table A1).

• Allow each learning team sufficient time to prepare a joint presentation for the rest of the class on an INGO or NGO involved in nonviolent social change.

• Student presentations might include short talks, videotaped interviews, mindmapping, and dramatization around a theme, such as "What practical insights are gained about the way people may contribute to making their preferable futures more probable and their feared futures less probable?"

Table A1. Investigating an International Nongovernmental Organization (INGO) or a Nongovernmental Organization (NGO) Involved in Nonviolent Social Change

Some focus questions:

1. What are the visions of this organization or group?
2. What specific methods does it use in trying to translate its images for a better world into action?
3. What obstacles does it encounter?
4. What successes has it had?
5. What story does it tell about "people's power"?
6. How can I/we learn from the experiences of this organization or group in dealing more effectively with situations that concern me/us?

Discussion

Among the important follow-up points to raise is the issue of the sense of powerlessness and even fatalism that many young people have about the future, particularly the big problems.

- Are ordinary people essentially powerless to change their world for the better? Is the future like a rollercoaster in which we hurtle along determined by forces beyond our control?
- Do our studies of case material and field research confirm or question such assumptions? Are our worst fears for the future more likely to become self-fulfilling prophecies if we assume we can do nothing?
- How adequate are the orthodox and alternative concepts of power? What are the practical implications of each for what we do or would like to do in our daily lives?

Other points to highlight include the relative effectiveness of varying methods of nonviolent social change in different situations (e.g., letter writing, petitioning, lobbying, green bans, consumer boycotts, use of public access radio, and student representative councils).

Extension

Select someone past or present to study involved in nonviolent social change (see Table A2). Collect and research information about the life and work of this person. Role play an interview with this person. One student can take the role of the reporter and the other the role of the person involved in nonviolent action.

Table A2. Nonviolent Social Action

Example Role Model	Example NGOs, INGOs, and Social Change Movements Past and Present
Gandhi	Independence movement, India
Emily Pankhurst	Suffragist movement
Martin Luther King, Jr.	American Civil Rights movement
John Seed (Rainforest Information Centre), Bob Brown (Wilderness Society, Australia), and Aila Keto (winner of United Nations environmental award)	Conservation movement
Chicko Mendez (Rubber Tappers Union, Brazil)	Union movement
Archbishop Desmond Tutu (Nobel Peace Prize winner)	Anti-Apartheid movement, South Africa
Aung San Suu Kyi (Nobel Peace Prize winner)	Democratic movement, Burma
Bill Mollison (Alternative Nobel Peace Prize winner)	Permaculture and ethical investment movement
A spokesperson from Community Aid Abroad/Oxfam	Freedom from hunger and social justice movements
Stella and Helena Cornelius (Conflict Resolution Network, Australia)	Peace movement, Women's International League for Peace and Freedom, United Nations Association
Mum Shirl Smith (social justice worker), Joan Winch (WHO Sasaka prize winner), Kev Carmody (musician and songwriter), Pat O'Shane (Chancellor, University of New England)	Aboriginal social justice and land rights movement
A spokesperson from Amnesty International	Human rights movement
A spokesperson from Greenpeace, Worldwide Fund for Nature, Australian Conservation Foundation	Ecologically sustainable futures movement

Note. NGO = nongovernmental organization; INGO = international nongovernmental organization.

PEABODY JOURNAL OF EDUCATION, 71(3), 63–83

Peace Education in an Urban School District in the United States

Ian M. Harris

My kindergarten students at Sherman Multicultural Arts School in Milwaukee were dealing with the trauma of growing up in a violent society. Their personal encounters with violence were reflected daily in their journal dictations, class discussions and peer conversations. It was difficult for them to understand why Mom had been robbed, a bike had been stolen, an uncle was in jail.

I wanted to engage them in an activity that would make them aware of peaceful alternatives. Using Martin Luther King Jr. as a role model, we had enthusiastic discussions on how to bring peace into their lives. We decided to compile their ideas into a "big book" and entitled it "Living Together Better Peace by Peace."

Each page in the book concentrated on one area of the students' lives—family, school, neighborhood and world. They composed peaceful rules to live by, such as: "Don't get mad and throw things." "Stay away from guns." "Help old people clean up their yard." Their colorful drawings enlivened the text on each page.

IAN M. HARRIS *is Professor in the Department of Educational Policy and Community Studies, School of Education, University of Wisconsin–Milwaukee.*

Requests for reprints should be sent to Ian M. Harris, Department of Educational Policy and Community Studies, Enderis 529, School of Education, University of Wisconsin, P.O. Box 413, Milwaukee, WI 53201.

Students then signed a pledge at the end of the book: "I promise to be a peacemaker in my family, in my school, in my neighborhood, and in my world. I promise when I am old I will not forget to be a peacemaker."

Students read the book again and again, and we constantly referred to it when dealing with conflict resolution. A substitute teacher was impressed when one student reminded others to behave better because "we are the peacemakers." The children brought relatives and friends to school to see the book. When it won first place in the citywide Martin Luther King Jr. writing contest, the children were ecstatic.

Violence continued in our community—a young man was killed next to the peace mural on our playground. Our book seemed to be a comfort to the students at this time. All year, individually and as a group, they reached for the peace book more than any other. (Leahy, 1995, p. 7)

In a postmodern world, American children are being exposed to more violence than ever before (Children's Defense Fund, 1991). As violence from home and community creeps into elementary, middle, and high schools, school personnel in the 1990s throughout the United States have been constructing elaborate lessons about peace, violence, and conflict resolution. Problems created by the prevalence of handguns are particularly worrisome to teachers in urban school districts: "One out of every three children in metro Atlanta knows someone who has brought a gun to school. And one in five worries about falling victim to a gunshot at school" (Loupe & Shepard, 1993). In 1990, 2,162 young Americans were killed in school by firearms, and 5.3% of students carried a gun to school ("It's Not Just New York," 1992). A Justice Department survey in 1989 indicated that 7% of students said they were victims of violent crimes at school (Celis, 1993). In 1992, every school day 100,000 students toted guns to school, 160,000 skipped classes because they feared physical harm, 40 were hurt or killed by firearms, 6,250 teachers were threatened with bodily injury, and 260 teachers were physically assaulted ("Every School Day," 1993). Some commentators have gone so far as to state that children in inner-city areas are suffering from stress disorders similar to what children in war-torn areas experience:

Today there are war conditions, and war effects, in many urban neighborhoods. A recent study found similar posttraumatic stress disorders in children in war-torn Mozambique, Cambodia, the West

Bank—and Chicago. The disorders may include inability to concentrate, persistent sleep disturbance, flashbacks, sudden startling and hypervigilence, nihilistic and fatalistic orientation toward the future, leading to increased risk taking. To be a witness to violence is to be a victim of violence. (Will, 1993, p. 48)

Many teachers are responding to increased levels of violence in punitive ways with tighter discipline and threats that include suspension, expulsion, weapons sweeps, locker searches, and even metal detectors (Harrington-Lueker, 1992). Others, who are concerned about violence in their students' lives, are teaching young people alternatives to violence. These peace educators rely on the principles of nonviolence to teach children how to manage conflict peacefully (Harris, 1988).

Interest in peace education has grown considerably since the 1980s. Teachers throughout the United States are using the insights of peace education under the following headings—school-based conflict management, environmental education, global studies, multicultural awareness, peer mediation, and violence prevention (Deutsch, 1991). In a postmodern world, teachers are starting to understand that children's deep concerns about violence are having a negative impact on their abilities to master cognitive assignments in schools (Craig, 1993). Some examples of peace education reform efforts include the following:

- In New York City in 1992, a violence prevention program in 100 schools is credited with reducing classroom fights by 71%.
- Created by Deborah Prothrow-Stith, assistant dean at the Harvard School of Public Health, an interactive course called "Violence Prevention Curriculum for Adolescents" is used by schools in 400 cities.
- In Chicago, a three-tier violence-prevention course involving students, teachers, and parents is being used by 4,000 students in 16 inner-city schools. (Holmstrom, 1993)

In 1988, the state of Oregon passed a law requiring all schools to teach about peace, and school districts in many large cities (Berkeley, CA; Hartford, CT; and Milwaukee, WI) have passed resolutions mandating peace studies. In describing this recent growth in peace education activities, Helen Swan, a Kansas City, Missouri social worker and the creator of a conflict resolution curriculum used in more than 100 schools, says, "Over the past three years, many schools have initiated antiviolence programs from kindergarten through high school. A lot of state departments of education have mandated programs" (cited in Holmstrom, 1993). This concern about violence in schools has been reflected at the national level with the Goals 2000: Educate America Act, which states as one of its goals that by the year 2000 every school in the United States will be free of violence.

Peace education reform efforts in the United States take many different forms but have similar goals—to appreciate the richness of the concept of peace, to address fears, to provide information about security, to understand violent behavior, to develop intercultural understanding, to provide a future orientation, to teach peace as a process, to promote a concept of peace accompanied by social justice, to stimulate a respect for life, and to end violence (Harris, 1990).

This article will provide a case study of efforts by teachers in a large urban school district in the United States to address problems of violence by using peace education strategies. It will describe district-wide initiatives, summarize curricular reforms at the elementary and secondary levels, and mention how teachers in this urban district are teaching alternative dispute resolution techniques. These approaches to peace education help young people learn about the roots of violence, and create an appreciation for how nonviolence can resolve conflicts peacefully.

Peace Education in Milwaukee

In 1985, the school district in Milwaukee, Wisconsin adopted a resolution endorsing peace studies at all levels and developed a peace studies curriculum (Haessley, 1991). Although the peace studies curriculum in Milwaukee Public Schools (MPS) originally emphasized the threat of nuclear war, by 1990 teachers in Milwaukee were focusing their efforts on violence in schools, homes, and urban communities. Milwaukee, like many other urban areas in the United States, has experienced escalating levels of homicide, drug-related violence, domestic abuse, street crime, and gang violence. In 1993, 19 children under the age of 18 in Milwaukee were shot dead, and 144 were wounded (Bothwell & Lawrence, 1994). Numerous other children were traumatized by these events. Teachers in Milwaukee have been using this peace curriculum and a variety of other conflict resolution techniques to help resolve some of the tensions created by such high levels of violence. These peace education reforms have two goals. One is to help young people settle down in schools so that they will not be so distracted by violence that they cannot focus on their lessons. The other is to teach children coping mechanisms so that they can peacefully manage conflicts in their lives. Similar attempts to initiate peace education strategies are occurring throughout urban school systems in the United States (Bernat, 1993).

The MPS peace curriculum is divided into three sections—elementary, middle school, and high school. The elementary curriculum has activities that can be added to already existing lessons and is organized along the following lines:

* Kindergarten—friendship.
* First grade—people packages.
* Second grade—feelings, my own and others.
* Third grade—respecting the community and all those in it.
* Fourth grade—getting along and working together.
* Fifth grade—cause and effect in history and today.
* Sixth grade—getting along peacefully in the world. (MPS, 1985)

Each section has a selected bibliography and a glossary.

The MPS middle school peace education curriculum focuses on conflict resolution and problem solving. It provides strategies that include taking turns, negotiating, compromising, communication clarification, ventilating, apologizing, exaggeration, sharing, avoiding conflict, acknowledging feelings, and appeals to authority. It has a section on nonrecommended strategies and a section on helping students make decisions. It also encourages students and teachers to explore community, national, and global conflicts.

The original MPS high school curriculum directly addressed the nuclear threat. In a postmodern world, this curriculum has been rewritten to stress human rights, domestic violence, the contributions of peace movements, and nonviolence.

Seven years after MPS first created its peace studies curriculum, one fourth of the schools in Milwaukee indicated that over half their staff is teaching this curriculum (Harris, 1995). At 9% of the 160 schools in Milwaukee the entire staff is involved in efforts to teach about peace and nonviolence. In 1991, the whole school system adopted a set of goals (MPS, 1991) that include the following:

* Students will demonstrate positive attitudes toward life, living, and learning through an understanding and respect of self and others.
* Students will make responsible decisions, solve problems, and think critically.

- Students will demonstrate responsible citizenship and an understanding of global interdependence.
- Students will learn strategies to cope with the challenges of daily living and will establish practices that promote health, fitness, and safety. (p. 4)

These goals support peace education efforts by staff at an urban district located in the 18th largest metropolitan area in the United States. Teachers in Milwaukee have adopted a broad variety of peace education strategies at all levels from kindergarten to high school. The central office at MPS provides considerable support in the area of violence prevention and peer mediation. The school board and superintendent have been outspoken in their efforts to promote nonviolence in schools.

Elementary Schools With Peace Themes

Many elementary schools in Milwaukee have adopted peace themes and activities. Staff at 38th Street School emphasize the concept *peace works,* and recognize student peacemakers on a daily basis. Desmond Tutu, the Nobel Peace Prize laureate from South Africa, visited this school on May 15, 1995 and autographed his facsimile on a mural that contains depictions of 10 Nobel peace winners at the entrance to the school. At this inner-city school, students write about peace, discuss what attributes a peacemaker holds, and create art activities on peace themes. Students who are "stressed out" or are disruptive are sent to a "Self Direction and Responsibility Center," where they discuss in-depth their problems with an African American male safety aide attached to the school. Escuela Fratney, a bilingual school, has developed a thematic curriculum based on the following four themes: (a) we respect ourselves and others, (b) we communicate, (c) we make a difference on planet Earth, and (d) we tell our stories to the world. A new urban Waldorf school has a philosophy based on peace, as do two elementary Montessori schools. At Fairview School, all the teachers promote a program called "Stop and Think" that teaches three ways to respond to conflict: (a) call an adult, (b) walk away, and (c) talk it out. The principal credits this program with completely turning around the climate at Fairview. When she first came there 5 years ago, the school was chaotic and dangerous, with high rates of student turnover. Now there is almost no mobility and Fairview has a long waiting list of children who want to attend.

Several elementary schools in Milwaukee have adopted a special assembly that gives awards to students who have made distinguished contributions to keeping the peace. Other schools award the "good citizen for the semester," to a student who has taken leadership in promoting and encouraging peaceful behavior. Other schools have held pep rallies for peace. Such acknowledgment of peacemaking helps students feel that these are significant activities, and counterbalances public perceptions of peacemaking as being cowardly or weak.

Many elementary schools in Milwaukee are seeking ways to help children deal with the strong emotions associated with violence. At some of the Montessori classes, teachers start the day with a circle where students can say anything they like about their own lives. Often in these sessions pupils will mention violent episodes, and receive support for their feelings both from their teacher and their peers. A similar tactic is a family meeting in class, or even a "me" box, where students can write down personal issues, place them in the box, and then pull them out to discuss them. Such activities allow children to express their concerns about violence in nonthreatening ways. Some teachers post charts on their bulletin boards that demonstrate positive and constructive ways to deal with anger. Other teachers are working on self-esteem exercises and positive pledges that help counteract negative messages some children receive at home.

Peace educators try to create a safe space where children who come from violent homes and communities can express anger constructively, instead of it erupting destructively at teachers and other students. Staff at one inner-city school in Milwaukee wrote a grant to hire two art therapists to work with children who had been traumatized by high levels of violence. Peace educators appreciate the legitimacy of this anger and teach their students appropriate ways to express it. A research study has shown that the Montessori schools with their comprehensive peace philosophy have by far the most peaceful effect on students (Harris & Callender, 1995).

As part of its commitment to the peace education, the Division of Psychological Services at MPS has trained teachers in all 100 elementary schools in the district in the Second Step Curriculum (Committee for Children, 1989). This curriculum contains lessons on impulse control, emotional expression, perspective taking, problem solving, and anger management. This skill-based curriculum is designed as an insert into existing lessons. A teacher using the second step curriculum receives a series of 3×2 ft (0.9×0.6 m) posters, each of which shows a photograph exhibiting children in a conflict situation. On the backs of the photographs are a series of questions that teachers read to students to get them to improve their level of awareness of certain key components to peacemaking. Even though staff at all schools have received this training, not all staff are using it. At some schools, teachers are reluctant to try anything new, whereas at other schools individual teachers have enthusiastically endorsed this curriculum and claim it has helped reduce hostile, aggressive acts in their classes.

Junior High School Efforts in Peace Education

Many junior high school teachers in Milwaukee have been striving to help young people think about peace. In the 1987–1988 school year, Fritsche Middle School—which was a typical urban middle school with high rates of suspension, failure, and fighting—received a new principal committed to the principles of peace education. The next year he started a peer mediation program. In the 1991–1992 academic year, students at Fritsche Middle School provided peer mediation services with 273 mediations. In this time period, the suspension rate of his school has declined from 31% to 10%. A physical education teacher at Fritsche helps run support groups after school for children who have experienced a death of a family member, who have witnessed violent acts, or who have a relative in prison. A teacher aide runs a 10-week anger management group for students whose disruptive behavior puts them "at risk." The slogan of this school is "Where Knowledge Builds Peace." These efforts have completely turned around this school. The course failure rate has decreased from 10% of the courses failed in 1989–1990 to 4.4% of courses failed in 1992–1993. Parental involvement has increased and grade point averages have increased. Even more significant, the number of African American students who request Fritsche as their first choice has doubled from 67 to 131 in the past 3 years. (Fritsche is located in a White part of Milwaukee's south side where African Americans do not always feel welcome.) The principal's goal, at this school, was to help this middle school to achieve the same status as highly popular specialty middle schools. He accomplished this with a daily attendance rate of 86.7%, which is similar to the rate at specialty schools, and by the high number of students that request Fritsche as their first choice. He attributes his success to peace education.

Teachers at Grand Avenue Middle School focus on future education emphasizing different ways of thinking about peace and nonviolence. One teacher at this school has been assigned to spend her full day in a "Working Out Room," where teachers send referrals—students who have participated in or seen some horrible acts of violence and are too traumatized to participate effectively in normal classrooms. Walker

Middle School has an emphasis on international studies, human rights, the United Nations, multicultural education, and celebrations of holidays all from all areas of the world. Students there can study the following languages: Japanese, French, German, and Spanish. Each homeroom at Walker has a country it emphasizes. A unitized curriculum, with four teachers (English, math, social studies, and science) focuses on a particular country for each marking period. During one marking period in the eighth grade students focus on traditional peace issues.

Other junior high schools use the occasion of Martin Luther King, Jr.'s birthday (a federal holiday in January) to start a peace week, when they conduct activities like having each homeroom present an assembly to the whole school on peace themes. Junior high schools in Milwaukee have also been promoting mentoring programs with local businesses so that young men can learn positive, nonviolent notions of masculinity to offset some of violent images they see in the media. One junior high school, Parkman, established a "love wall" where students could place mementos of youth they knew who had died or been injured by handguns. Teachers were amazed at how quickly this wall filled up with pictures and poems about young people who had been killed or wounded. This exercise helped teach all people in the school compassion for the victims of urban violence.

These activities help young people develop beliefs so that they can appreciate how peace strategies can deal constructively with problems of violence. Junior high school students look to adults to construct their own ideologies. They can learn alternative dispute resolution techniques from teachers who promote peace. Thought patterns adopted by children in this age range, 10 to 13, will last a lifetime. Urban youth in the United States approaching adolescence are often immersed in violent behavior in their homes and inundated by violent media images. For those children who come from violent homes, crime-ridden neighborhoods, or both, the presence or caring adults who teach alternatives to violence can make a huge difference in how they respond to conflict. Young people who never learn about nonviolence will not know how to create a peaceful world when they are adults.

High School Responses

Adolescents in urban school districts in the United States face enormous challenges, confronting decisions about sex, pregnancy, alcohol, drugs, depression, and suicide. To gain approval from their peers, some have to be tough and even commit violent acts. At one high school in Milwaukee, half the students indicated that they knew someone who had been violently murdered. Even for those students who do not personally experience violence, news reports full of violent stories about young people being killed or wounded—some in deliberate gang-related deaths, some in random acts of violence—cause youth to fear for their lives. Urban adolescents in a postmodern world, often without the guidance of adults, help friends grieve tragic losses, as well as figure out how to achieve safety in communities where terrifying levels of violence pose a constant threat. Peace educators help teens address these challenges by empowering them to solve their problems, resolve conflicts nonviolently, express their feelings in healthy ways, and communicate effectively with parents, siblings, and peers.

In several Milwaukee high schools, students in "Stop the Violence" clubs act out their feelings about violence in role plays. They perform skits that involve young people in role plays where they can learn nonviolent ways to respond to violent street incidents where young people are being assaulted and killed for clothing. The Human Relations staff at Central Office has worked with high school students to give them an appreciation of differences and identify their biases. High school teachers in Milwaukee committed to the peace education curriculum attempt to move beyond tolerance by inviting students from different cultures to brainstorm solutions for the problems of violence.

At Riverside University High School, the open education program had in 1992 a curricular theme on peace and nonviolence. As part of this theme, 300 students spent 1 day at the University of Wisconsin–Milwaukee, where they heard a keynote speech on the power of love and attended workshops on different aspects of peace. They created a Haunted Hunger House and donated proceeds to the hunger task force. They also established a living museum honoring their African American heritage. During the spring they built a giant wall of peace, with each student adding a brick that had his or her wishes for peace. Students divided themselves into mock neighborhood councils to suggest solutions for violence in their communities and held a peace Olympics.

Several high schools have held classes specifically geared toward helping adolescents understand the causes of violence. At Pulaski High School, a history teacher offers a one semester course, "Alternatives to Violence," in which he encourages seniors and juniors to discuss problems of violence in their lives, inspires them to seek solutions, and lets them ventilate some of their fears. During the spring of 1993, at Washington High School a social worker from the Walkers Point Youth and Family Center cotaught a home economics class on nurturing. This class comes as a response from lobbying efforts by community clinics that have adopted for teenage parents a three-part nurturing curriculum that, in the 10th grade, teaches nurturing the self; in the 11th grade, nurturing family and community; and in the 12th grade, nurturing children (Bavolek, Dravage, & Elliot, 1992). These programs are offered on a counseling, as opposed to a didactic, format. Students meet in small groups and discuss stresses in their environment. They receive support from their peers, which helps heal wounds that can lead to hatred, frustration, depression, rage, and further violence. Nurturing programs also teach assertive skills, self-respect, respect for others, care taking, empathy, appropriate roles, and nonviolent, nonpunitive ways of managing behavior.

Two half-year classes at 2 of 12 high schools in Milwaukee do not represent a high proportion of teachers adopting peace education reforms. They are just a tip of the iceberg. "Stop the Violence" groups provide a vehicle for students to express their anguish about violence. High school teachers are infusing peace education concepts into their existing classes—teaching about the war in Vietnam in history classes, emphasizing the contributions of peace movements to U.S. history, choosing literature that speaks to the problems of urban violence in English, or teaching about ecological security in biology. Other teachers committed to peace education reforms are explaining the interdependent nature of the human species in a global village with shrinking resources and an instantaneous planetary communications system. There are many clever ways that teachers can teach peace concepts in contemporary high schools, that is, what does the situation in Somalia portend for residents in the United States? Many of the 14 high schools in Milwaukee have peer mediation programs and are receiving peer mediators trained in middle schools, whose skills at negotiating school hostilities are helping resolve tensions within the increasingly stratified nature of urban high schools, whose students are dividing into hostile, warring camps that are often armed.

Peer Mediation

By far the fastest growing and most widely accepted aspect of peace education reforms is peer mediation, which has "improved quality of life on the playground, in the lunchroom and halls, and in the classroom" (Gentry & Benenson, 1992, p. 101) by training students to be mediators, so that when students are facing conflicts at school, they don't need to go to adults to solve their conflicts. Rather, they can solve them nonviolently themselves using skills they have learned as peer mediators (Kreidler, 1990). School mediation programs were initiated in 1982 by the Community Boards program in San Francisco. Research studies about peer mediation have indicated results similar to those stated in the following: "The teachers reported that after the training conflicts among students became less severe and destructive. Conflicts referred to the teacher were reduced by 80 percent and the number of conflicts referred to the principal was reduced to zero" (Johnson, Johnson, & Dudley, 1992, p. 93).

Students in all school settings face daily conflicts that include put downs, teasing, playground conflicts, physical aggression and fights, academic work conflicts, and turn taking. Most youth are not taught how to manage these conflicts constructively. Research shows that young people taught alternative dispute resolution techniques in schools often take them back into their communities helping parents, friends, and relatives resolve conflicts nonviolently (Stichter, 1986).

Over half the schools in Milwaukee now have school-based conflict management programs. Peer mediations most frequently occur in problems where students are hassling each other, fighting, having disagreements, or spreading rumors. In a typical school, one staff member will be given release time to train and supervise mediators who are chosen sometimes by teachers, but often by peers. After these students are trained, they mediate conflicts in the school. Students will write a note about a conflict and place it in a box in their classroom. At a regular time each day the teacher will collect these notes and assign the students who have the conflict to go to the area of the school set aside for peer mediation and let the students work out a solution.

School mediation programs have been especially successful in school yards and in dealing with bullies who lack empathy and want authority over others. Peer mediators assigned to playgrounds are given T-shirts so that they are easily identified. When the mediators spot a nonphysical conflict they approach the pupils involved. If there is a physical conflict, the mediators don't get involved. When they approach a nonphysical conflict, they must first introduce themselves and then ask those involved if they would like help solving their problem. If one or more of the parties do not want help, the mediators walk away. If parties agree to accept help, the mediators take the disputants through a structured process to resolve their conflict.

Mediation requires students to use active listening skills to mirror back to disputants their disagreements. This process teaches positive communication and problem-solving skills that help improve a school's environment. Mediators help young people listen to each other to keep conversations going, encourage disputants to find a solution, and serve as witnesses to any agreement reached (Johnson & Johnson, 1991). One principal involved in this program at a Milwaukee elementary school—who saw a 50% drop in the number of problems referred to his office—suggested that all students should go through the peer mediation program because it teaches leadership, communication skills, and conflict resolution, along with many other necessary skills students need to live and work with others.[1] A Milwaukee teacher who is the peer mediator trainer at her elementary school made the following comment:

> There was a fight in the hall today between two eighth graders. I was just trying to conduct traffic when I overheard some other students saying that those fighting should try to work something out and that it is stupid to fight. I also saw an improvement in attitudes of those students who are peer mediators. It was not only the "best" students (the quiet ones who turn in their homework and never cause trouble) that become peer mediators. Some were students who seem to be involved in so many of conflicts at school and now see themselves as having an important role in the school.[2]

Peer mediation and school-based conflict management programs help put out fires in schools. Research has shown that these programs can make schools safer (Burrell & Vogl, 1990). Student mediators at Fritsche Middle School reported to this investigator that their lives with family members and friends were less violent because of the peer mediation training. Several reported that they had been called on to mediate disputes with their friends, but that it "doesn't work with strangers."[3] Peer mediation helps create a more positive school climate, teaches students with skills to manage conflicts constructively, and provides students with a technique to address violence their lives. One principal in Milwaukee—who attributes peer mediation with greatly improving the climate at his school—told this investigator that peer mediation helps students internalize appropriate behavior, as opposed to having adults telling children how to behave (see Footnote 3). Through alternative dispute mechanisms, students learn practical skills about how to put out fires, but do not necessarily address the larger question of why these fires get started in the first place. Mediation is a tool that empowers young people to solve their conflicts. Instead of using force, they use their hearts and brains to reconcile differences.

[1] Reported by a teacher who ran the peer mediation program at that school.
[2] From a paper submitted by a graduate student to meet the requirements of a course, "Peace Education," taught by Ian M. Harris.
[3] From an interview at Fritsche Middle School, January 6, 1994.

I. M. Harris

System-Wide Training in Nonviolence

Staff at the MPS central office committed to the principles of peace education reform have been addressing problems of violence in the schools. The guidance staff has developed a change curriculum that teaches positive communication skills, self-esteem, decision making, problem-solving skills, and anger management. The human relations staff has been providing peer mediation training, offering curricula dealing with conflict prevention, and giving workshops for students in communications and cultural awareness. The office of psychological services at MPS has been promoting a Second Step violence prevention program that targets elementary schools in an effort to decrease the underlying propensity toward violence and the use of violence as a coping strategy for youth.

For the past 4 years, the staff development academy at MPS has sponsored inservice workshops for teachers on peace education. These workshops acquaint teachers with peace education curricula and challenge them to consider how they can apply the insights of nonviolence to their classrooms. They also require teachers to develop peace education lesson plans for their classes.

Most recently, the Milwaukee Board and School Directors and Superintendent established "Schools Against Violence Week," which began on January 16, 1994 with a moment of silence in memory of 30 children who were slain during 1993:

> Superintendent Howard L. Fuller will offer advice to parents on how they can demonstrate non-violent behavior at home. He will also advise parents on how to manage their anger when disciplining their children. ... Children will be encouraged to offer suggestions on how to make their communities safer. ... One aim of the anti-violence week is to inspire students to supply ideas themselves. ... Students will also write reports and create banners based on a theme of nonviolence. (Lawrence, 1993, p. B1)

Most recently, in August of 1995, the Milwaukee School board of Directors passed a resolution expanding these efforts by endorsing a peace month that goes from December 10 (the anniversary of the signing of the Universal Declaration of Human Rights) until January 15 (the anniversary of Dr. Martin Luther King, Jr.'s birthday).

Despite recent budget cuts, the Milwaukee School Board and superintendent have preserved efforts to promote peace in the schools. They realize that peace education activities are badly needed to give students who come from extremely violent backgrounds a positive view of the future. Education is, after all, a future-oriented activity. Juveniles who despair about their futures will not be motivated to get an education. How are taxpayers benefitting from their investment in public schools if youths are shot, killed, maimed, or become cynical and despairing because they cannot manage violence in their lives?

Principles of Modern Peace Education Reform

Many contemporary school reform efforts fail to address the impact of violence on education. Children who are either traumatized or distraught by violence cannot focus clearly on the cognitive tasks presented in school settings and hence are either failing or at risk of failure. This article has demonstrated how school personnel in a large district in the United States have responded to escalating levels of violence by promoting peace education. Results from Milwaukee indicate that peace education reforms can improve urban schools. When the principal and staff adopt these reforms, schools have shown an increase in attendance, grade point averages, parent involvement, and a decrease in suspensions and expulsions. Administrators committed to the goals of peace education rely on a nonpunitive approach to discipline, where students learn to take responsibility for their actions and seek alternatives to violence. At schools committed to these reforms, student mobility rates have declined. Schools that are peaceful have long waiting lists of students. The word gets out into the community. Parents want their children to attend schools that have a reputation for being nonviolent.

Despite the important gains made by peace education reforms at some Milwaukee schools, not all school personnel are embracing these reform efforts. Peace education in Milwaukee works best where a strong principal motivates staff to pursue alternatives to violence. In most schools, teachers and administrators still use punitive measures to punish students distraught by violence who are acting out in classrooms. Many of the professional staff do not believe in the power of peace to address the problems of school failure in an urban area. Adults who believe in retribution resort to suspensions and expulsions to get rid of troublesome students. They believe that punishment provides security, and do not take time out from teaching traditional curricula to teach children about nonviolence and peace. Many teachers who feel inadequate to handle the psychological trauma brought on by violence in their students' lives do not create spaces in their daily routines for children to talk about the impact of violence on their lives. Others have neither the time nor inclination to learn new conflict resolution skills so they can teach them to children. Beset by many demands, they have no energy to adopt new reforms. As mentioned earlier, despite a board mandate promoting peace education, the majority of teachers in the MPS system are not involved in peace education reform efforts. Many teachers, faced with angry, hostile students, are growing cynical and bitter. They see no way out of the endless cycles of violence that seem to be engulfing both them and their students.

Reflection on 10 years of peace educational practice in the MPS system provides some principles for peace education reform: All children can benefit from peace education, violence has a profound emotional impact on young people, peace education has a broader realm than conflict resolution, all courses can incorporate peace concepts, and all teachers can use a peaceful pedagogy.

All Children Can Benefit From Peace Education

Although this article has highlighted peace education efforts in an urban school district, violence presents problems in schools in many different communities. Suburban and rural communities are struggling with how to deal with weapons in school. Young people raised in dysfunctional homes need adult care and compassion to help them develop a sense of security. Ignoring problems caused by violence can contribute to despair on the part of youth preoccupied with problems of violence. Peace educators do more than teach people how to stop violence. By spelling out conditions for positive peace, they provide all children with hopeful images for their future.

Violence Has a Profound Emotional Impact on Young People

Compassion, caring, nurturing, and friendship are some of the many tools of peacemaking that should be taught in schools to help overcome the academic failings in a postmodern world where high levels of violence cause youth to despair about the future. Peace educators provide important role models for students troubled by violence who have been wounded either physically or psychologically. Teachers who encourage students to talk about their experiences with violence can, through active listening, heal some of the hurt of these wounds. To help their students manage their anger, teachers have to be skilled in effective educational techniques. Children distraught by violence need adult nurturing to overcome their fears so that they can focus on cognitive tasks in schools.

Peace Education Has a Broader Realm Than Conflict Resolution

School-based conflict management techniques provide skills to help students deal with anger in productive ways, but peace education explores the roots of violence. Peer mediation can make schools a safer place, but peace education implies much more than learning how to solve conflicts. Peace educators teach about ways to create just social and personal relations that preclude violence. They instruct their students about the causes of violence, both physical and structural. They enlighten their students about the skills of peacemaking, but not only in the spirit of trying to promote better behavior in schools. Peace education teaches nonviolent alternatives to solve problems of violence in the broader society, not just in the schools.

All Courses Can Incorporate Peace Concepts

The experience of Milwaukee has shown that peace education can be infused throughout the curriculum. Classroom teachers use the insights of peace education to help pupils deal with conflicts in all classrooms. Young children can learn peacemaking skills, even though they may not be able to articulate abstract thoughts about peace. Up to the age of 10, young people tend to personalize enemies, but after age 10 young people are more interested about conflicts between groups. After age 13, young people start to ask questions about why there are so many conflicts. Teachers in all classes can figure out how to get students to articulate concerns about violence and teach different aspects of peace to youth who often become cynical and despairing about a world sinking into more desperate levels of violence.[4]

---

[4]It should be noted that Milwaukee was the home of Jeffrey Dahmer, one of the most nefarious mass murderers in the U.S. history, who ate the remains of his victims.

I. M. Harris

All Teachers Can Use a Peaceful Pedagogy

Peace educators do not rely on domination, but rather establish democratic classrooms where teachers and students together explore the impact of violence on their lives. These teaching methodologies, by using the principles of cooperative learning, motivate students and result in better student retention. Being in a secure environment will increase the ability of students in today's schools to learn cognitive material. The emphasis on competition—in school reform proposals advanced during the 1980s—has increased student insecurity about the future. In a postmodern world with fewer and fewer good-paying jobs, schools have become a vicious track meet with the losers being placed on the slag heaps of humanity. Peace pedagogy encourages students to share concerns and pool resources to seek solutions to the terrible problems of violence they see all around them.

There exist many excellent resources for teachers and school personnel who want to learn about peace education. Teachers do not have to invent the wheel in order to infuse peace education curricula into their classes. After 20 years of practice, many fine curricula demonstrate how to teach peace in age-appropriate ways (see Appendix A). There are also many organizations that can provide training and resources for practitioners (see Appendix B).

Contemporary calls to restructure schools and even privatize schools overlook a responsibility of adults to provide a secure environment for young people. Teachers adopting peace education reforms are attempting to live up to that responsibility, although their efforts are often overwhelmed in a culture where 80% of the parents believe it is appropriate to use physical punishment (spanking) and the media is replete with violent images. Peace education, which provides students with information about how to deal with conflict nonviolently, can contribute a small part to the solution to the problems caused by school failure in a postmodern world. However, it is not a panacea. As peace researchers have pointed out, the problems of violence in the modern world are structural. In its impact, peace education in many ways parallels sex education. Many young people who learn about safe sex practices in school choose to ignore them. Likewise, a young person who has learned conflict resolution techniques in school may not use them on the street—especially when he or she looks at the adult world, which is well armed, and resorts to peace through strength to resolve its conflicts. Peace through strength uses force to destroy, subdue, or intimidate enemies. Peace educators assume that humans can be educated to behave in civilized ways.

References

Bavolek, S. J., Dravage, K. A., & Elliot, L. D. (1992). *Developing nurturing schools: A school based curriculum for senior high school.* Oak City, UT: Family Development Resources.

Bernat, V. (1993). Teaching peace. *Young Children, 48*(3), 36–39.

Bothwell, A., & Lawrence, C. (1994, January 2). Gunfire takes a huge toll on kids—320 injured in past two years here. *Milwaukee Journal,* p. 1.

Burrell, N., & Vogl, S. (1990). Turf-side conflict mediation for students. *Mediation Quarterly, 7,* 237–250.

Celis, W., III. (1993, April 23). School crime. *New York Times,* p. 9.

Children's Defense Fund. (1991). *The state of America's children.* Washington, DC: Author.

Committee for Children. (1989). *Second step: A violence preparation curriculum.* Seattle, WA: Author.

Craig, S. E. (1993). The educational needs of children living with violence. *Phi Delta Kappan, 1*(74), 67–71.

Deutsch, M. (1991). Educating beyond hate. *Peace, Environment and Education, 2*(4), 3–19.

Every school day ... . (1993, January 25). *Time,* p. 23.

Gentry, B. G., & Benenson, W. A. (1992). School-age peer mediators transfer knowledge and skills to home setting. *Mediation Quarterly, 10,* 101–109.

Haessley, J. (1991). Peace education in Milwaukee. *Peace in Action, 5*(1), 36–39.

Harrington-Lueker, D. (1992). Blown away by school violence. *Education Digest, 58*(11), 50–54.

Harris, I. (1988). *Peace education.* Jefferson, NC: McFarland.

Harris, I. (1990). The goals of peace education. *Peace Review, 2*(2), 1–4.

Harris, I. (1995, February 2). Ten years of peace education in Milwaukee Public Schools. *Shepard Express,* pp. 10–11.

Harris, I., & Callender, A. (1995). Comparative study of peace education approaches and their effectiveness. *The NAMTA Journal, 20,* 133–145.

Holmstrom, D. (1993, September). The art of undoing violence is finding its own place in classrooms and streets. *Christian Science Monitor,* p. 8.

It's not just New York ... . (1992, March 9). *Newsweek,* p. 35.

Johnson, D. W., & Johnson, R. T. (1991). *Our mediation notebook.* Edina, MN: Interaction.

Johnson, D. W., Johnson, R. T., & Dudley, B. (1992). Effects of peer mediation training on elementary school students. *Mediation Quarterly, 10,* 89–97.

Kreidler, W. (1990). Conflict resolution land: A round trip tour. *ESR Journal, 1*(1), 41–45.

Lawrence, C. (1993, December 22). Schools to remember 30 slain children. *Milwaukee Journal,* p. B1.

Leahy, J. (1995). Peace by peace. *Teaching Tolerance, 4*(2), 7.

Loupe, D., & Shepard, B. (1993, April 13). A common sight for students: Guns at school. *Atlanta Constitution,* p. A1.

Milwaukee Public Schools. (1985). *Peace studies guide for elementary teachers: Activities for facilitating a more peaceful and harmonious classroom, school, and world.* Milwaukee, WI: Department of Curriculum and Instruction.

Milwaukee Public Schools. (1991). *K–12 teaching and learning: A working document.* Milwaukee, WI: Department of Curriculum and Instruction.

Stichter, C. (1986). When tempers flare, let trained student mediators put out the flames. *American School Board Journal, 173,* 41–42.

Will, G. (1993, March 22). "Medicine" for "724 children." *Newsweek,* p. 48.

Appendix A

Following are some of the many fine curricula that will provide teachers with ample resources to begin teaching peace education concepts:

Alternatives to Violence (Cleveland, OH: Friends Meeting, 1984)

Children's Creative Approaches to Conflict (Nyack, NY: Fellowship of Reconciliation, 1983)

Conflict Management: A Curriculum for Peacemaking (Denver, CO: Cornerstone, 1983)

Creative Conflict Solving for Kids (Miami, FL: Grace Contrino Abrams Peace Education Foundation, 1985)

Choices: A Unit on Conflict and Nuclear War (Washington, DC: Union of Concerned Scientists, 1983)

Decision Making in a Nuclear Age (Weston, MA: Haycon House, 1983)

Dialogue: A Teaching Guide to Nuclear Issues (Cambridge, MA: Educators for Social Responsibility, 1983)

Education for Peace and Justice (St. Louis, MO: Institute for Peace & Justice, 1981)

Elementary Perspectives 1: Teaching Concepts of Peace and Conflict (Boston, MA: Educators for Social Responsibility, 1990)

Keeping the Peace: Practicing Cooperation and Conflict Resolution With Preschoolers (Philadelphia, PA: New Society, 1989)

The Friendly Classroom for a Small Planet (Wayne, NJ: Avery Publishing, 1978)

Learning Peace, Teaching Peace (Philadelphia, PA: Jane Addams Peace Association, 1974)

Learning the Skills of Peacemaking (Rolling Hills Estates, CA: Jalmar Press, 1987)

Let's Talk About Peace: Let's Talk About Nuclear War (Oakland, CA: Parenting in Nuclear Age, 1983)

A Manual on Nonviolence and Children (Philadelphia, PA: New Society, 1984)

Milwaukee Public Schools Curriculum (1985)

One World, One Earth: Educating Children for Social Responsibility (Philadelphia, PA: New Society, 1993)

Our Future at Stake (Oakland, CA: Citizens Policy Center, 1984)

Peace Works: Young Peacemakers Project Book II (Elain, IL: Brethren, 1989)

Second Step: A Violence Prevention Curriculum (Seattle, WA: Committee for Children, 1990)

Starting a Conflict Manager Program (San Francisco, CA: The Community Board Program, 1992)
Watermelons Not War! (Philadelphia, PA: New Society, 1984)

Appendix B

Some of the leading organizations in the United States that provide resources in this field are:

The Community Board Program, 1540 Market Street, Room 490, San Francisco, CA 94102. (415) 626-0595.

The Consortium for Peace Education, Development, and Research (COPRED), George Mason University, Fairfax, VA 22030–4444. (703) 993-3639.

Educators for Social Responsibility (ESR), 23 Garden Street, Cambridge, MA 02138. (617) 492-1769.

The Grace Contrino Abrams Peace Education Foundation, P.O. Box 19–1153, Miami Beach, FL 33139. (305) 576-5075.

Humanity House, 513 West Exchange Street, Akron, OH 44302. (216) 864-5442.

The National Association for Mediation in Education (NAME), 205 Hampshire House, The University of Massachusetts, Amherst, MA. (413) 545-2462.

PEABODY JOURNAL OF EDUCATION, 71(3), 84–94
Copyright © 1996, Lawrence Erlbaum Associates, Inc.

Australian Aboriginal Constructions of Humans, Society, and Nature in Relation to Peace Education

John Synott

The Indigenous Contexts of Peace Issues

My interests in exploring the themes of this article are both theoretical and practical. With more than 250 million indigenous peoples in the world today (Burger, 1990)—comprising perhaps more than 3,000 distinct cultures (Nietschmann, 1988)—their involvement in war and other forms of conflict is extensive.

It is estimated that there are, more or less currently, some 86 conflicts around the planet involving indigenous communities, comprising some 72% of total global conflicts (Nietschmann, 1988). Furthermore, of the approximately 120 total global conflicts, 98% are in the Third World and 75% of these involve struggles between nation-states and Fourth World indigenous communities. In almost every conflict situation, the indigenous community is pitted against a more powerful foe, armed not only with modern weapons but the ideological apparatuses

JOHN SYNOTT *is a member of the Oodgeroo Unit for Aboriginal and Torres Strait Islander Education, Queensland University of Technology, Brisbane, Australia.*

Requests for reprints should be sent to John Synott, Oodgeroo Unit, Aboriginal and Torres Strait Islander Education, Queensland University of Technology, Kelvin Grove, Brisbane, Queensland 4059, Australia. E-mail: j.synott@qut.edu.au of the legal systems, the media, and the education systems. Frequently in these arenas, the indigenous communities are depicted as "rebels," "guerrillas," "communists," "fundamentalists," "terrorists," or some other expression of subversives. In Papua New Guinea, for example, there is a generic colloquialism used for resisters, a blurring of distinctions between indigenous communities struggling to retain or regain control of their lands against developers in the rural countryside and the gangs of dislocated urban youth in cities like Port Moresby: They are all called "rascals," criminal gang members whom the police can shoot on sight. The rascal gangs that have terrorized the urban centers, often very violently, are a different (though not unrelated) social issue to the struggles of the 80% of the New Guinean population to survive and determine their own future in the face of rapacious development. Such generalizations applied to subordinated people's identity are not surprising to scholars of colonialism. As Albert Memmi (1957/1990) once commented, "At the basis of the entire construction, one finally finds a common motive; the colonizer's economic and basic needs, which he substitutes for logic, and which shape and explain each of the traits he assigns to the colonized" (p. 149).

In the contemporary world, whether in Burma, against the Karen, Mon, and Lahu peoples; in Chile in the oppression of the Mapuche; or in the valley of the Narmada River in India, the resistance of indigenous peoples is portrayed by the oppressors and invaders as the actions of criminals and subversives. In this respect, the practices in the late 20th century have shifted little from those of two centuries ago. When the British arrived in the land that became Australia in 1788, they promptly declared the local inhabitants to be British subjects, so any resistance was henceforth construed as criminal behavior.

The Australian Aboriginal history of genocide and resistance has been substantially documented by now, although the full story has hardly been revealed to the Australian public (e.g., Blomfield, 1988; Lippman, 1988; Reynolds, 1981; Rowley, 1970). Only recently has the Aboriginal view on history been accorded legitimacy (Broome, 1991; Harvey, 1988). The ongoing deaths of Aborigines and Torres Strait Islanders at the hands of the so-called criminal justice system in Australia has been so enduring that, in 1987, a special Commission was instigated to investigate Aboriginal Deaths in Custody. Despite a 2-year inquiry and a national report (Commonwealth of Australia, 1991) running to four long volumes and hundreds of recommendations for reform, the deaths in custody continue at the rate of two a month. Instances of internal colonialism abound in the international indigenous communities. In another context, in the United States, for example, we have witnessed the past maneuvers to influence indigenous communities to accept the storage of spent nuclear waste on their tribal lands (Taliman, 1994).

If there is ever to be any resolution to these conflicts, enduring efforts need to be made to understand what the indigenous peoples of the world are striving to defend. Any inquiry into the conflict between indigenous peoples and invaders worldwide quickly recognizes a vast difference in the understanding and meaning of the stakes in the conflicts, from the indigenous and invader perceptions. Moreover, some comparative analysis reveals a large degree of congruence between the assertions and claims of indigenous peoples in different parts of the globe, even though they have had few contacts with each other, apart from local trading and cultural exchange activities.

Theorizing Indigenous Ontologies

Earlier social science explained away these parallels by the notions of "stages of development." It was argued by anthropologists from Tylor onwards, in paradigms based on Social Darwinism, that the indigenous communities—with their particular social and economic systems and cosmologies—had reached a certain "stage" of human evolution, which was primitive and well below that of the "civilized" Europeans (Bohannan & Glazer, 1973; Tylor, 1930). These theories, long the scientific and ideological bulwarks of racism, have been appropriately rejected in social science theory (Turner & Beeghley, 1981).

In an odd twist of fate, or intellectual reinvention ("a good idea that refuses to go away"), the notion of stages of inevitable advancement resurfaced in positivist "economic development" theory (e.g., Baran, 1957; Rostow, 1960; Sahlins & Service, 1973) and, once again, indigenous communities were subjected to demands for surrender of their cultures and resources in acceptance of the requirements of a higher stage of development, namely that of "modernization," still equated with "civilization" (Larrain, 1989). However, apart from a general acceptance of the doctrine of "cultural relativism" in social science, little has been done to make contemporary sense of indigenous ontologies and common features in their orientations to the world.

As in the case of social relations worldwide, where indigenous peoples are repressed and denied the right to distinctiveness of cultural identity, expression, and maintenance (not to mention the direct theft of their lands and resources; Burger, 1990), similarly, in the realm of intellectual discourse, the knowledge values of indigenous cultures remain marginalized. This is not only the case in arenas such as positivist science (e.g., medicine) where paradigms of the technology of the body dominate the discourse and practice of medicine, but the neglect of indigenous knowledge is also apparent in intellectual forums emerging from what I might describe as *postindustrial humanism:* the critical traditions within social science, psychology, political economy, and history, meshed with environmental awareness into globally oriented systems-navigated paradigms for human emancipation.

Peace education is one such field where a project of global human emancipation is sustained on theories of inalienable human rights, human ecology, and, generally, notions of the person–planet nexus, drawn from the intellectual and ethical traditions of Judeo Christianity, Ghandiism, Marxism, and the rationalist claims of advocates such as Sharp (1980) and Galtung (1980) for an internationalist distributive justice, further legitimated by the assertions of an empiricist environmentalism (e.g., Bjerstedt, 1992; Bose, 1994; Calder & Smith, 1991; Carey, Di Masi, Rickard, & Spokes, 1987; Haavelsrud & Galtung, 1983; Hicks, 1991; Toh & Floresca-Cawagas, 1990).

Worldwide, one of the areas of concern for peace educators is the conflict involving indigenous peoples. Social justice for indigenous peoples is generally supported by peace educators. However, the notion is tacitly assumed that the affirmation of indigenous rights is achieved somewhere "out there" outside the circle of peace educators and our theories, in other realms of social space and social discourse. It is my contention, however, that the knowledge constructions of peace educators and the peace movement generally need to place indigenous epistemology within the central understandings and representations of our discourse. Indigenous peoples could well claim that their knowledge is as marginalized by the peace education movement as by any other group. Omission and silence are strategies of oppression as much as active oppression, as well the feminist movement has shown us. It is my assertion that the paradigms of peace education need to be inclusive of indigenous perspectives on the nature of the world and appropriate human actions within it, if they are to achieve the truly global currency they seek.

The *Tjukurrpa* in Aboriginal Cultures

In the remainder of this article, I present an introductory description of some of the salient features of the holistic knowledge of the groups of Australian Aborigines who live in the desert regions of Central Australia. Pitjatjanjara, Aranda, Walbari, and Pintubi are just some of the communities in this region who use the common term that is discussed here. Throughout Australia, Aboriginal people share forms of knowledge, with different modes of expression in the 300 or so local languages. This representation of the *Tjukurrpa*, has been historically misunderstood and mistranslated as "the Dreamtime." The naming is important here and requires some explanation. When the earlier generation of structural-functionalist anthropologists (e.g., Radcliffe-Brown, 1931) explored Aboriginal society, they impressed their own understandings of the origin of the world on the stories that were told to them by the Aborigines. They invented the notion of the Dreamtime, which endured in anthropological, educational, and popular discourses as some Aboriginal parallel to the Biblical Garden of Eden or Greek mythology's Golden Age, events of the primitive—perhaps formative—but now irrelevant past. In fact, generations of missionaries set out to replace, quite forcibly, the notion of the Dreamtime with that of the Garden of Eden. The meaning-making frames these colonial intellectuals imposed on the Aboriginal worldview were quite inappropriate. The distorted views on the Dreamtime actually facilitated the theft of the land and the efforts to destroy Aboriginal cultures. The reassertion of the term *Tjukurrpa* is a reclaiming of the knowledge itself by Aboriginal people, and an affirmation of the conceptual clarity of Aboriginal languages in understanding the world.

The core understandings that inform the various elements of this ontology are those of relatedness and process. The Aboriginal world is a systemic one, where the central nodes of the physical, human, and sacred worlds are mutually constructed and sustained. Even these categories are heuristic rather than actual for, in the *Tjukurrpa*, there are very flexible boundaries between the physical, human, and sacred worlds. They interpenetrate and identify with each other. The features of nature, such as landscape, do not represent but are spiritual phenomena, just as the people's sense of self is formed by the forces of nature and the spiritual realm. In the Aboriginal worldview, for instance, the land can be literally addressed as "mother"—from whom the people come and by whom their lives are sustained. This is not just an ecological recognition of the "mother earth" variety, but goes beyond that, to a profound understanding of the sacred character of the land and one's kinship with it, entailing both rights and responsibilities.

This understanding has been symbolized in the stories of Ancestral Beings, creative powers who traveled to the unformed landscape and established its features and relationships as they moved around it, metamorphosing into a multitude of forms throughout the continent: plants, animals, minerals, and rocks; water; the winds; indeed anything within the natural environment, including humans:

in the time of *tjukurrpa* ... the essence of life stirred in the land and beings arose from the earth in which they had always been inherent. They moved, as humans do, making camp, finding water, initiating the young, growing old, and quarreling. In them was the kurunba or life-essence of all the animals, and all humans. (Mack, cited in Jacob, 1991, p. 11)

In this way, life and the world were summonsed into being. The Ancestral Beings subsequently molded themselves into visible features of the landscape, from which their presence and influence has continued. All things, including the people, were interrelated. Because the land was sacred and the source of life, all human activities were oriented toward its proper maintenance. Moreover, the land provided evidence of their origins, the rules for life, and a stable, loving avenue through which the cultural expression of humans could be pursued:

He came from the north of Collie, turning his big body, forming the hills and making the river. ... At the place we call Minninup Pool he gave his final turn releasing his people—the Wilmer. He gave them the laws and languages and what they were to do. These people are still here today. (Wilmer Aboriginal Community, cited in Jacob, 1991, p. 21)

Also central to this set of fundamental relationships is the ongoing existentialism of the system. Unlike the lock of Western cause and effect determinism into linear time and the inevitable entropy, whereby in both our science and our dominant religion are the notions of a foreseeable end of the world, the Aboriginal view is dominated by an understanding of the continuity of the world: The emphasis is not on the creation but the process of shaping and the practice of maintaining the world. The spiritual forces that shape the world and give it life are as present and compelling now as they were 50,000 years ago, when the knowledge was first transmitted in song cycles that remain contemporary today. These song-cycles, called *inma*, are rich narratives that contain the concepts of a profound order in the world (Layton, 1986).

This realization of the fundamental interrelationship of the human with other realms of phenomena also contained a vision for wholeness and survival. For, accompanying the philosophic grasp of the interrelatedness of being was also a recognition of interdependence—that the conditions of wholeness are sustained by the agencies of the various forms of life and, in this, the spirits have their parts and humans have theirs. Thus, the maintenance of the *Tjukurppa* is a dynamic process of response and creativity, conducted by all forms of life from each generation to the next. For instance, each of the life cycles of the animal world contribute to this maintenance of the *Tjukurrpa*. Every form of life, from the smallest and short-lived to the largest contributes, in their living out of their natural way, to the making and sustaining of the *Tjukurrpa*. So, also, it is the case that destroying the landscape and ridding it of its insect and animal life destroys the *Tjukurrpa*.

In turning to the human world, we need, again, to suspend our learned notions of what a person is, and of how individual and group identity are formed and expressed. In the *Tjukurrpa*, each person is established in an identity that centrally locates them within the system of reality. Alienation is impossible except through ritual exile, whereas belongingness is constructed along a principle of being owned as well as owning: Thus, a community who "owns" a certain area of land, in the sense of enjoying exclusive economic and cultural rights to it, also belongs to the land. Their rights have reciprocal duties as custodians of the land.

The activities within the human domain are identified and regulated by the powerful establishments of the Law, which underlies and governs all aspects of social relations and behavior: "It's not our idea, it's a big law. ... We have to sit down alongside of all that Law like all the dead people who went before us" (Myers, cited in Jacob, 1991, p. 56). The Law entails the process of maintaining the central identity in the *Tjukurrpa* of the human, physical, and sacred worlds. The Law exists outside of time, neither past nor future, but the functional mechanism of regulating the correct codes of human behavior and relationships:

> *The Dreaming does not end; it is not like the whiteman's way.*
> *What happened once, happens again and again.*
> *This is the Law.*
> *This is the power of the Song.* (Marshall-Stoneking, 1990, p. 30)

The Law recognizes the existence and problematics of human agency: "The *Tingarri* (ancestral spirits) gave us Law. To be strong, you have to hold that law tight" (Tutama Tjapangarti, cited in Marshall-Stoneking, 1990, p. 91). Thus, the complex prescriptions on social relations (e.g., in respect to kinship) reside in the Law, whose purpose is the peaceful coexistence of all living, physical, and spiritual forms. Kinship includes forms of distribution of responsibility for the maintenance of the *Tjukurrpa*, as well as locating one's identity within it. All knowledge was contained within and circumscribed by the Law. Knowledge was of the Law, the "way," and embraced every aspect of life from birth to death. Upholding the Law meant that the *Tjukurrpa* and the balanced well-being of human and other life forms and the natural, physical world were sustained. Within the *Tjukurrpa*, also, were the appropriate methods of transmission of knowledge, the education of the people, based around notions of "readiness" and "life-long learning." Moreover, the Law prescribed the methods of conflict resolution, again with a view to sustaining the fundamental relationships on which survival and well-being depended. Consensus in decision making, education in self-regulation, and collective responsibility—along with clear, largely nonviolent sanctions, often involving "shaming," avoidance, and humor—served to maintain social harmony.

Given that Aboriginal culture healthily survived for 50,000 years, it should be noted that the *Tjukurrpa* was a dynamic and flexible system, adaptable to the vast range of geographical, climatic, and human diversity across the continent of Australia over this vast time. Aboriginal cultures were characterized by interaction and change, far from being a static maintenance of conservative primitivity over many thousands of years. However, in many respects, Aboriginal societies have been depicted as an extended "dark ages," prior to the coming of the dynamic European "light."

This feature applies nowhere more so than in that of technology. The technology of Aborigines has been held to be primitive indeed, when compared to the inventions of the Europeans. However, in technology, as in all forms of human activity, the principle of working within the domain of the *Tjukurrpa* was maintained. In made objects of all kinds, whether they be ceremonial artworks or tools for survival, resided the same spiritual essences as in the landscape. Trade around the continent, or daily gathering of sustenance, or the activities of decoration and painting or singing, were all alike in their shared identity of belonging within the *Tjukurrpa*.

Conclusion: Dreaming Peace Education

This discussion has set out to convey the fundamental notions underlying the discourse on being or ontology of the Aboriginal people of Australia, taking the language of the groups of Aboriginal people in Central Australia in using the term *Tjukurrpa* as a clearer notion than the more common Western phrase of "the Dreaming." My intention has been to attract the attention of peace educators to an awareness that the insights of a holistic, systemic, interdependent world of humans and other forms of nature, which underlies the socially critical and transformative project of peace educators, has parallels and experiential precursors not only outside the domains of Western social theory, but within societies that the West continues to oppress and destroy; that the indigenous people of the world are struggling to preserve and assert the very values and forms of social organization that peace educators are trying to promote.

I have used an example from Aboriginal cultures in Australia but, as I suggested earlier, there are many points of commonality between the epistemologies of the world's indigenous cultures. For example, the four principles of the code of life of the *adivasis*, indigenous people currently threatened by the Narmada River hydroelectricity project in India, have a strong congruence with those of Australian Aborigines: *susangat*, the fundamental principle of harmonious coexistence with the environment; *samanta*, being equality of people; *samuita*, indicating collective action with mutual consent; and *sharkaria*, meaning cooperation (Schechla, 1993, pp. 1–6). Similarly, the Mapuche people of southern Chile, or the indigenous peoples of America assert similar values. The central relationships expressed in the diagram of the *Tjukurrpa* have been understood by these cultural nations for thousands of years.

The concerns of this article have been predominantly theoretical in their focus on worldviews and paradigms of peace education. I have suggested that there is an imperative for peace educators to include indigenous perspectives in their theorizing, at the very least to end the ethnocentric bias in what claims to be a global paradigm. I have also indicated that the holistic paradigms of indigenous peoples have a lot to offer peace educators in their insights and approaches to appropriate and sustainable societies.

I would like to conclude by recognizing that much of the work of peace educators is of direct and indirect benefit to indigenous peoples engaged in often solitary struggles for survival. Promoting issues such as universal human rights, antiracism, exposures of the arms trade and state terrorism, educating about protecting the environment, opposing debilitating development and tourism, the promotion of cultural diversity, examining the conditions and effects of colonialism and the contemporary neoimperialism of multinationals, and insisting on the rights of women—all of these and the many other concerns of peace educators are directly relevant to the causes of indigenous peoples.

Returning to the realities of the many global conflicts involving indigenous communities, with which this discussion opened, a recognition of indigenous worldviews, of how the land that the people struggle—usually nonviolently—to retain, forms such a central dimension of their identities and ways of life, of how they must resist invasion, destruction of the environment, and their cultures—understanding of these things can only contribute to the task of peace educators in promoting knowledge that can bring the world through its current predicaments to be a safer, sustainable place for all to share.

References

Baran, P. (1957). *The political economy of growth.* New York: Monthly Review Press.
Bjerstedt, Å. (1992). *Conceptions of the future and education for responsibility* (Peace Education Report No. 4). Malmö, Sweden: School of Education.
Blomfield, G. (1981). *Baal Belbora: The end of the dancing.* Chippendale, Australia: Apcol.
Bohannan, P., & Glazer, M. (1973). *High points in anthropology.* New York: Knopf.
Bose, A. (1994). [Review of J. Galtung's *The way is the goal: Gandhi today*]. *Peace, Environment and Education, 5*(3), 53–62.
Broome, R. (1991). *Aboriginal Australians: The Australian experience.* Canberra: Australian Institute of Aboriginal and Torres Strait Islander Studies.
Burger, J. (1990). *The Gaia atlas of first peoples.* London: Gaia.
Calder, M., & Smith, R. (1991). *A better world for all.* Canberra: Australian Government Publishing.
Carey, D., Di Masi, P., Rickard, J., & Spokes, J. (1987). *A peace of the action: An annotated bibliography and teacher guide on peace education.* Collingwood, Australia: Friends of the Earth.
Commonwealth of Australia. (1991). *National report: Royal commission into Aboriginal deaths in custody* (Vols. 1–4). Canberra: Australian Government Publishing Service.
Galtung, J. (1980). *The true worlds: A transnational perspective.* New York: Free Press.
Haavelsrud, M., & Galtung, J. (Eds.). (1983). The debate on education [Special issue]. *International Review of Education, 29*(3).
Harvey, M. (1988) *"The Dreaming" in Yanguwa country: The Yanguwa people of Boroloola tell the history of their land.* Richmond, VA: Greenhouse.
Hicks, D. (1991). *Exploring alternative futures: A teacher's interim guide.* London: Global Futures Project.
Jacob, T. (1991). *In the beginning: A perspective on traditional Aboriginal societies.* Perth: Ministry of Education Western Australia.
Larrain, J. (1989). *Theories of development.* Cambridge, England: Cambridge University Press.
Layton, R. (1986). *Uluru: An Aboriginal history of Ayers Rock.* Canberra: Australian Institute of Aboriginal Studies.
Lippman, L. (1988). *Generations of resistance.* Ringwood, Australia: Penguin.
Marshall-Stoneking, B. (1990). *Singing the snake.* Sydney, Australia: Angus & Robertson.
Memmi, A. (1990). *The colonizer and the colonized* (H. Greenfield, Trans.). London: Earthscan. (Original work published 1957)
Nietschmann, B. (1988). The third World War. *Cultural Survival Quarterly, 11*(3), 1–15.
Radcliffe-Brown, A. (1931). *The social organization of Australian tribes.* Melbourne, Australia: Macmillan.
Reynolds, H. (1981). *The other side of the frontier.* Ringwood, Australia: Penguin.
Rostow, W. (1960). *The stages of economic growth: A non-communist manifesto.* Cambridge, England: Cambridge University Press.
Rowley, C. D. (1970). *The destruction of Aboriginal society.* Ringwood, Australia: Penguin.
Sahlins, M., & Service, E. (1973). *Evolution and culture.* Ann Arbor: University of Michigan Press.
Schechla, J. (1993). More dam "progress" in India's Narmada Valley. *Fourth World Bulletin, 2*(3), 1–6.
Sharp, G. (1980). *Social power and political freedom.* Boston: Extending Horizons Books.
Taliman, V. (1994). Mescalero sign nuclear waste storage deal with Northern States power. *Fourth World Bulletin, 3*(2), 18–19.

J. Synott

Toh, S., & Floresca-Cawagas. (1990). *Peaceful theory and practice in values education.* Quezon City, Philippines: Phoenix Publishing.
Turner, J., & Beeghley, L. (1981). *The emergence of sociological theory.* Homewood, IL: Dorsey.
Tylor, E. (1930). *Anthropology.* London: Watts.

PEABODY JOURNAL OF EDUCATION, 71(3), 95–110
Copyright © 1996, Lawrence Erlbaum Associates, Inc.

Early Tendencies of Peace Education in Sweden

Bengt Thelin

In the early 1980s in Sweden, as in so many other countries, the Cold War provoked a deep fear of a potential war of annihilation. The peace movement grew stronger and stronger and also affected schools and education. The National Board of Education (NBE), at that time the central school authority in Sweden, felt an obligation to meet the demands of many schools for advice and guidance on how to deal with "the peace question." As a Director of Education at the NBE with special responsibility for international issues, it fell to me to carry out this new task. Although we had for many years been dealing with "Third-World solidarity" and "international understanding" in our work with curriculum development and instruction, "peace education" was for me and my colleagues something fairly unknown.

BENGT THELIN *served between 1969 and 1989 as a Director of Education at the Swedish National Board of Education. Currently, he is Vice President of the International Baccalaureate Organisation.*

Requests for reprints should be sent to Bengt Thelin, Sommarvägen 24, SE–183 62 Täby, Sweden.

However, after a couple of years, peace education became a more or less established concept and an issue in which many schools, teachers, and students were involved. Our working methods at the NBE for the several years ahead were to publish articles, produce service materials, and arrange workshops and conferences for teachers and principals on peace education (Bjerstedt, 1986; Thelin, 1991). It did not take long until we realized that the enterprise that we, a little unsuspectingly, had launched was a rather controversial one. As in several other countries peace education was an intensively, if intermittently, debated topic in the media. One thing that evidently distinguished the situation in Sweden from that one in most other countries was that peace education had been initiated and was supported by the central state school authority (Bjerstedt, 1988, pp. 30–32). It meant that schools, teachers, and students devoted to peace and peace education could have their activities officially sanctioned and legitimized.

Another factor relevant to this article is that we who worked with peace education at the NBE in the 1980s were unaware that this topic had a history. Of course, I myself—like so many others who became teachers in the 1950s—was very interested in the developing countries, upset by their poverty and hard conditions, and possessed with an ambition to "do something." Knowledge about the Third World gradually became an element in subjects such as Civics, History, and Religion and included in the centrally issued curricula for different levels of the school in Sweden. International solidarity and international understanding became frequent terms and concerns. We called it *internationalization* and *internationalism*. These concepts referred almost exclusively to the Third World (unlike the situation today, when these terms have acquired a very strong European and economic meaning).

To sum up, we worked with international education and our direction was North–South. But we did not work with—or even use the term—*peace education*. As stated previously, it was not until the beginning of the 1980s that this topic and this term became a reality and our work acquired an East–West direction. After some time, we also realized that these two directions—international education with its North–South orientation and peace education with its East–West orientation—were closely interrelated. But let us return to the forgotten past of peace education and to what, in the title of this article, is referred to as "early tendencies." The reason why I discovered this past was my intention to write a book with a description and an analysis—a "survey of knowledge"—of what peace education stands for. My plan was to begin my writing with a very brief historical background covering the years of my own personal involvement. However, from my initial research in the material I was carried further and further backward. To my surprise I found that there really exists a history of peace education with both similarities and differences compared with our own time. The similarities depend on a common origin and the idea that education has a role to play in safeguarding the peace. The differences, on the other hand, are due to the different political, social, and pedagogical contexts. Nevertheless, there is a common thread, an identity that deserves to be unraveled. This thread represents an unknown or neglected part of our history of education as a whole.

What I am presenting here are some summarizing glimpses from my Swedish manuscript. The book, *Knowledge, Feeling, Action: Some Reflections on Peace Education in History and Today* is scheduled to be published in Swedish. My sources mainly consist of journals, magazines, and pamphlets published by Swedish trade unions of teachers and peace associations, and of textbooks and curricula. As all this material is published in Swedish and is in addition difficult to find, I have, writing for an international public, to a large degree limited my references. Interested readers for whom Swedish is an understandable language are referred to my forthcoming book.

From the second part of the 19th century, peace ideas and peace movements grew stronger and stronger in Europe and in the United States. Aggressive nationalism, militarism, and war heroism were severely criticized. Diplomacy and arbitration were called for instead of violence and weapons to solve international conflicts. As a result of improved communications and a more effective news distribution, even people living far from the different theaters of war—there were many of them during the second part of the 19th century—became familiar with the cruelty and barbarism of war. Florence Nightingale's work during the Crimean war in the 1850s, and Henri Dunant's experiences from the French–Austrian war some years later and his book *Un souvenir de Solferino* (1862) strongly affected public opinion. The same, if not more so, goes for Bertha von Suttner's *Die Waffen nieder* (1889). A new way of thinking on peace and war slowly came about, possibly the beginning of a universal change of paradigm in which we find ourselves today, the conclusion of which could take mankind centuries to reach—if ever.

Visible manifestations of the force of peace ideas—and I am now first and foremost talking about the time before World War I—were a profusion of international and national conferences, proclamations, and programs on peace. Many peace associations were founded, in all more than 400 by the turn of the century. Concrete results among others were The Interparliamentary Union (1889) and The International Peace Bureau (1891). The establishment of the Nobel Peace Prize in 1896 was an event of great importance for peace ideology. Official recognition of this ideology came with the Hague Conferences in 1899 and 1907. In previous centuries, governments had negotiated over treaties to end wars, but the Hague Conferences were the first international conferences between governments that were convened to discuss how to preserve peace. These conferences represent important steps toward the idea that international conflicts must be solved by peaceful mediation and not by weapons. They were part of a process that led to the International Court of Arbitration (*World Encyclopedia of Peace*, 1986, p. 630).

It is also important to note that women increasingly set out to walk at the head of the peace movements and join together in associations and groups. Not infrequently, their call for peace went hand-in-hand with the call for universal women's suffrage.

In all these peace activities in Sweden and elsewhere I have, for this particular period so far, found only a few references to education and its potential role in peace promotion. I can imagine that there are three probable reasons for this. Firstly, public education in most countries, Sweden included, was still fairly undeveloped. It had not yet developed an opinion-building power. Secondly, democracy and universal and equal suffrage were still rare phenomena. The popular masses were lacking political influence. Thirdly, peace ideas were very controversial and met with suspicion and hostility from the greater part of the political and military establishment. In such circumstances to call for regular peace education in the schools is likely to have been entirely futile. In the European states and in their educational objectives, if such documents existed at all, "God and the Fatherland" was still the dominating and solely accepted ideology (Tingsten, 1969). As for Sweden, it was not until 1919 that there appeared, in the centrally issued curriculum, a certain deglorifying of war and war heroes.

Despite what has just been said, it is nonetheless possible to find at least some examples of proposals and ideas indicating that "peace" should also be a concern for education and for young people.

At an international peace congress in Paris in 1849, where Victor Hugo was one of the most famous participants, a statement was adopted that has been characterized as the first program of the international peace movement (Fogelström, 1983, p. 16). It also contains a paragraph in which the participants are requested to work, in their respective countries, for eradicating political prejudices and "hatred that has been learnt." This can, among other things, be achieved by improvements in the upbringing of the younger generation.

Looking at Sweden, an early example of the link between peace idealism and education in this country worth mentioning is a teacher training college for young women that was founded in Stockholm in 1861. Behind this initiative we find the famous author Fredrika Bremer, a very prominent figure both for the early feminist and peace movements. There are no particular traces of what could be called a peace education program in the syllabi of this school. Nevertheless, it has been testified over the years—by many of the young women trained there—that the dominating idea and atmosphere, the culture of the school, was peace, reconciliation, and dissociation from violence and war. This peaceful attitude was, among other things, obvious in the manner of instruction of such subjects as history and literature. It is in this connection interesting to compare this women's college with the state grammar schools, which at this time were available only for male students. Here we can observe a totally different spirit and atmosphere with a rather one-sided emphasis on force and virility, war, and war heroes (Ekbom, 1991; cf. Florin & Johansson, 1993, pp. 47–53). (Thanks to Ekbom's book, this heritage from Bremer is rescued from oblivion.)

Many young women who had been trained at this college received important political and cultural positions later on in their careers. One was the author Selma Lagerlöf, Nobel Prize winner of literature in 1909. Peace and altruism are salient features in most of her writings. Another was the teacher and school principal Matilda Widegren, who in 1919 together with some other women initiated a Swedish section of the Women's International League for Peace and Freedom (WILPF). She also founded a teacher association for peace about which I will give some information later. A third example is Inga Thorsson, a famous politician and diplomat with a great number of international assignments both for the United Nations and the Swedish government. She was especially involved and active concerning disarmament matters. Among other things she functioned as the chairperson of a group of 27 governmental experts, which in 1981 produced a report on the relation between disarmament and development (Ekbom, 1991; Thorsson, 1984).

Let us turn back to the 19th century and more precisely to the 1870s, which is the decade when the continental peace movements started to obtain a footing in Sweden. In the vanguard we find some journalists and members of parliament belonging to the liberal and socialistic camps. The Swedish Peace and Arbitration Society (SPAS) was founded in 1883 and is regarded as the oldest, still-existing peace association of the world. There is no reference made to the school system in its oldest program. However, from a peace conference some years later there is a statement saying that one of the most immediate tasks of the Nordic peace associations is to reach the younger generation and their teachers to "at least in the future" achieve a better understanding on talking about arbitration and neutrality (Fogelström, 1983, p. 50). In my opinion, this wording, with its reference to the future, reflects the moderation and realism already mentioned and which the early peace advocates had to observe in making links between peace and education.

Of greater importance for the years to come was a pamphlet published in 1886 titled "Hermann Molkenboer: The School and the Peace Thought" (Berg, 1886). It has an introduction by Fridtjuv Berg, one of the central figures of Swedish educational history, president of the Swedish Teacher Trade Union and editor of its journal. Molkenboer was a Dutch teacher. He drew attention to double standards in education. Love, even toward one's enemies, is taught in religious education whereas the instruction in history is characterized by national pride and hatred toward other peoples. The cleansing and ennobling of patriotism is a task for the school. If this is to be brought about, instruction in history has to be reformed. "The friends of peace and humanity" have to cooperate in the different countries. Peace associations that would establish contacts beyond the national frontiers must be founded. The final goal should be to establish an international "Upbringing Council" assigned with the task of working for the "harmonizing of history and geography instruction with morality."

Berg said, after his account of Molkenboer's ideas and activities, that "we are now at the beginning of a movement, which in the future will be regarded as one of the most remarkable events of our time" (Berg, 1886, p. 6). How right Berg was, or will be, in his predictions depends, of course, on what we mean by "the future." However, I think we can all agree that peace education, after more than 100 years, still has a long way to go!

There are several things worth noting with respect to Molkenboer's—and Berg's—thoughts and proposals. The first is that this little book deserves to be respected as one of the oldest elaborations of a program for peace education. The second is the importance for a peace element to be introduced into history instruction. This is a feature characteristic of peace education efforts until our own time. The third is Molkenboer's grounding in the Christian faith and the great importance he attached to religion for peace education. This linkage has to a large degree disappeared in the efforts of our own secularized time to work for peace education. The fourth is his idea of an "Upbringing Council," which prefigures both the League of Nation's early efforts to improve textbooks in history and geography and still more UNESCO and its more effective work of this kind. The fifth point, finally, to which I would like to pay attention is the firm conviction that school and education have a real role to play when it comes to contributing to peace and to changing the world. "Peace educators" today, hopefully, have—despite the reduced possibility of education to influence public opinion—kept this conviction but in a more realistic and modest way.

Molkenboer's ideas, conveyed by the influential Fridtjuv Berg, obviously had an encouraging and clarifying impact on educators engaged in the peace movement. His criticism of double standards in education between religious and history instruction recurs frequently in discussions in subsequent years. The way to resolve this tension is to reform history instruction and to "cleanse" it of chauvinism and one-sided war heroism. Very little was said, from a peace point of view, about how to reform religious instruction despite the many accounts of wars, to which the children were exposed when reading texts from the Old Testament.

To say that there was a very swift flood of articles, conference resolutions, and declarations on peace education in the Swedish educational debate would be an exaggeration. The vast majority of teachers, officials, and politicians on different levels responsible for education were probably ignorant or strongly hesitant of any change in line with the thoughts of the peace advocates. I believe this especially goes for the teachers of the grammar schools, where the political and cultural conservatism had a stronger hold than among the teachers of the compulsory schools. I have found hardly any references to peace education in the magazines of their trade union.

However, the fact that "the peace question" in education could be debated in daily newspapers as early as 1898 is illustrated by the following episode. In that particular year, the first peace association for women was established in Sweden. In the program that was adopted, the following was stated as the first point: "Upbringing has to be cleansed from war elements. War plays and war toys must be banned. The same goes for glorifying of the warriors and wars of which both literature and history are guilty" (Larsson, 1985, p. 26). Instead of being dominated by wars, history instruction must pay attention to the cultural and peaceful development.

In one of the conservative newspapers in Stockholm, this program was met by great indignation (Larsson, 1985, p. 28). Above all, there was opposition to the proposal that children should be taught to admire peaceful achievements more than those carried out by war heroes like Alexander, Gustavus Adolphus, or Napoleon. The article, in an indirect but clear way, compared love for peace with treason, and preparation for war with patriotism. Reading this, one easily recalls the vulgar and ironic slogan from the Cold War in the 1970s and 1980s: "It's better to be dead than red."

Because of the tension between Sweden and Norway, linked together in a political union and ruled by the same king, the turn of the century was a very critical period in Nordic history. However, in 1905 a peaceful agreement was reached and the union dissolved without war. It would be of interest, of course, to know to what degree either war or peace propaganda occurred in the classrooms during the critical months prior to the agreement. The Swedish people were divided into hawks and doves. But the teacher magazines are very silent on this topic. Although the debate was probably intensive both among teachers and students, the sources available do not, as far as I have found, give any information on this. The teachers are likely to have imposed moderation on themselves.

An attempt made by some nationalistic Swedes to boycott a Nordic teacher conference in 1905 with participation by Norwegians was a failure. The conference took place in Copenhagen with a great number of Swedes present. Referring to the aforementioned contradiction between a Christian spirit of reconciliation and an aggressive nationalism in education it is evident that, in this particular situation, the former luckily proved the stronger.

To what degree teachers devoted to peace played a role in forming public opinion is, of course, difficult to know. Worth saying, however, is that the previously mentioned Fridtjuv Berg was one of the most influential doves. He was also appointed minister of education at this time.

The women's peace association, to which I have already made reference, worked on indefatigably. For instance, they established a "pedagogical section" to, among other things, fight for a reformed subject of history. Like other "peace friends" they were highly inspired by Bertha von Suttner, who visited Sweden several times. Her friendship with Alfred Nobel is well known. So is her role in Nobel's decision to set up a special peace prize, which later on, in 1905, was given to von Suttner, who in Sweden was honored as "the queen of the peace friend's empire."

A person greatly influenced by the Austrian author was the famous feminist and author Ellen Key. She presented and interpreted von Suttner's thinking in several articles. In one of them, she gave an account of von Suttner's conviction that an ethical and social evolution will take place leading to an end of all wars (Key, 1899). The means to reaching this goal is "a slow change, generation after generation, during which fostering peace love will take place in the same way as, in times past, there existed a fostering war love" (pp. 3–4). Through this process of upbringing, the old ideals, according to von Suttner's view, will gradually wither away and the new ideals will increase their vital force. War is not a natural force and von Suttner pleads for arbitration courts and neutrality.

Central to the thoughts of von Suttner, like so many others, is the discussion over the contradiction between patriotic love and love of mankind. She believed in the possibility of fostering generations to "the peace thought" and she opposed engaging young people and children in the defense movement. Concerning women, she held them jointly responsible for war because they had not stopped the men. In a lecture some years later, she expressed her belief in education "as the first means to prevent war" and to eradicate "the wild beast heritage" in which wars have their origin (Key, 1914, p. 4).

The outbreak of World War I in 1914 caused tremendous distress and disappointment to all people engaged in war prevention work. In particular, those working for a reformed and peace oriented education in the different countries, which were mostly women, must have experienced the outbreak of the Great War as a tragic defeat. It is even more surprising and admirable then that the women, when the initial paralysis had worn off, succeeded in arranging a conference with more than 2,000 participants from 12 countries (Larsson, 1985, pp. 69–84). One of the leading figures of the conference, which took place in the Hague in 1915, was the American woman Jane Addams, who in 1931 was awarded Nobel's peace prize.

From Sweden about 15 women took part in the conference, among them the pacifist journalist and author Elin Wägner, who wrote reports on what was going on in the Hague for a Swedish magazine. Another was the previously mentioned teacher Matilda Widegren, who now more and more appears as a leader and organizer of the peace-minded Swedish teachers.

The Hague Conference passed a great number of peace resolutions that were delivered by special delegations to the belligerent and also to the neutral states after the conference. One of the resolutions was titled "The education of children" and reads as follows: "This International Congress of Women urges the necessity of so directing the education of children that their thoughts and desires may be directed towards the ideal of constructive peace" (Larsson, 1985, p. 285). In my opinion, a resolution of this kind was an effective way of putting education for peace on the international agenda. I also think it is correct to say that the Great War functioned as a driving force in convincing public opinion to look upon education as a means for bringing about a changed mentality, a mentality directed toward a world released from war.

At least in Sweden there are indications that efforts were now being intensified to make peace education more visible and active, maybe also a bit more self-confident. In fact, the last years of the 1910s and the first of the 1920s meant something of a change. A threshold was crossed. I now intend to support this statement with some examples of events and actions taken and then, finally, to summarize, describe, and analyze the situation up until the end of the 1930s.

At a congress in 1915, the SPAS passed a resolution among several others—resolutions were at that time a frequently used way of influencing public opinion—in which a "change of education and upbringing" emphasizing the solidarity and fraternity of different peoples and individuals and also a realization of the principles of democracy was requested (Fogelström, 1983, p. 148). At the same congress, SPAS pointed to "the military education of the peoples" as one of the causes of wars. For their youth organization, one of the goals mentioned was fighting against "false virility and perverted femininity." The youth members should rather be occupied with planting trees and bushes and taught to honor nature (Fogelström, 1983, pp. 149–150). Although SPAS was evidently not very successful in putting these principles into practice, their idea of a connection between "peace and nature" in upbringing is worth noting as a very early example of what today, by many "peace educators," is regarded as a both necessary and self-evident linkage as instanced today in the name of our PEC magazine "Peace, Environment and Education." A Swede who, very early, paid attention to the close relation between these two concepts was the previously mentioned author Elin Wägner.

Influenced by the Hague Conference and the resolution passed there, which has already been quoted, two of the participants, Matilda

Widegren and Fanny Petterson, established the Peace group of Swedish Female Teachers in 1916. In that way the peace education movement in Sweden got a particular organization—no matter how small it was—from which it could carry out its activities such as information lectures and discussion meetings. After a few years, male teachers also wanted to be members of the group, which made it necessary to change the name to The Swedish School's Peace Association (SSPA; Svenska skolornas fredsförening).

At the same time, in 1919, a new national curriculum (undervisningsplan) for compulsory school was issued by the government. From a general perspective, this curriculum resulted in an important modernization both for the content and method of Swedish school education. Of special interest in our connection are goals and guidelines formulated for the subject of history. In the goal, it is stated that instruction shall be adopted according to the age and mental development of each child and that their teaching should make them familiar with personalities and events that have contributed to *cultural* development. A basis should be laid for a *sound* patriotism and for good citizenship (italics added; Undervisningsplanen, 1919, p. 100). For the first time on this level it is prescribed that some time shall also be given to world history (Undervisningsplanen, 1919, p. 101). In the guidelines, it is said that history instruction has to be carried out in such a way, "that its leading thread is peaceful cultural and societal development." Children should be informed that war is suffering, but also be made aware of the differences between defensive war and war waged to conquer other states. The history teacher shall endeavor to counteract hatred and hostility toward other peoples and promote the insight that peace and mutual understanding is a primary condition for the common advance of mankind. Children must be taught that in history there also exist peace heroes, brave personalities who have promoted the development of their country and therefore deserve its gratitude and admiration (Undervisningsplanen, 1919, p. 106).

There is also an interesting reference to the mother tongue teaching. "Reading texts" glorifying war shall be avoided, because such texts can counteract the endeavors to peaceful coexistence between individuals and peoples (Undervisningsplanen, 1919, p. 52). The 1919 curriculum and the syllabi of history and the mother tongue can certainly not be regarded as the only official response to the peace-minded teachers. Peace and war preventing work attracted much public interest in the years after World War I. Nevertheless, it seems to be evident that their work effectively contributed to an awakening of a common awareness and also to a focusing on the central role of history instruction. As demonstrated earlier, this had been a central topic of the peace education movement for half a century.

Articles and information paragraphs on peace and peace education in the magazines of the teacher's trade unions now started to become more frequent. Above all this goes for "Lärarinneförbundet," which was edited by the Association of the Female Teachers. In fact, this publication was a main source for peace education during the 1920s and 1930s.

An early initiative taken by the SSPA, led by Matilda Widegren, was to introduce a special Peace Day for Swedish schools. The association got this idea from the United States, but still more from Wales. There, starting in 1922, an annual message called the Message of Peace and Good Will was delivered (from 1924, also broadcasted) to a great number of overseas countries. The day chosen was May 18, because on this date the first Peace Conference opened in the Hague in 1899. This initiative is one of the oldest examples of an international network for peace among youth. The Swedish association immediately jumped at the idea, and every year since 1923 the Message of Peace and Good Will was translated and delivered to schools in Sweden to be cited at the morning prayers on May 18.

The Peace Day meant that traditional and nationalistic commemorations, which were celebrated in schools, above all the anniversaries of the death of the kings Gustavus II Adolphus (November 6) and Charles XII (November 30), were complemented. It has not, however, so far been possible to find out how many schools took up the new day in their commemoration calendar. That it was celebrated, at least in some places, as late as at the beginning of the 1960s is evident by oral testimony given to me. Other days with a peace content, annually celebrated in several schools, were the day of the armistice of World War I (November 11) and the day in September when the League of Nations assembled.

An initiative taken by the SSPA was a questionnaire "to the educators of our country" on peace education delivered in 1920. Unfortunately, I can say here only a few words about this interesting project, thoroughly presented in a booklet published by the SSPA (Fredsundervisning inom skolan, 1923). Of the 150 teachers answering the questionnaire, only 6 wanted peace education to be an independent subject in its own right. This problem, with which we are often confronted today, is consequently an old one. Among the reasons presented against a separate subject was the view that such a subject could run the risk of being "tendentious," abstract, and wrenched from its natural context, evidently the history.

An interesting aspect of the questionnaire, which was delivered to different types of schools, is that more than two thirds of the answers emanated from male teachers. This surprises the rapporteur, who is well aware of the leading role female teachers played in promoting peace education. He cannot find any explanation, but says that the female answers show an "intensive interest" and that they, from a qualitative point of view, are "rather valuable." Could an explanation of the male dominance be that the female teachers still had a more subordinated position among their colleagues, especially when it comes to functioning as a representative of the school?

Another activity of the SSPA was a series of booklets on peace and international topics. These booklets had an important role to play as information material for teachers. It is likely that neither the teacher training colleges nor the universities paid any special attention to anything called peace education. It was all the more important, then, for the SSPA to provide some sort of in-service teacher training for interested colleagues.

Another instrument was summer courses arranged every second year during this period, sometimes in cooperation with sister associations in other Nordic countries. Some opportunities were also given, however, to leading peace educators to address colleagues other than those with a special interest in peace matters. This can be verified by printed reports from the big general teacher congresses and school meetings during this period, both Swedish and Nordic.

The 1930s were troubled years for the peace education movement, as for the peace movement as a whole. The shortcomings of the League of Nations, on which so much hope and optimism had been attached, caused disappointment and pessimism. The growth of dictatorships and aggressive nationalism were worrying phenomena and impaired the "market" for peace and reconciliation education in schools. Instead, defence education was introduced, which caused a dilemma for some peace-minded teachers.

There is much more that could be said from a peace education perspective about this particular situation and also more about the activities during the earlier more auspicious period, before the clouds of a coming second world war began to darken the European scene. I have to be content, however, with the glimpses given, hoping that there will be subsequent opportunities to deal with these "early tendencies" in a more thorough way.

Concluding Reflections

A characteristic of the peace education movement, particularly in the 1920s, was its deep confidence in education as an effective instrument for the prevention of war and the safeguarding of peace. An indication of this was the concentration on the subject of history. The conviction was very firm that a reformed instruction in history in the long term could make a very valuable contribution to eliminating an ancient war and weapon culture. Today, we may have some difficulties in imagining how strong this culture was and what a grip it had on people's minds two or three generations ago. For contemporary peace education this concentration on history is normally not a main concern, but I think it is correct to say that the pioneers of peace education in this respect contributed to a new way of thinking.

It was not only the devoted peace teachers who had a confident and optimistic view of education as an instrument for peace. At an international teacher congress in Edinburgh in 1925, arranged by the World Federation of Teachers' Associations, the conviction was expressed that if five million teachers of the world were against wars they could also effectively contribute to prevent them. At the same congress the title of one of the lectures was "The Hope of Mankind Lays in the Upbringing for Peace."

I have used the terms "peace-minded teachers," "peace educators," and "peace teachers" several times in this article to denote this particular category of people. A question to pose is how far did they go as teachers to promote their ideals in their daily work. How much did they dare to demonstrate and put into practice their engagement? Were their concerns more of peace than of education, and were their energies primarily directed outside of the school? The sources available do not, as far as I have found, tell us very much about their didactic practice or their professionalism with respect to the peace topic. My impression is that peace education at that time had more of a pleading and preaching character than a pedagogical one. However, these are certainly questions still worth considering for our generation when we are dealing with peace education in theory and practice.

Finally, let me also say that peace education during all the years covered in this article is concerned exclusively with peace and war on the macrolevel. It is the open, bloody war that was the concern. Only in exceptional cases were references made to the microlevel, to war and to violence within societies and families. What these peace pioneers worked for was, in other words, first and foremost what we today would call the negative peace.

In addition, peace education, like other pedagogical tendencies, has passed through a process of development. It has a history of its own. This history remains, to a large degree, unwritten, at least in Sweden. Nevertheless it forms an important, although neglected, part of our educational history. What I have presented here are only some glimpses. This history is worth research and investigation, and can certainly be of great value for the peace educators of today when it comes to getting a perspective on their efforts.

References

Berg, F. (1886). *Hermann Molkenboer: Skolan och fredstanken* [Hermann Molkenboer: The school and the peace thought]. Stockholm: Sveriges Allmänna Folkskollärarförening.

Bjerstedt, Å. (1986). *Fredsorienterande skolaktiviteter: Några glimtar från debatt och FoU i Sverige* [Peace-oriented activities in school: Glimpses from debate and R&D in Sweden] (Särtryck och Småtryck No. 530). Malmö, Sweden: Lärarhögskolan Malmö.

Bjerstedt, Å. (1988). *Peace education in different countries* (Educational Information and Debate No. 81). Malmö, Sweden: Lärarhögskolan Malmö.

Dunant, H. (1862). *Un souvenir de Solferino* [A memory of Solferino].

Ekbom, I. (1991). *Den kvinnliga fredstanken: Fredrika Bremer och andra i kamp för fred* [Women's peace thought: Fredrika Bremer and others fighting for peace]. Helsingborg, Sweden: Carlssons.

Florin, C., & Johansson, U. (1993). *"Där de härliga lagrarna gro ... ": Kultur, klass och kön i det svenska läroverket 1850–1914* ["Where the glorious laurels do grow ... ": Culture, class and gender in the Swedish grammar school 1850–1914]. Kristianstad, Sweden: Tiden.

Fogelström, P. A. (1983). *Kampen för fred: Berättelsen om en okänd folkrörelse* [The fight for peace: Report about an unknown popular movement]. Stockholm: Svenska Freds- och Skiljedomsföreningen.

Fredsundervisning inom skolan: En rundfråga bland vårt lands pedagoger [Peace education in the school: An inquiry among teachers in our country]. (1923). Stockholm: Svenska Skolornas Fredsförening.

Key, E. (1899). *Fredstanken—Fredsrörelsen och försvarsrörelsen. Fredens förverkligande. Två uppsatser* [The peace thought—The peace movement and the defense movement. The realization of peace. Two essays] (Småskrifter utg. af Sveriges Kvinnliga Fredsförening No. 2). Stockholm: Sveriges Krinnliga Fredsförening.

Key, E. (1914). *Kriget, freden och framtiden* [War, peace, and future] (Svenska Fredsförbundets Skriftserie No. 11). Stockholm: Swedish Peace Association.

Larsson, M. (1985). *De arbetade för fred: Kvinnoföreningar i Sverige med fred på sitt program 1898–1940* [They worked for peace: Women's associations in Sweden with peace on their agenda 1898–1940]. Stockholm: Författares Bokmaskin.

Thelin, B. (1991). *A tentative introduction from a Swedish perspective* (Peace Education Report No. 2). Malmö, Sweden: Malmö School of Education.

Thorsson, I. (1984). *In pursuit of disarmament: Conversion from military to civil production in Sweden: Vol. 1A. Background, facts and analyses.* Stockholm: Liber Allmänna Förlaget.

Tingsten, H. (1969). *Gud och fosterlandet: Studier i hundra års skolpropaganda* [God and the fatherland: Studies of a hundred years of school indoctrination]. Stockholm: Norsteds & Söners Förlag.

Undervisningsplan för rikets folkskolor den 31 oktober 1919 [Curriculum for the Swedish elementary schools October 31, 1919]. (1919). Stockholm: Svenska Bokförlaget P.A. Norsted & Söner.

von Suttner, B. (1889). *Die Waffen nieder!* [Lay the arms down!].

World encyclopedia of peace (Vol. 1). (1986). New York: Pergamon.

PEABODY JOURNAL OF EDUCATION, 71(3), 111–127

Nonviolent Conflict Resolution in Children

Diane Bretherton

There is increasing concern about the level of violence in our community. Within Australia, National and State committees have been established to investigate the dimensions and causes of violence. Mugford (1989) noted, "There are devastating consequences of violence to individuals and their implications for health, welfare and criminal justice provision are staggering. In 1986–1987 refugee funding in Australia cost $27.6 million and this is the tip of the iceberg" (p. 4). The National Committee on Violence (1990) estimated that one homicide costs the Australian Community a million dollars, money that could be better spent on the prevention of violence or the promotion of effective relationships.

This concern about the level of violence has led to the introduction of conflict resolution programs in schools, a measure that seems to be both sensible and cost effective. But to what extent do such programs actually grapple with the fundamental issues of violence prevention? And, given the variation in such programs, how might a program be best tailored to this end? There are a number of unknowns: what the

DIANE BRETHERTON *is Associate Professor in the Department of Psychology, University of Melbourne, Parkville, Australia.*

Requests for reprints should be sent to Diane Bretherton, Department of Psychology, University of Melbourne, Parkville, Victoria 3052, Australia. E-mail: d.bretherton@psych. unimelb.edu.au

111

essential ingredients of such a program are, where it might best be located, what age groups might most benefit, what teaching methods should be used, and so on. Also, unless such programs are evaluated, there may be a gap between what adults think they are teaching the children and what the children are actually learning.

In this article, I explore some of the research that describes the process of growing up to be violent, review a typical conflict resolution program, and describe an action research project that provides some pointers to developing conflict resolution programs which address the problem of violence in greater depth.

Growing Up To Be Violent

Several researchers accept that attitudes toward conflict, and the skills we acquire in resolving it, are initially learned at home. The family is the forum in which most people learn how to communicate, solve problems, and work cooperatively. Eron (1982) found, in terms of interaction between parent and child, that those parents who punish their children physically and express dissatisfaction with their accomplishments and characteristics have the most aggressive children. An aggressive response may be defined as an intentional act that injures or harms another person. It involves using power to violate the legitimate rights of others and is the insistence upon expressing one's own thoughts and feelings, or getting one's own way, regardless of the feelings or rights of others. Following Straus (1979), aggression and violence can be seen as ranges on a continuum, with smaller actions such as pushing or hitting being termed *aggression* and more extreme actions such as shooting being judged *violent*. As women's groups have stressed, aggression and violence need not be this overt and may take more subtle forms, but the research on children makes use of observable behavioral indicators.

According to Lefkowitz, Eron, Walder, and Huesmann (1977), "The literature on aggression is monotonous in the consistency with which it reports sex differences" (p. 89). Within the family the idea of separate sex roles is established (Maccoby & Jacklin, 1974). Children are tagged with social cues as to gender, such as their clothing and name. Whereas adults attribute different treatment to the needs of the child, a baby dressed as a girl elicits different behaviors from care givers than the same baby dressed as a boy, who is provoked to more physically aggressive play. Boys are discouraged from expressing vulnerability, whereas girls are constantly reminded of their dependence in small ways. Smith and Green (1974) found greater amounts of aggression (verbal and physical) expressed by boys than girls. Omark and Edelman (1975) reported that male children from preschool to third grade were significantly more aggressive (hitting and pushing) than females. According to Cairns (1979), five times as many adolescent boys as girls are arrested for violent crimes such as homicide, robbery, and assault. The National Committee on Violence (1990) noted that the most probable perpetrator of violence is a male between the ages of 18 and 30.

As the child grows, the gendered nature of behavioral differences is reinforced by television, toys, books, and games. The Australian College of Paediatrics (1992) Policy Statement on Children's Television stated that television has become entrenched as the most important socializing influence in Australian Culture. The causality can be seen as bidirectional. Children who are aggressive become socially isolated and watch a lot of violent television (Eron, 1982). Watching violent television reinforces and condones their aggressive attitudes, and those who are already at risk are most vulnerable to the effects of television. War toys and their associated television scripts are gendered and reinforce the idea that males are active and females are passive. Action for boys is confused with violence, for example "action man" is a military figure, and "action movie" is a euphemism for fast and copious slaughter with special effects. Girls, on the other hand, are offered dolls to care for rather than being encouraged to take adventurous risks. Both boys and girls love action, color, and transformation, but this does not have to be linked with violence.

Walker and Browne (1985) suggested that sex role training that encourages girls to be passive creates a sense of helplessness. Seligman (1975) showed that animals who experienced helplessness early in life were vulnerable to helplessness later in life and hypothesized that the same principle might apply to humans. Walker and Browne (1985) concluded that,

> if women are to escape violent relationships, they must overcome their tendency to helplessness by, for instance, becoming angry rather than depressed, active rather than passive and more realistic about the likelihood of the relationship continuing on its aversive course rather than improving. In doing so, they must also overcome the sex role socialisation they have been taught from early childhood. (p. 192)

Conflict strategies that are learned at home may be brought to school and affect the incidence of aggression in the classroom. Slaby and Guerra (1988; Guerra & Slaby, 1990) argued that boys and girls develop sex role-related cognitive standards for seeking, interpreting, and responding to aggression. Their model integrates internal factors such as the individual's temperament or constitutional propensities, and the external factors such as sex role expectations and physical punishment. They hypothesized that antisocial aggressive adolescents, who had been incarcerated for violent offenses, were more likely, and low aggressive individuals less likely, to solve social problems by (a) defining problems in hostile ways, (b) adopting hostile goals, (c) seeking few additional facts, (d) generating few alternative solutions, and (e) anticipating few consequences for aggression. As well as documenting differences in problem-solving skills, they found antisocial aggressive individuals were more likely to hold beliefs legitimizing the use of aggression: that victims don't suffer, that aggression increases self-esteem, and that victims deserve aggression. That is, they showed a link between cognitive mediators (social problem-solving skills and attitudes toward aggression) and behavioral indicators of violence (such as being convicted of a violent offence).

The effect of television and popular culture on the minds of the young can be considered in the light of these cognitive mediators of aggression and violence. Material that reinforces the idea that the world is a frightening and hostile place might incline young people to a more hostile interpretation of interpersonal events. Plots that suggest that force can only be met by force justify beliefs in the legitimacy of aggression. Stories that suggest violence is the end of the story and the solution, rather than the start of a new cycle of violence, undercut an appreciation of the need to consider the consequences and costs of using violence. The idea that there is no choice forecloses on the search for other nonviolent solutions. In other words, possible harm lies not only in seeing aggression and violence modeled by heroes, but also in the message about the type of problem-solving techniques that are used. A cultural ethos of machismo, the "Rambo" genre, tends to narrow down the options. The emphasis is on winning. The alternatives to violence and the possible costs of violent solutions are not explored. Violent television and toys promote the idea that the enemy is less than human and that force is the way to solve things. Carlsson-Paige and Levin (1990) gave some tips on handling children's war play that teachers and parents find helpful.

Review of a Typical Conflict Resolution Program

The "Dealing With Conflict" course (Bretherton, Hooper, Hooper, Nancarrow, & Sedgman, 1989) was initially compiled in 1986 to be a "typical" conflict resolution program. A group of people experienced in teaching conflict resolution and mediation skills to young people pooled their knowledge to help teachers who wished to introduce conflict resolution into their classroom—as a contribution to the International Year of Peace—by providing them with a curriculum. The endeavor was to document the practical tried-and-true favorites, activities that seem to work consistently in workshops. These "grandmother's recipes" could be shared with other teachers. These were structured, printed up, and made available for use in schools. Teachers using the program would differ in terms of their prior experience of the concepts and methods. The aims of the course are to develop the students' awareness of the causes of conflict in their lives, and to build skills in the positive management of conflict. The program was designed for senior secondary school students, between 15 and 17 years of age, and has four phases.

The first step is "Assessing the Group." The teacher runs some introductory activities such as name games and ice breakers. An example of an activity is the line game. The group is to imagine a line running down the center of the room. Students place themselves along this imaginary line according to a number of bipolar dimensions (such as whether they live more than a 1-hr drive to the school or next door to the school, have their birthday at the start or the end of the year, know a lot about a certain film or have never heard of it and so on). This activity gets the group moving and fosters communication. The teacher observes how the group handles the introductory activities. For example, are all students included in activities? Do girls and boys mix with each other? Do the different ethnic groups mix? Do the students listen to each other and treat each other with respect? Before moving on to the next step the group negotiates the rules by which it will work. The class might be broken into subgroups that write up their ideas on how a classroom should operate, then share these in the larger group with a scribe writing down all the ideas. The teacher then uses his or her knowledge of conflict resolution strategies to ensure that integrative solutions are found. For example, if students suggest an unworkable rule, the teacher can ask the class to consider what the consequences of such a rule might be. This session might stretch the teacher's patience, but is necessary if the program is to be true to its own principles. It is also an opportunity for the teacher to demonstrate conflict resolution skills in action.

The second stage, "Building the Group," is designed to develop a trusting and trustworthy climate. If the group has effective communication skills and social cohesion, this phase may be brief. However, if the group is unresponsive, clique ridden, or denigrates members, then students will not be free to discuss conflicts. Conflicts over domestic detail or peer pressures (such as who does chores or whose preferences determine which television program is selected) are the meat of conflict resolution programs and are usually dealt with in a lighthearted way. Occasionally, a more serious issue, calling for a sensitive response, may emerge from these scenarios. To ensure the group is ready to respond aptly, the program provides the teacher with a bank of cooperative games, self-esteem activities, and listening skill exercises that can be used to improve the group awareness. An example of an activity at this stage is the body language exercise. Students work in pairs with one person talking and the other listening in turn. The teacher directs the listeners to vary their behavior. For example, sit back-to-back so the speaker can't see the listener, sit very close, speaker looks into the eyes of the listener, listener fiddles and is inattentive, listener remains unresponsive and poker faced. The group as a whole can discuss the feelings associated with the different conditions and list behaviors that signal that a listener is interested. More generally, the class can discuss the effect of nonverbal cues on personal interactions.

The third phase, "Dealing With Conflict," is the core content of the program and consists of nine lesson plans. Students are asked to give some of their own scenarios to define what conflict is, to discuss a videotape that shows some typical adolescent conflict scenarios, to talk about the conflicts they experience, and to keep a conflict diary. The causes of conflict are discussed in relation to self-concept, peer pressure, power, racial and cultural differences, and the magnification of small conflicts and family hassles. Students are taught that

> often in a conflict the people involved both try to win without thinking about what needs to be changed. Concentrating on being a winner only leaves both people angry and the problem not solved. People need to work together to find a solution that both are happy with—then both people are winners. Conflicts are helpful to us because they let us know that there is a need for change. (Bretherton et al., 1989, p. 43)

Three conflict styles are identified: avoidance, aggression, and assertiveness. Role plays are used to help students identify the differences between them. Problems (such as, You notice that one of your younger neighbors is shoplifting from the milkbar—what do you do? One of the teachers writes on the board in letters that are too small for you to see properly from the back of the room, where you like to sit. What should you do?) are posed so the students can practice the analysis and assertive resolution of conflict.

The fourth phase, "Communication," provides five lesson plans for further practice in communication skills. For example, in Lesson 4 students work in triads and are given topics such as "Should schools have uniforms?" "school violence," or "drug use and abuse" to discuss. Person A practices using open-ended questions, reflective listening, and summarizing skills to draw out the concerns and opinions of person B. Person C observes and gives feedback, which necessitates using assertion. Finally, there is a questionnaire that teachers can use to evaluate the program as a whole.

An evaluation of the program was conducted (Bretherton, Collins, & Ferretti, 1993). The study used a social-cognitive model to examine the perceptions and beliefs of secondary school students in relation to aggressive behavior and investigated the effectiveness of the 10-week training program. Eighty-nine adolescents with an average age of 15 years, in four inner-Melbourne schools, participated. Three classes received one session per week of the training and the fourth acted as a control group. A peer rating (Walder, Abelson, Eron, Banta, & Laulicht, 1961) and the Straus (1979) conflict tactics scale were used to classify students as either high, medium, or low aggressive. The students' perceptions, problem-solving skills, and beliefs relating to aggression were tested before and after the training, using the Slaby and Guerra measures (1988; Guerra & Slaby, 1990). The training group was compared with the control group to investigate any change in these cognitive mediators of aggression or in their self-reported conflict tactics.

There were significant differences found between high and low aggressive students. High aggressive students were significantly more likely to choose a hostile goal than were low and medium aggressive students. High aggressive students were significantly more likely to perceive aggression as a legitimate response. There were no other significant differences in the cognitive mediators found between the aggression groups. Gender differences in aggression were found with males being more likely to report using physical violence. On the pretest the boys were found to be significantly more likely than the girls to agree with the belief that aggression increases self-esteem, helps to avoid a negative image, and that victims deserve their victimization. There was no significant difference between the boys and girls regarding the belief that aggression is a legitimate response or that victims of aggression don't suffer. However, there was no significant change on the five beliefs measures as a result of doing the training.

Analysis of the effectiveness of the dealing with conflict program revealed a decrease in both hostile perception of problems and hostile goal selection for the training group. After completing the program, students reported a decreased use of physical violence.

Although the decreased use of physical violence reported was encouraging, this could be reflecting the fact that the scale is a self-report measure. Students may have been less frank in reporting the use of physical violence rather than actually changing their day-to-day behavior. Further, there is a difference in being able to resolve conflicts nonviolently in one context and being motivated to do so in another. For example, studies of domestic violence, such as the one by Hatty (1987), show that offenses occur across occupational ratings, suggesting that having effective managerial skills in the workplace does not ensure that a man will refrain from coercive or violent behavior in the home. The finding that the belief that aggression increases self-esteem in males was not challenged by the program suggests a serious shortcoming in the approach.

Another limitation of the program was its overemphasis on the written word. The program itself takes the form of a written curriculum, and participants in the program felt that there were too many worksheets. If more innovative teaching methods are to be used the adults who run the program may need training in ways of encouraging a more active style of learning; more creative evaluation techniques might be necessary.

Although most students reported that the course was useful and enjoyable, observers commented on the derivative nature of some of the classroom role plays. Although it is important to link the conflict resolution curriculum to fields outside the classroom, and encourage a critical analysis of how conflict is handled on television, it is not very useful to simply reproduce scenes from the soap operas. How role plays are discussed is an important issue. If aggression can be learned, and the social cognitive approach suggests that it can, then teachers need to consider how to talk about aggression and violence without reinforcing it.

In discussions with the teachers, the relation of the conflict resolution program to the school curriculum also emerged as an issue. Time within the school day tends to be committed to timetabled subjects, and the organizational structures do not necessarily support the methods and concepts of conflict resolution. Also, there is a contradiction for the teachers who will need to loosen the reins if students are to be empowered, but are judged by other teachers on the extent to which they are seen as being in control of the children.

An Action Research Project

Action research follows a cycle of planning, implementation, and reflection; with the reflection feeding into the planning for the next cycle.

Planning

It followed from the aforementioned situation that a conflict resolution program for children should address the issue of gender, should be experiential, should include training for the teachers, and should be monitored and provide feedback for the teachers so that teachers as well as children are seen as developing learners. Given that conflict resolution programs urge teachers to empower children, and yet trainee teachers may be expected to demonstrate an ability to control children—and that there are pressures to get through a set curriculum in the classroom—we decided to locate our training in afterschool care.

Out-of-school-hours care is based either in schools or in community halls and differs from the classroom in that attendance is voluntary. Some child care workers believe there should not be a structured program because the children have a full day in school. Our (Allard, Bretherton, & Collins, 1992) observations in setting up the program were that spontaneous play scripts were heavily influenced by aggressive themes from popular culture and that free play situations in child care could result in vulnerable children being bullied. Child care workers informed us that as boys grew they tended to see afterschool care as babyish and to drift on to the streets, increasing the risk of contact with delinquent subcultures. The prevailing attitude among the workers seemed to be that "boys will be boys" and that aggression is natural. We decided it would be important to include child care students and workers in the program along with the teacher trainees. We also felt that gender should be a central issue, not only in the children and their relationships with each other, but also in the gendered behavior of the adults, largely women, who care for the children. Given that our program for change was to deal with conflict resolution in relation to gender, aggression, and violence it was a little difficult to think of a succinct title. The children themselves call afterschool care "Afters," and so when our program was implemented the children named it simply Afters.

Implementation

The Afters program provided the means to address gender issues through conflict resolution strategies on two levels: first, through working with the adults, who will be termed teachers, and second, with children. The adults were 20 third-year B.Ed (Primary) students and child care students who were offered a special training over a 6-week period. Through a series of activities they were taught awareness of gender issues and conflict resolution skills. The teachers then worked in pairs to develop these skills in 10 groups of children, with group sizes ranging from 4 to 20 children, in four afterschool care centers. The children ranged in age from 5 to 12 years. These figures are approximate. One of the features of child care that disconcerted us was the fluid drop-in and drop-out rate of child care programs. The groups, consisting of pairs of teachers working with their children, were videotaped over a 10-week period. During this time, the teachers kept a weekly journal in which they reflected on their experiences of working with children. Each pair of teachers was free to tailor a curriculum through negotiating with their group of children. The teachers were visited in the child care settings, by the research team members, to discuss progress and provide support. Several teacher meetings were held back at the university, to allow teachers to share experiences; their final evaluation meeting was audio taped and transcribed.

The videotapes were used to give teachers feedback about the way they ran their groups and to help them understand how their own gender behavior and beliefs affected their interactions with children. Waiting patiently, doing the major share of the food preparation and clean up, and looking after the little ones were expectations that they applied more to girls than to boys. Girls who were more assertive, which is after all what the program was trying to teach, tended to be labeled "bossy boots" or "madam." Cooperation in girls tended to be taken for granted rather than rewarded. Boys tended to be given more attention, be it praise or blame, called by name more often, given first choice of equipment, given more help, and excused for their aggressive behavior (e.g., "boys will be boys," "he is just having a bad day," or "he's bored"). Although the teachers we had trained learned not to use aggressive computer games, war toys, violent videos, and television programs as a way of keeping the boys quiet, it was not easy to let go of valuing activities that are traditionally seen as "masculine" (e.g., building rockets) over those traditionally seen as "feminine" (e.g., sewing puppets).

The videotapes were edited into a 28-min documentary, "Afters: Gender and Conflict in After School Care." The aim of the videotape, and its accompanying booklet, is to present the information in a manner that is accessible to people working with children who would not necessarily read academic articles. The following discussion will be more meaningful to readers who are able to view it. The videotape, then, is on two levels; the edited tape, which will be referred to in the singular, and the naturalistic footage, which will be referred to in the plural form.

We used the "Dealing With Conflict" course (Bretherton et al., 1989) as a starting point for the conflict resolution content of the course for both the teachers and the children. Activities suitable for younger children, such as puppet making and plays, were used to teach nonviolent resolution of conflict. With young children, activities like cooking, puppet making, and movement games such as Tangles and Fruit Salad worked well. Other activities that teachers listed in their journals as being successful included: The Love Tree, Chinese Whispers, Story Telling, Feeling Box, Painting & Drawing, Self Advertisement, Special Person, Freeze, Pass the Parcel, and Building a Machine (see Bond, 1989; Borba & Barba, 1978; Callister, Davies, & Pope, 1988; Canfield & Wells, 1976; Connor, 1988; Cutting & Wilson, 1992; Judson, 1983; Kniedler, 1984; Kruper, 1973; Prutzman, 1978; Wichert, 1989; Wilson & Hoyne, 1991; and Women Against Violence Communications, 1984, for such activities). This fun approach was necessary in child care where a more didactic approach would be seen as inappropriate. The teachers also became adept at modifying traditional games to more cooperative forms, such as musical chairs where children do not go out, but must all fit onto a decreasing number of chairs.

We found that young children can learn conflict resolution techniques, and show this on the videotape. For example, in one scene Doris, the teacher, has set Rose and Jemima a problem: There are two puppets in the play but only one ruler. Rose and Jemima explore a number of different ways of dealing with the conflict this has posed. A wide variety of common methods of dealing with conflict are acted out by Rose and Jemima in the spontaneous puppet production, offering various solutions to the problem of the ruler. Their suggested solutions are listed here with the category of solution in parentheses:

"Cut the ruler in half" (compromise)
"Sooky baby" "You've got yukky hair" (insult)
The children enact hitting (physical violence)
"Boo hoo" (crying)
"I'll do a suicide" (threat)
"Goodbye" (withdrawal, avoidance)

"Come on sucker, make my day" (imitating television)

"I'd like to say sorry" (apology)

"Let's be friends and let's share the ruler" (sharing is the integrative solution)

Doris shows great patience, asking the children, "does that solve the problem?" until finally they arrive at a just and effective solution. The tape shows how young children are capable of generating a variety of creative responses to conflict and making informed judgments about the efficacy of different solutions. That is, it supports the idea that young children have the cognitive ability to learn conflict resolution techniques. The tape also illustrates how children incorporate aggressive scripts from popular culture: the implied revenge shooting "come on sucker, make my day," and two threats of suicide. This is a timely reminder that there are many influences on a child's thinking. Television, videos, rock clips, and other popular media present a particular view of conflict and problem solving that runs counter to the ethic of nonviolence. They build a notion of masculinity that is based on aggression, violence, and domination.

The Afters program drew on the experience of Andrea Allard in designing gender-inclusive curricula. The assumption underlying the Afters program is that problem-solving skills can be learned, giving the person a range of response options to choose from in any given situation, but—because aggression is culturally condoned in boys, whereas girls are encouraged to be submissive—the teaching of assertion to boys will differ from teaching assertion to girls. The dichotomy between "masculine" and "feminine" is not set in stone, but must continually be learned and relearned (Clark, 1989; Davies, 1988). How "successful" one is may be determined by others' reactions to specific behavior and interactions. When children do "cross over" in their behaviors, that is, move outside of what is seen as appropriate to their gender, their peers and adults often will perceive that behavior as outside the norm and in need of correction. Thus, when a girl exhibits loud, demanding behavior, because this is not widely understood as gender appropriate, she may well be viewed as an aggressive girl and treated with dismissal or disapproval. However, when similar behavior is exhibited by a boy, this may be read as gender appropriate. Similar actions by a girl or a boy may receive dissimilar responses. For example, Louise is seen as bossy and pushy by her teachers and many viewers. However, a careful analysis of the videotape shows her as being very conscientious and so ready to obey the teacher that she occasionally even anticipates commands.

Reflection

The videotape shows all too vividly that even adults who are trained in gender awareness behave toward the children in ways that perpetuate discrimination. Even when teaching listening skills, the teacher can listen to boys and ask girls to wait, and attend to the aggressive boys while expecting the girls to remain silent. The videotape highlights the difference between espousing a belief, such as equality, and enacting it in interaction with children. The video demonstrates that some children, mainly boys, individually demanded and received far more than their fair share of the resources. Other individuals, mainly girls, sat patiently waiting for a fair share. The educational goals for boys and girls were the same. For example, both boys and girls needed to learn cooperative behavior, active listening, assertive speaking, problem-solving strategies, and negotiation. However, in developing these skills with children, the teachers needed to keep in mind that girls and boys, because of their gendered experiences, had different starting points. Different skills needed to be emphasized for different children. For example, many girls had already learned cooperative behaviors but needed more practice in assertively speaking about their needs. On the other hand, boys required more work in active listening skills because many boys are not used to practicing these.

Unlike many programs that address gender issues, the Afters program emphasized the need for girls and boys to learn and practice communication skills together. If girls learn about assertion in groups with other girls, we are not teaching the boys to actively listen to the girls when they assert their needs. The conditions of assertion in a girls-only group will differ from those in a mixed group. There is no reason to assume that the skills will automatically transfer, particularly because girls tend to be ignored in mixed groups anyway. Conversely, if boys are isolated in all-boy groups, the message that boys only need to listen to other boys is reinforced. Skills built and practiced in the context in which they will be used tend to be applied more effectively than if they have been learned in a different context. The videotape showed that children who had learned the skills in a mixed group of boys and girls are able to use them to create more equal relationships even in the absence of adult guidance. The value of teaching these skills in mixed groups is especially relevant with primary school age children because this is the time when most boys and girls cease to play together (except in private).

The videotape provided a useful means of reflecting on what was happening in the group, what worked well, and what needed to be changed. For example, the videotapes indicated that when teachers began working with the groups of children there were some shared common misunderstandings about conflict resolution strategies. These included confusing children's politeness with active listening, confusing being nice to the children with effective group management, insisting on cooperation at the expense of addressing conflict within the group, and confusing compliance on the part of the children with effective resolution of conflict. As the teachers were predominantly female, reflecting the predominance of women in early childhood care and education, this can be seen as a gendered interpretation of what conflict resolution is. In line with their own socialization as women to be pleasing, the teachers interpreted the subject matter as being pleasant. On the other hand, the two male teachers who undertook the program found it very difficult indeed and are not shown on the tape.

On the basis of video evidence, the teachers' abilities to fully utilize the conflict resolution processes and to make the links between the suggested activities and the children's skill development varied greatly. The source of this variance was not only the ability to work with children but also the ability to be open to change in oneself. Some teachers were more able to "see" the videotape and reflect on their own behavior patterns than were others. Just as the program was ending the teachers reached the stage of being comfortable with the group looking at each other's tapes. This was very useful as it allowed an analysis of what was happening, and for rerunning the tapes to decide if an intervention was well timed, could have been handled differently, and so on. This gets past the habit teachers have of saying "I tried it and it doesn't work," for clearly "it" works for some of the people some of the time.

Journal keeping was important in giving the teacher a chance to state her or his own perceptions, to give the inner voice expression. The interplay of the inner intention as expressed in the journal, and the outer view as recorded by the camera, proved to be a much richer source of information gathering and personal change than did the more conventional research approaches of questionnaires, quantitative analysis, and so on. For example, one of the male teachers wrote in his journal that the children threatened his authority, while his behavior as illustrated by the tape was to literally stand over the children.

The teachers often commented on the advantage of working in pairs. This enabled them to share their thoughts and to reflect together on the progress of the group. A number of them chose to monitor each other's interactions with the children as a way of exploring the group dynamics. By providing each other with support and understanding, they were better able to grapple with difficult and complex issues and together were more willing to take risks in trying out new ideas. This cooperative approach was integral to the Afters program and enabled the adults to share their reflections, through the use of the videotapes that they were able to monitor themselves to check if what they were actually doing matched their intentions, and to reflect on their actions.

Several helpful suggestions for the teacher of nonviolent conflict resolution flow from the Afters program. There needs to be a shift from a didactic instructional mode to an interactive mode that is monitored, through working in pairs and through recording and replaying class interactions. The next step in an action research cycle might be to recognize that some of the elements that the teachers found most helpful were not replicated at the children's own level. The focus for children was on learning the conflict resolution skills through play. The children did not have activities in gender awareness, or opportunities to reflect on the videotaped interactions, or some equivalent of the journal process. Although this may be appropriate given the age of the children, it is possible that this underestimated their capacity for reflection and did not challenge their ideas about gender roles.

Implications

The evaluation of Dealing with Conflict found that the program was popular with staff and students, and that students reported a decreased use of violence as a conflict resolution strategy after participating in the program. However, the fact that the program did not challenge deeper attitudes toward gender and aggression was highlighted by the evaluation. The observations of the Afters program—which demonstrate that conflict resolution skills may be taught in a way that is gender biased—converge with the research literature on violence, which emphasizes the centrality of gender to understanding its incidence. Experiences from this program provide a cautionary note for practitioners and researchers. Although conflict resolution techniques have potential as a means of reducing violence in society, this will not be realized if they are taught in a superficial or biased way. The Afters program provides some pointers. Both teachers and children need to be seen as entering the group with habitual ways of relating that reflect the wider social structures. Observations need to be made of how conflicts are in fact being handled by the group. We need to monitor, reflect, and learn from our efforts to teach conflict resolution. Conflict resolution involves the tacit assumption that we are preventing violence but perhaps it is timely to make the link between conflict resolution and the theory of nonviolence overt and explore it more fully. This entails shifting conflict resolution from a bag of techniques to a philosophy of relationships. As the teachers in the Afters program reflected, one might begin by thinking a short course will make a difference but really "its more of a life long process."

References

Allard, A., Bretherton, D., & Collins, L. (1992). *Afters: Gender and conflict in after school care* [Videotape and booklet]. (Available from the International Conflict Resolution Center, Behavioral Science, University of Melbourne, Parkville, Australia 3052)

Australian College of Paediatrics. (1992). *Children's television policy statement.* Parkville, Australia: Author.

Bond, T. (1989). *Games for social and life skills.* London: Hutchinson.

Borba, M., & Barba, C. (1978). *Self-esteem: A classroom affair. 101 ways to help children like themselves* (Vols. 1–2). Minneapolis, MN: Winston.

Bretherton, D., Collins, L., & Ferretti, C. (1993). Dealing with conflict: Assessment of a course for secondary students. *Australian Psychologist, 28,* 105–111.

Bretherton, D., Hooper, A., Hooper, J., Nancarrow, L., & Sedgman, C. (1989). *Dealing with conflict: A course for young people.* (Available from the International Conflict Resolution Center, Behavioral Science, University of Melbourne, Parkville, Australia 3052)

Cairns, R. B. (1979). *Social development.* San Francisco: Freeman.

Callister, E., Davis, N., & Pope, B. (1988). *Me and you and others. Class and group activities for personal development.* Victoria, Australia: Brooks Waterloo of McPherson's.

Canfield, J., & Wells, H. (1976). *100 ways to enhance self-concept in the classroom. A handbook for teachers and parents.* Englewood Cliffs, NJ: Prentice-Hall.

Carlsson-Paige, N., & Levin, D. (1990). *Who's calling the shots? How to respond effectively to children's fascination with war play and war toys.* Philadelphia: New Society.

Clark, M. (1989). *The great divide. The construction of gender in the primary school.* Canberra, Australia: Curriculum Development Center.

Connor, G. (1988). *Self-esteem: Teachers hold some keys. A resource supporting social development and self-esteem in schools.* Perth: Western Australia Ministry of Education.

Cutting, L., & Wilson, J. (1992). *Squashed bananas, mouldy sultanas: A diet of chants.* Melbourne, Australia: Oxford University Press.

Davies, B. (1988). *Gender, equity, and early childhood.* Canberra, Australia: Curriculum Development Center.

Eron, L. (1982). Parent–child interaction, television violence, and aggression of children. *American Psychologist, 37,* 197–211.

Guerra, N., & Slaby, R. (1990). Cognitive mediators of aggression in adolescent offenders: Intervention. *Developmental Psychology, 26,* 269–277.

Hatty, S. E. (1987). Women battering as a social problem: The denial of injury. *Australia and New Zealand Journal of Sociology, 23,* 36–46.

Judson, S. (1983). *A manual on nonviolence and children.* Philadelphia: New Society.

Kniedler, W. J. (1984). *Creative conflict resolution. More than 200 activities for keeping peace in the classroom. K–6.* London: Scott, Foresman.

Kruper, K. (1973). *Communication games.* New York: Free Press.

Lefkowitz, M., Eron, L., Walder, L., & Huesmann, L. (1977). *Growing up to be violent: A longitudinal study of the development of aggression.* New York: Pergamon.

Maccoby, E. E., & Jacklin, C. N. (1974). *The psychology of sex difference.* Stanford, CA: Stanford University Press.

Mugford, J. (1989). *Domestic violence.* Canberra, Australia: National Committee on Violence.

National Committee on Violence. (1990). *Violence: Directions for Australia.* Canberra: Australian Institute of Criminology.

Omark, D. R., & Edelman, M. S. (1975). Formation of dominance hierarchies in young children: Attention and perception. In T. Williams (Ed.), *Psychological anthropology.* The Hague, The Netherlands: Mouton.

Prutzman, P. (1978). *Friendly classroom for a small planet.* Philadelphia: New Society.

Seligman, M. (1975). *Helplessness: On depression, development and death.* San Francisco: Freeman.

Slaby, R. G., & Guerra, N. G. (1988). Cognitive mediators of aggression in adolescent offenders: 1. Assessment. *Developmental Psychology, 24,* 580–588.

Smith, P. K., & Green, M. (1974). Aggressive behavior in English nurseries and playgroups: Sex differences and the response of adults. *Child Development, 45,* 211–214.

Straus, M. (1979). Measuring intrafamily conflict and violence: The conflict tactics (CT) scales. *Journal of Marriage and the Family, 41,* 75–88.

Walder, L., Abelson, R., Eron, L., Banta, T., & Laulicht, J. (1961). Development of a peer-rating measure of aggression. *Psychological Reports, 9,* 497–556.

Walker, L. E., & Browne, A. (1985). Gender and victimisation by intimates. *Journal of Personality, 53,* 170–195.

Wichert, S. (1989). *Keeping the peace; practicing cooperation and conflict resolution with preschoolers.* Philadelphia: New Society.

Wilson, J., & Hoyne, P. (1991). *Cooking with class: Celebrating festivals with cooking.* Melbourne, Australia: Oxford University Press.

Women Against Violence Communications. (1984). *Building bridges. Co-operation activity for the classroom.* Blackburn, Australia: Dove Communications.

PEABODY JOURNAL OF EDUCATION, 71(3), 128–150
Copyright © 1996, Lawrence Erlbaum Associates, Inc.

Exploring Peace Education in South African Settings

Valerie Dovey

Peace doesn't form a picture in my mind because I haven't experienced complete peace.
—South African high school student, 1992

The Youth Project of the Centre for Conflict Resolution (CCR)—formerly known as the Centre for Intergroup Studies, an autonomous institute associated with the University of Cape Town—focuses on the field of constructive conflict resolution and peacemaking empowerment for young South Africans and is one of the pioneers in this field in South Africa. In 1992, the Human Sciences Research Council initiated a cooperative research program into South African youth and the problems and challenges they face. Among the program objectives were the initiation and support of research into South African youth, and the generation of academically sound research results with significant policy implications.

CCR was commissioned to participate and submit a report titled "Conflict Resolution and Peacemaking Among Youth." The report was

VALERIE DOVEY *is Youth Project Coordinator at the Centre for Conflict Resolution, University of Cape Town, Cape Town, South Africa.*

Requests for reprints should be sent to Valerie Dovey, Centre for Conflict Resolution, Private Bag, University of Cape Town, Cape Town, Rondebosch 7700, South Africa. E-mail: vjdovey@ccr.uct.ac.za compiled by myself (Valerie Botha Dovey), as Youth Project Coordinator, and by an associate, Adele Kirsten, and presented in May 1993 (Botha & Kirsten, 1993). The report aimed to promote the development and implementation of conflict resolution and peacemaking programs for young South Africans, and worked toward equipping them with resources and skills that encourage an ethos of constructive conflict resolution and peacemaking.

In exploring peace education in South African settings, this article provides a synopsis of aspects of our research report. It does this in three sections that look at (a) the needs of our children and youth, (b) the range of initiatives already working in this field, and (c) some suggested future directions.

For the purposes of our report, the term *peace education* is used in a generic sense and encompasses the fields of conflict resolution and peacemaking.

The Needs of South African Children and Youth

In looking at the needs of South African children and youth, the article draws from the empirical component of our research that had two components—a Western Cape and a Johannesburg-based survey. In both surveys, groups of young people and educationists were involved.

In the Western Cape, questionnaires were completed by 189 young people between 12 and 30 years of age. The sample represented a variety of ethnic backgrounds and home languages, and youngsters who were at school, studying further, working, and unemployed. The Johannesburg youth sample involved 107 pupils from Standard 4 and Standard 8 levels at 10 representative schools in the wider Johannesburg area. Our research material emanated from group discussions generated around a series of pictures depicting conflict situations and questionnaires.

A number of educationists and others working in youth-related areas were interviewed. We also included input obtained from consultations and discussions initiated by the CCR with people around the country as part of our ongoing peace education promotion work. The "educationists and other" category thus represents a variety of fields and—besides academics, teachers, curriculum specialists, and researchers—includes health and welfare professionals, lawyers, and members of grassroots and community organizations. Our discussions focused largely on establishing whether there is a need for peace education for South African children and youth, and if this is indicated, how best peace education could happen. This article summarizes what our respondents had to say in response to specific questions and focuses on common themes that emerged.

Our report prefaced the section on the needs of South African children and youth by looking at the context in which they are growing up. Mokwena (1992) reminded us that South Africa is one of the most violent places in the world. A culture of violence permeates the society—not merely in the overt political violence reported in the world's media, but also in the entertainment media, the spiralling levels of crime, road and work accidents, and domestic violence. And those most directly affected by our country's violence have been the children (McKendrick & Hoffman, 1990).

What Do Our Young People Say?

The young people in our survey tell us that South African children and youth from all walks of life are living in a conflict-ridden culture—whether it be at intrapersonal, interpersonal, intergroup, or broader societal levels. In our questionnaire, many of their associations with the word *conflict* referred to states of violence, war, fighting, and death, and situations characterized by friction, chaos, hurt, and a lack of peace. They were predominantly related to negative situations and provided graphic illustrations of this: "Guns—fire—people running around crying"; "Broken, uptight, unravelled and hurt"; "Unhappiness in my home—not ever feeling wanted or longed for."

The vast majority of our respondents spoke of experiencing conflict in their own lives, with family-related conflicts featuring significantly. A predominant theme in the family conflicts experienced was the feeling that parents showed lack of respect for children as individuals and that parental decisions were imposed rather than discussed. Many issues had to do with ineffective parental communication with children, and with disagreements about issues such as freedom to make choices, the suitability of friends, and careers. Sibling-related conflicts centered inter alia on jealousy, provocation to get attention, arguments about home duties, and a lack of respect for possessions.

Many of the older respondents referred to the prevalence of intrapersonal conflicts in their lives. These had to do inter alia with fear of failure and making mistakes because of ignorance; feelings of being out of control; inability to solve problems and make decisions; trouble handling criticism; matters of salvation, trust, and conscience; and concerns about how to make progress in life and make friends. Some respondents spoke of conflicts related to lack of self-understanding and self-confidence, inability to communicate effectively, and the expression of individuality in the face of strong influence by others: "My greatest conflict is with myself. I have conflicting ideas of what my life in general is really about"; "Not being able to express myself well enough to be understood the way I want to be."

Other common conflict areas centered around friends, teachers, politics, and racial discrimination. Social problems areas mentioned focused mainly on drug and alcohol use and abuse, as well as problems such as AIDS, gangs, poverty, inadequate housing, unemployment, township terror, and sexual harassment: "Young people in South Africa are under a lot of pressure."

Conflicts related to education were prevalent for many of the Black youngsters surveyed. They mentioned issues such as the high cost of education, the South African education system, and the disruption that has characterized their school careers.

Our survey group as a whole was highly supportive of the idea of young people learning to deal with conflict constructively. Accompanying comments spoke of conflict being everywhere, and of young people being "prisoners" of their internal and external conflicts—often not knowing how to deal with different conflict situations effectively. Some respondents mentioned suicide and engaging in other negative behaviors as a result of being ill-equipped to handle conflict. Some felt that the prevalence of family disintegration and domestic and societal states of alienation, chaos, and violence—and their effects on young people—make this kind of training imperative. Its importance in equipping young people for their roles in a changing South Africa was highlighted: "We all have conflict and must all learn to deal with adverse situations and stop repressing and building anger which leads to hatred."

In terms of the anticipated benefits of conflict resolution programs, the composite picture emerging from the survey was that young people would be equipped with lifeskills and constructive bases for problem solving and decision making. These programs would help young people to (a) develop self-confidence; (b) develop understanding of themselves and others; (c) develop mutual respect, tolerance, and appreciation of differences; (d) express their feelings and communicate more effectively; (e) take greater responsibility for their actions; and (f) become equipped to deal with conflict in constructive ways.

The consequent development of personal and interactive skills could reduce the incidence of violence, crime, gangsterism, suicide, drug abuse, and broken relationships, and generally contribute to the creation of a more peaceful present and future society. Conflict would be transformed into "something good": "That might bring peace in the country. People who [have been] taught about this program are the ones who are going [to] teach others who haven't [had] the opportunity"; "The benefits will obviously lead to peace because teaching a young person [is] teaching the whole nation."

Motivating comments for conflict resolution programs being part of a school curriculum or presented in school settings suggested inter alia that (a) this was the forum for reaching the greatest number of young people, (b) every child would have the opportunity to learn conflict resolution skills, (c) there were ongoing opportunities to interact with other young people, (d) skills could be taught and progressively reinforced in school settings, and (e) a subject like conflict resolution was a component of "all-round" education. Some respondents, however, expressed concerns that the introduction of additional programs might interfere with their schoolwork.

Respondents stressed the importance of children growing up with the correct knowledge and skills that they can apply throughout their lives. A number of respondents suggested that teaching should commence "as soon as children can understand" or as early as possible—while they are still "open" and before they become set in their ways: "If you want to build a house you start with the foundation"; "This is a starting point to enrich our societies for a better life, South Africa and world."

There was a general feeling among the young people surveyed that they have a vital part to play in the peacemaking process in South Africa and they welcome opportunities that enable them to do this. They see themselves as being an energetic, enthusiastic, creative, vibrant, spirited, gregarious, and a powerful force. They are tomorrow's leaders and parents and they should be equipped for these roles while they are still young. They could be positive role models for their parents, peers, community leaders, and the rest of South Africa: "The new generation believes in peace."

Suggestions about how young people could work toward peace included: interacting with other young people and promoting peace among themselves, changing their attitudes, encouraging White youth to visit Black townships, taking active roles in community projects, and using effective strategies and channels (e.g., youth groups, church activities, political organizations, and rallies). Youth should also crusade actively against discrimination, and work to alleviate social problems such as gangsterism and drug abuse. Some respondents spoke of a need for youth to start with developing self-respect, self-determination, self-confidence, and assertiveness, and to "liberate their minds" so that they could focus on new horizons.

The need was expressed for young people to be taught about responsible decision making and constructive conflict resolution and peace-making, and to be motivated to apply this learning confidently and effectively in their lives. Supportive education in their homes, schools, and communities was important.

The contributions of adults, friends, churches, schools, governments, political organizations, and professionals (e.g., psychologists and psychiatrists) to help youngsters deal with the repercussions of conflict were valued. Family involvement was also mentioned. Working closely with, and showing respect for, parents was seen to be important and families could make a valuable contribution by, for example, establishing effective and fair "discipline" strategies and platforms for constructive discussion: "Parents have a lot of 'ammunition' that was propaganda from the past. They find it hard to understand the plain love and acceptance that young people naturally have."

The institution of a nonracial, unitary education system was seen as essential by some respondents. Educational programs, training workshops, leadership training, holiday activities, inter-youth camps, and conferences—organized with regular follow-ups so that contacts and friendships could be promoted and mutual understanding encouraged—were suggested by many respondents. Training and outreach programs should happen in all communities and a special plea was made for initiatives to reach youth in rural areas. Organizations working in the peace education field were seen to have an important role to play in the empowerment of young people: "If parents, teachers and everyone in the community start to address this, a huge change will be seen."

What Do Educationists Say?

Questions about the kinds of conflicts perceived to be facing young South Africans today drew a wide variety of responses, and backed up what the young people surveyed had to say in this regard. Young people in South Africa today are experiencing conflicts ranging from ones that are related to sociopolitical issues, to those on more personal levels. The fact that intrapersonal, interpersonal, and family conflicts are prevalent in many young lives should not be lost sight of in our preoccupation with the more macrosocietal problem areas and their impact on the young.

Our respondents saw youth as flexible and creative people who have vision, hope, optimism, energy, and a desire to make a contribution to the peacemaking process in South Africa. Many of them are far more assertive and "verbal" than their parents were at their age, but they are often insufficiently equipped to channel their idealism constructively. They need to have opportunities to understand, question, and challenge how society operates and how they can influence peaceful change in a positive way.

Youth should be empowered to take responsibility for themselves, to relate to others in constructive ways, and to deal effectively and positively with conflict situations in their schools, homes, streets, communities, and at wider societal and national levels. The needs of youth should be taken cognizance of holistically.

The need for peace-education-type programs for children and youth was endorsed by all respondents. Such a need is a critical one—in view, particularly, of our violent heritage and the multitude of challenges being presented to our young people today as members of a society in transition.

In terms of introducing such programs, the approach should be an all-embracing one, involving schools, families, and communities. School-based programs would help filter concepts of peacemaking and constructive conflict resolution to the community at large. South African pupils and teachers were seen to have a critical role to play as effective agents of change in our society.

The school ethos is an important consideration. Peace must be manifest in school procedures, and principals and teachers should work to promote this by assessing whether peace education is compatible with a school environment that shows signs of injustice and allows little opportunity for student participation and exercise of responsibility.

The climate is conducive to experimentation. Education departments have become less rigid and teachers have been encouraged to become more creative. Many schools have the leeway to introduce new programs and take responsibility for curriculum development. Some schools have developed a core curriculum of examinable subjects and are showing flexibility as they introduce other subject areas into a more general curriculum. This could be a place for peace education. "Social problem" issues are increasingly finding their way into school curricula, and many teachers are becoming aware of the need for courses in conflict resolution. There are already practical examples of how the principles of subject correlation in education are being applied to incorporate new ideas, and teachers should be given practical guidelines regarding infusion of peace education concepts.

Curriculum planners and textbook designers should be actively involved and publications designed to suggest bases for debate and peace-related themes should be developed. Support from outside facilitators and experts should be solicited and cooperation with projects already existent in school and other settings encouraged.

Some of our discussions suggested that a key issue would be methodology related rather than content related. Much of the material presupposes an established sense of identity among young people. Many of them would have difficulty talking about their own identity, let alone talking about "what it means to be a South African!" Methodology should be such that students are encouraged to become actively involved in the program, and a process of interdependence and cooperation among students stimulated.

In terms of focus, peace education should be looking at personal empowerment that cannot, however, be divorced from political empowerment. Peace education was seen to be a political as well as an educative matter and content should relate to practical issues affecting youth. The enhancement of self-esteem should be a core component of any such program.

Links of school-based peace education with the home and broader settings should be made explicit and school programs supplemented by youth involvement in community outreach activities where their input will be seen by them as "making a difference" and having a lasting effect. Community support for and involvement in the introduction of peace education programs is important and could suggest other entry points for peace education. Cross-cultural interchange opportunities should be provided for young people of all races and cultures in an effort to promote a wider culture of peace.

An Overview of Peace Education Initiatives

The field of peace education might be relatively new in South Africa, but the very existence of a wide and exciting range of initiatives indicates that the need for the promotion of a culture of peace among our young people is being regarded seriously by practitioners, educationists, and researchers alike. This article looks at some of our programmatic and research initiatives and refers to certain recent developments not included in our research report.

Programmatic Initiatives

There are a number of institutions and organizations making important contributions and advances to the overall field of peace education in South Africa. Some, like the CCR and the Quaker Peace Centre, have been pioneers exploring and working in this area for some time now.

CCR houses its own youth project that works to encourage the development and implementation of conflict resolution and peace education programs for South African children and youth. For the past 3 years the project has directed its activities in the areas of training, research, resource collection, local and international networking, and public awareness. Its primary focus is training the teachers and other "trainers" of young people.

The formal start of the project was launched in 1991 with research for a publication, *Interactive Skills for South African Youngsters* (Botha, 1991b), which aimed to provide the CCR with an overview of the existent range of programs and approaches operating to equip South African youngsters with interactive lifeskills, and identify any focus on conflict resolution in such programs. A definite need for this type of training to be offered emerged from our research.

The Quaker Peace Centre's team of peacemakers encourages the creative, nonviolent resolution of conflict through promoting awareness, cooperation, and empowerment. Promoting peace education and nonviolent conflict resolution among young people in school and community settings is an important focus of its work. In 1992, the draft of the first *South African Handbook of Education for Peace* was printed and distributed by the Quaker Peace Centre (1992). The handbook is designed for use by teachers, youth leaders, and others interested in promoting peace education. Both the Quaker Peace Centre and the CCR youth project have developed comprehensive resource collections of programmatic and other materials.

Other endeavors have been initiated by inter alia grassroots and nongovernmental organizations, individual schools, teacher bodies, education departments, university-linked agencies, the media, and welfare organizations. Their programs do not always have a specific peace or conflict resolution focus, but their youth-related work is targeted in some or other way toward the empowerment of young people and those working with them.

Throughout the country today, there exist projects and programs that aim to provide young people with opportunities to develop lifeskills of some kind. These include programs providing exposure to the concept and practice of democracy (Institute for a Democratic South Africa [IDASA]), empowering children through creative expression (The Open School), teaching listening skills through the medium of oral history (Joint Enrichment Project), and involving young people in decision-making learning processes (church youth groups).

The area of tolerance is receiving increasing attention. The education for tolerance/anti-racism project, currently being undertaken jointly by the departments of Education and Psychology at the University of

Cape Town, for example, aims to assist teachers to reduce racism and intergroup hostility in South African schools. Also working in the area of promoting tolerance, IDASA's media department has published an educational youth booklet, *Long Live Tolerance.*

The Anne Frank in the world exhibition, touring South Africa during 1994, has provided a teaching vehicle for many subjects raising issues such as human rights, tolerance, use and abuse of power, stereotyping and propaganda, and discrimination. Special teacher workshops have been held to introduce locally designed teacher packages focusing on six themes: The Holocaust, Nazi Germany, The Diary of Anne Frank, Apartheid, Human Rights, and Making Choices.

Besides CCR and the Quaker Peace Centre, there are a number of organizations providing conflict resolution training for young people and teachers. These include The Community Dispute Resolution Trust; the National Institute for Crime and Rehabilitation of Offenders; the Independent Projects Trust; Vuleka Trust; the Institute for the Study and Resolution of Conflict, based at the University of Port Elizabeth; and the Lifeskills Project attached to the University of Cape Town.

Certain schools (e.g., in the Natal Education Department) have included conflict resolution components in their piloting of Life Orientation programs. Other schools are experimenting with ways and means of introducing peace education and conflict resolution into formal and informal curricula. Claremont Primary School in Cape Town, for example, has infused principles and practices of peace education in creative ways, and Riebeek College in Uitenhage has developed a peace education curriculum that it uses as part of guidance teaching for Standards 6 to 10.

Among the areas of focus of the Catholic Institute of Education have been the development of an integrated studies curriculum, and a program for students from Standards 1 to 5 that aims to build bridges between young people of different cultural backgrounds.

A teacher organization's initiative was the launching of the Peace Committee of the South African Teachers' Association (SATA) in 1991 to investigate the need for peace education in South African schools. This committee subsequently recommended to SATA that peace education should be a component of the school curriculum and inform a broad spectrum of school activities. A number of pilot primary and high "Peace Schools" have introduced peace education into their schools and members of the committee have designed peace education manuals for use at high, primary, and preprimary school.

Supporting the introduction of peace education into school settings are initiatives such as that of the school library section of the Cape Education Library Service, which has distributed seven annotated bibliographies devoted to peace education to 1,000 schools in the Cape Province this year. It has also organized conference exhibitions of pupil-oriented fiction and nonfiction books that can be used in peace education.

Some endeavors are focusing specifically on principal and teacher groups. One example is the Centre for Cognitive Development in Pretoria and Cape Town, which aims to empower teachers to empower learners to become skilled, responsible, confident, critical, and creative problem solvers. Another is the Centre for Educational Development, based at Stellenbosch University, which has developed a support program for teachers in multicultural schools. A team of academics at this university is currently working on a peace education curriculum for teachers.

The Centre for the Study of Violence and Reconciliation, associated with the University of Witwatersrand, focuses on research into violence around questions, such as "How do we recover and reconstruct?" It has an education component that offers education and training workshops for children and teachers around violence-related issues. Special skills-based programs equip teachers with basic counselling skills for victims of violence.

There are also initiatives underway to promote the introduction of democratic approaches to school management. The Transvaal branch of IDASA, for example, has been cofacilitator—with the Vista University Mamelodi branch of the Union of Democratic Staff Associations—of a project aimed to facilitate a culture of learning and teaching at a pilot Mamelodi high school that can then be used as a model for transformation by other schools. The Parent–Teacher Student Association (PTSA) movements in many of our Black schools see themselves as structures of democratic control, striving for quality in education within the context of the broader school community.

During the ongoing process of transformation of educational systems in South Africa, a number of initiatives have drawn up submissions to bodies looking at new education policies. CCR, for example, sent a recommendation to the Convention for a Democratic South Africa after a group of educationists from formal and informal sectors met at the CCR in January 1992 to discuss a draft document, "Education for a New South Africa" (Botha, 1991a), and to share ideas about peace education and related areas. CCR has also sent documentation to the National Education Training Forum and the African National Congress Education Desk about the need for peace education.

There are a number of active law-related endeavors, one of which is the South African Street Law program that is taught to Standard 9 and 10 pupils throughout South Africa, usually incorporated into the school guidance curriculum and taught by final-year Bachelor of Laws students. Use is made of student and trainer manuals published by the Centre for Socio-Legal Studies and the Association of Law Societies. These focus on issues such as juvenile justice and criminal law, and alternative dispute resolution strategies such as negotiation, mediation, and arbitration.

Lawyers for Human Rights have a Human Rights Education Project that seeks to help create a human rights culture and establish political tolerance through national outreach to inter alia formal education structures (i.e., Standard 9 and 10 school pupils and university students), and community-based organizations. A set of *Human Rights for All* (McQuoid-Mason, O'Brien, & Greene, 1991) student texts and teacher manuals has been developed with a specific peacemaking and nonviolent conflict resolution component.

The Community Law Centre (CLC) affiliated with the University of Natal works with rural communities, including primary and high school pupil groups. CLC's recent publications, *Waiting for Democracy* (Wilson, 1992) and *Human Rights* (Baekey & Gabriel, 1992), have been designed in a way that will allow access for those who are not literate.

There is a growing emergence of peer trainer and support-type programs, particularly in the area of AIDS and substance abuse education, and these focus heavily on the development of personal and social skills. Phuting College near Johannesburg has, for example, pioneered a peer support program that aims inter alia to break down cultural barriers; develop self-esteem and self-confidence; develop negotiation, mediation and leadership skills; and equip pupils to contribute toward the development of a peaceful society. All pupils are trained as facilitators and have the opportunity to serve as such during their senior years.

Other youth development, leadership, and interaction programs include the Leadership South Program whose Facilitator Training Program empowers youth to become facilitators and organizers of community development projects in urban and rural Western Cape areas. Leadership South has helped establish a FutureLinks–South Africa program by coordinating a trip to the United States for 15 South African youth leaders for a period of intensive conflict resolution skills training with professor Dudley Weeks at the American University in

Washington, DC. FutureLinks–South Africa is a group of young, trained conflict resolution facilitators whose purpose is to promote community-based and national conflict resolution services and skills transference in South Africa. It is now the first chapter in the Global FutureLinks Network.

Peace Visions, another youth empowerment initiative, is a creative peace education program initiated by six organizations involved in social, political, and cultural work. Young people between 15 and 18 years attend weekend programs on Robben Island exploring "peace with the past–present," before participating in workshops on conflict transformation, interactive drama, and mural painting. Youth are trained as cofacilitators in the program and encouraged to create "ripples" in their own communities.

The South African Youth Symposium Programme aims to bring high school students and teachers of all races together in an informal atmosphere; focus on the development of self-esteem, basic lifeskills, and conflict resolution skills specifically; and encourage students to play a more active role in influencing positive changes in a society in transition. The Youthreach Project of Women for Peaceful Change Now, as part of its aim to improve intergroup relations and promote peace and democracy, brings Standard 9 pupils of all races together for weekend programs that include conflict resolution training and practice. An important area of IDASA's work has been leadership training and the facilitation of interactive and joint learning processes among youth.

Organizations concerned with early learning are also playing their part in promoting peace education. The Early Learning Resource Unit has incorporated peace education principles and conflict resolution training in its nonformal adult and teacher training programs and developed an Anti-Bias Project focusing on curricula, materials, and practice. The South African Association for Early Childhood Educare (SAAECE) has developed a Peace Pack containing a poster, "Recover From Violence," which highlights (a) ways to create peace and rebuild community life, (b) ideas for activities, articles, and cartoons on conflict resolution, and (c) resource information for people who work with young children.

In the area of parenting, The Parent Centres in Cape Town are examples of organizations working to promote healthy family relationships and to contribute toward the prevention of physical and emotional abuse of children in all communities. Their parents' lifeskills training program includes components on effective family communication, the enhancement of self-esteem, and constructive conflict resolution.

There is growing evidence of peace-related media initiatives. *Upbeat,* a monthly magazine aimed at South African youth, for example, has produced an eight-part cartoon series on conflict resolution with each issue having a skills-based focus. "Peace Radio" now broadcasts daily on one of our radio channels; it aims to facilitate peace, reconciliation, reconstruction, and tolerance, and structures its programs around community needs. "Peace Cafe" is a relatively new youth television program initiated by the Cape Town-based Media Peace Centre in support of the National Peace Secretariat's Peace and Development Program. It encourages youth to speak their minds and participate in the country's peace and development processes.

The contributions being made by these kinds of initiatives are invaluable. Dunn (1992) referred to this very process as a necessary stage in the wider process of generating a more holistic and coherent program, that is, in some sense, more general. He saw a complementary approach as an institutional or governmental one, which tries to produce a structure within which these individual efforts are coordinated or legitimated, "where the general concept of allowing education to contribute to community relations, peace studies and conflict resolution is acknowledged and systematised" (Dunn, 1992, p. 1).

Research Initiatives

We gave attention to three different kinds of current research endeavors in our report, and reference will be made to these here. The first overviews research material relating to South African youth and politics, the second relates to academic postgraduate research work, and the third is a study of adolescent risk-taking behavior. Two individuals who have been pioneer researchers in the field of peace education are Professor Cedric Taylor at the University of Port Elizabeth, and Professor Jannie Malan who works with the African Centre for the Constructive Resolution of Disputes (ACCORD) organization.

Ian Liebenberg's cooperative research program report on South African youth and politics (1987–1992) looks at research material on issues relating to youth and politics during that period. In terms of youth-related peace and conflict research, he mentioned a number of initiatives aimed at facilitating contact, interaction, and dialogue between South African youth. He stated that, while hopefully promoting the development of an atmosphere conducive to peaceful interchange, these initiatives did not generate much research.

As yet, no thorough nationally coordinated programme on peace research on the South African youth has been initiated or undertaken. There exists a great need in this field for research programmes as well as the implementation of proposals emanating from research. (Liebenberg, 1993, p. 13)

A number of recent research initiatives related to the field of peace education have been undertaken in partial fulfillment for Master's and Doctoral degrees. This body of research has been school based and includes initiatives focusing on principals' conflict-handling styles, organizational conflict in high schools, management practices and tasks of principals when dealing with unrest situations, prejudice-related conflict among students, the role of education in improving intergroup relations, the implications of multicultural education for the school community, the prevention and management of intergroup conflict, mediation of conflict in nonracial schools, and Cooperative Learning.

It is encouraging that the areas of conflict resolution and peacemaking, and structuring positive intergroup contact, are being given increasing attention by South African researchers such as these. Their recommendations highlight the need that exists for these areas to be addressed further in terms of both research and practical application. A striking commonality among these recommendations was that attention be given to the incorporation of conflict resolution training for teachers at undergraduate, graduate, and in-service levels.

Our report also noted research undertaken jointly by the Centre for Epidemiological Research in Southern Africa and the Department of Psychiatry at the University of Cape Town (Flischer, 1993). The study was motivated by the fact that although a number of researchers have investigated the psychological and social consequences of exposure to violence in South Africa, the extent to which our "culture of violence" manifests in individual behavior has not received much attention.

Violent behavior was thus included as part of a larger prevalence study among adolescents—adolescence being seen as a critical period for the acquisition of health-promoting behavior and attitudes. Risk-taking behavior patterns of 7,340 Cape Peninsula high school students was investigated as an initial step in the design of appropriate interventions. Suggested strategies that may reduce the prevalence of violent behavior specifically include school-based programs encouraging nonviolent coping strategies and tolerance, education on the relation between sex-role stereotyping and violence, opposing the use of physical punishment in the school and home setting, reducing the exposure of children and adolescents to violence in the media, and revising firearm legislation and discouraging the carrying of weapons as a means of self-defence. The researchers highlight the need for the development of preventive programs within the social context of health-damaging behavior.

The Way Forward

Our considerations of the way forward involved asking ourselves how best young South Africans can be provided with a range of empowering experiences that will equip them to play their roles as conflict resolvers and peacemakers in their everyday lives, and how to motivate them to play these roles accordingly? We also asked how best conditions can be facilitated for young people to develop personal and interpersonal processes that will contribute to the promotion of a culture of peace?

The continued growth of the field of peace education in school and other South African settings will take time, energy, and dedication. As peace educators, we need to experiment, explore, evaluate, and learn from our own experiences, as well as those of others, use existing frameworks, and look for new avenues during this process.

In the light of our research, we suggested certain policy guidelines. This article presents a summary of these under the following headings: Peace Education for South African Youngsters, Some Cautionary Thoughts, And Research Directions.

Peace Education for South African Youngsters

We would like to see our research project as an initial phase of a long-term comprehensive Peace Education Plan aimed not only at young people, but at all South Africans—a process that should be accompanied by fundamental sociopolitical structural change if peace education programs are to have lasting value and effectiveness.

A way forward might be the constitution of a National Commission to formulate a Peace Education blueprint that would give attention to the promotion, development, implementation, and evaluation of educational endeavors of a formal, informal, nonformal, and community character in a coordinated and structured manner. The establishment of a Network Association, which would provide communication and interaction opportunity among all those working to promote peace education among youth, should be an integral part of this.

Our report suggests that peace education programs for South African children and youth should be introduced, developed, and implemented in a variety of settings. We believe that peace education should begin in the home, starting at birth and having a central place in the development of our children, that parents have a critical role to play in this regard, and that the concept of "parenting for peace" should be promoted.

The school. Schools are the most central and obvious channel for peace education and they should be encouraged to take on this role. Peace education, with a specific focus on conflict resolution, should be introduced, developed, and implemented in South African primary and high schools for the benefit of all students in a school and pilot programs should be initiated in a variety of schools. This should be regarded as a long-term process that requires flexibility and openness rather than adherence to rigid preset agendas with schools taking account of their own needs, capabilities, and characters. A range of support mechanisms should be activated to encourage effective implementation and ideally this means involving the whole school community. Student empowerment cannot develop constructively in isolation.

This would mean engaging the sanction and support of Departments of Education and School Management Boards, principals and teachers, student populations, Student Representative Councils, Parent–Teacher–Student Associations and other parent bodies, and, where appropriate, agencies in the wider school communities. Enlisting technical, financial, and administrative support is important, as is the utilization of organizations like the CCR for consultation, training, resource material, and general support.

We offered some guidelines with regard to equipping teachers for their roles as peace educators:

• In-service training opportunities, focusing on peaceful classroom management, peace education, conflict resolution, and cooperative learning strategies, should be provided for all principals and teachers.
• Teachers should become involved in designing educational and training programs, contribute to their development, and take responsibility for running them.
• Principals and teachers should make opportunities to discuss among themselves areas such as conflict resolution, peace education and diversity, and the use of constructive techniques with which they

can and do approach situations of conflict and discrimination in their schools.

• The basic principles of peace education, conflict resolution, and peaceful classroom management should be components of teacher training courses at universities and training colleges, and theoretical and practically structured courses on conflict and its resolution should be compulsory components of postgraduate university courses in Education.

Our suggestions regarding the teaching of peace education included the following:

• The school context should be influenced by, and conducive to, the spirit of peace education and characterized inter alia by relationships of dialogue between teachers and students, tolerance, constructive conflict resolution and discipline strategies, cooperative procedures, and supportive mechanisms for those in need. A peace education curriculum, in contrast to that of a more academic subject, cannot really stand on its own.

• Peace education should ideally be accommodated in the whole school curriculum with the approach being both subject-oriented and integrative (i.e., creating dimensions that provide an opportunity to explore issues in different ways, with different groups, and in any subject).

• A classroom-based program should provide all students with the opportunity to develop important lifeskills, and a safe training ground on which students can try out these skills and deal with conflicts creatively.

• Peer mediation programs should be piloted and introduced where appropriate but ideally as supplements to classroom-based learning.

• Pedagogic models for peace education should reflect the historical reality, the cultural specificity, and the aspirations of young South Africans.

• School-based peace education should extend to include community outreach initiatives to promote a wider culture of peace.

• The media should be encouraged to support the concept of peace education in school and other settings with topical and practical peace education and conflict resolution programs for presentation in high-profile prime-time television and radio slots.

• The medium of "distance education" should be used to reach, and provide exposure for, youth and teachers in rural and other relatively inaccessible areas.

The wider community.   Peace education initiatives should also be directed at reaching young people who are not in formal learning situations, and providing "habilitative" and rehabilitative support for those who have been impacted by the ravages of daily violence and had no opportunity to develop constructive social skills.

The involvement of a wide range of organizations, institutions, and agencies (e.g., youth and service organizations, churches, trade unions, women's groups, publishing houses, grassroots theater, art and dance initiatives, and private sector enterprises) should be activated to promote, and do advocacy work for, peace education. Cognizance should be taken of the needs expressed by the young people surveyed for more interaction opportunities among youth of different races and cultures.

Besides young people, teachers, and principals, peace education should be targeted at inter alia education departments, parent associations, community structures, political parties, governmental bodies, military institutions, health and welfare organizations, and churches. Transformations from top to bottom are essential if we are to achieve sustainable peace in South Africa.

Ways to encourage and support professional and other educators to teach peace education should be explored and use made of organizations working in the peace education and conflict resolution field, for consultation, training, and resource material. The social responsibility role and the positive potential of the entertainment media should also be given attention.

Some Cautionary Thoughts

Our report highlighted certain "caution areas" or areas of challenge. Attention is given to some of these under three headings: Terminology, Schools, and Parents.

Terminology.   The words *peace, peace education,* and *conflict resolution* have confusing and negative connotations for many people and this could militate against acceptance of the need for peace education and support for its introduction in school and other settings.

Some of the people interviewed for our survey, particularly those involved in the education field, were uncertain about the actual meanings of these words. They felt that they mean different things for different people and that we need words or concise sentences that will give more clarity to the concepts. Some expressed reservations about the words because of historical associations (e.g., "peace" terms were often used in South Africa's past by people who simultaneously condemned the antiapartheid movement for using violence and yet condoned the structural violence of the state). Among the students surveyed, particularly those at primary school level, there were some who struggled to understand the concepts and wondered why we didn't just talk about how "not to fight."

We need to promote the concept of peace as a realistic and challenging option in the lives of all South Africans, as a necessary component of a societal model built on democratic principles, and as a process that is action-centered and appealing rather than one that is bland and passive, with soft option connotations. We need terminology that will describe accurately, and in "accessible" language to all our people, the concepts of peace, peace education, and conflict resolution.

Schools. Introducing a new process such as peace education will fundamentally challenge the system and teaching model of many schools. This implies change, adaptation, and also the possibility of resistance. The authoritarian nature characterizing the management of many of our schools may militate against introducing a peace education process that tries to involve the whole school.

Principal and teacher resistance, suspicion, and nonsupport could negate the effectiveness of peace education. Some teachers may question the value of or feel threatened by peace education. Some may feel that peace education will interfere with formal learning—that timetables are already full and teacher resources stretched to the limit and that after all the disruptions to many of our schools, teachers really need to get on with the business of "teaching" in traditional terms.

Many schools today are being inundated with requests to introduce new programs such as AIDS awareness, Multicultural Education, and Education for Democracy, and they might be wary of yet another "good idea" that they feel will require additional energy, effort, and resources to implement.

Parents. Some parents might resist the whole idea of peace education in schools, viewing it with suspicion and unease. Parents who are unable to deal with conflict constructively in their own lives might feel threatened if their children come home with new ideas that they try to put into practice in the home environment. This might be particularly true for parents who feel that physical punishment is an appropriate way of dealing with conflict. It is also likely that some parents might feel that schools should focus on academic subjects that pave the way for further education and career direction, and that peace education is a waste of children's time. Part of our challenge is to familiarize parents with the concept of peace education and to encourage them to play active roles as peacemakers and peace educators.

Research Directions

This article gives attention to some of the research directions our report suggests, the main one dealing with the development of appropriate materials. We need to design and develop culturally relevant program and resource materials appropriate for use in South African settings, rooted in a context that is meaningful for our youth and grounded in their own experience.

Materials and training modules should reflect language and cultural diversity, and we need to be wary of methodological and cultural biases built into Western models of conflict resolution in our program design. We need to gather a body of knowledge about traditional formal and informal patterns of problem solving and peacemaking among South African ethnic and other groups so that these can be applied to training materials. The value of giving attention to "tradition" in peace education programs should be explored.

South African pupils and teachers could be encouraged to critique particular training models and adapt them to fit in with their own traditions and situations, discuss how people can make themselves understood across language and cultural divides, and provide a wealth of relevant scenario and role-play material from their own experiences as we build up a body of South African resources.

Materials should be designed and developed for use by and with those young people who do not have well-developed reading and writing skills, and the educative potential of cartoons and other graphic material, for example, should be explored.

Among the other research directions suggested are:

- Identifying appropriate and acceptable terminology.
- Investigating how peace education could be incorporated into teacher training curricula.
- Identifying appropriate organizations and community services that can be actively involved in promoting peace education in communities and other-than-school settings.
- Undertaking a more comprehensive survey on attitudes to and understanding of violence and conflict among South African youth,

especially those in communities that have experienced extreme levels of violence.

•   Understanding the importance and kinds of coping mechanisms employed by children, and identifying the factors that assist them to overcome stresses and strains in the family and wider environments.

•   Investigating further the extent to which, and how, the South African culture of violence manifests in individual behavior among children and young people.

•   Supplementing existing research to increase our understanding of the role of key factors such as self-esteem, self-confidence, and trust in the central core of the personality.

Conclusion

It is not easy to work for peace in a country that has been geared for physical and emotional confrontation. Achieving sustainable peace in South Africa is going to involve transforming its people, its societal conditions, and its development models, and as peace educators, we might sometimes experience disillusionment and skepticism as we wonder about the effectiveness of what we are doing. But at these times we should remember the voices of the young people in our survey. They have spoken to us from their hearts and from their experiences of growing up in a turmoiled society.

The time has come to stop the violence, the psychological maiming, and the enormous waste of our children's talent and potential. Peace educators have a responsibility to help develop a new generation of South African citizens and leaders who understand that peace is a positive and alternate reality to violence and war, and who are equipped to deal effectively and constructively with resolving conflict—on personal, community, and political levels.

It is important that our children, from an early age, develop resources and skills that will facilitate and encourage an ethos and practice of peacemaking and constructive conflict resolution. It is also important to instill in our children a sense of being able to positively impact the social structures and attitudes in today's society—a sense that they can, and do, effect change, and that we, as adults, desire, recognize, and value their contributions in this regard.

We need to give our young people the opportunity to ensure sustainable futures for themselves and South Africa and commit ourselves to investing in this valuable, but unexploited and largely neglected, resource in our country—our children and youth. We need to look seriously at peace education. We owe it to them.

References

Baekey, C., & Gabriel, A. (1992). *Human rights/Litekelo tsa mantlha tsa botho.* Durban, South Africa: Community Law Centre.

Botha, V. (1991a, November). *Draft discussion document: Education for a new South Africa.* Cape Town, South Africa: Centre for Intergroup Studies.

Botha, V. (1991b). *Interactive skills for South African youngsters: A resource guide* (Conflict and Peace Studies Series No. 3). Cape Town, South Africa: Centre for Intergroup Studies.

Botha, V., & Kirsten, A. (1993). *Conflict resolution and peacemaking among youth.* Cape Town, South Africa: Cooperative Research Programme for South African Youth, Centre for Intergroup Studies and Human Sciences Research Council.

Dunn, S. (1992, July). *Peace education and structural change.* Paper presented at the EN-CORE European Summer School, "Values in Conflict—Education for Change," Magee College, University of Ulster, Coleraine, Northern Ireland.

Flischer, A. (1993, January). *Adolescent risk taking behavior—A neglected area.* Paper presented at the seminar, "Towards a National GOBI–FFF Programme for South Africa," Cape Town, South Africa.

Liebenberg, I. (1993). *Research on South African youth and politics.* Pretoria, South Africa: Human Sciences Research Council.

McKendrick, B., & Hoffman, W. (1991). *Violence in South Africa.* Cape Town, South Africa: Oxford University Press.

McQuoid-Mason, D., O'Brien, E., & Greene, E. (1991). *Human rights for all: Education towards a rights culture.* Cape Town, South Africa: David Phillip.

Mokwena, W. (1992). Living on the wrong side of the law. In D. Everatt & E. Sisulu (Eds.), *Black youth in crisis* (pp. 30–50). Johannesburg, South Africa: Ravan.

Quaker Peace Centre. (1992). *The South African handbook of education for peace* (Draft ed.). Cape Town, South Africa: Author.

Wilson, J. (1992). *Waiting for democracy/Ukulindela intando yeningi.* Durban, South Africa: Community Law Centre.

PEABODY JOURNAL OF EDUCATION, 71(3), 151–169

Educational Violence and Education for Peace in Africa

Clive Harber

Formal education is not inherently or inevitably an enhancing and liberating experience. The following three quotations are perceptive observations on this unfortunate reality:

> Children who are lectured to learn how to lecture; if they are admonished, they learn how to admonish; if scolded, they learn how to scold; if ridiculed, they learn how to ridicule; if humiliated, they learn how to humiliate; if their psyche is killed, they will learn how to kill—the only question is who will be killed: oneself, others or both. (Alice Miller)
>
> But good gracious you've got to educate him first. You can't expect a boy to be vicious till he's been to a good school. ("Saki"—Hugh Hector Munro)

CLIVE HARBER *is Professor at the School of Education, University of Natal, Durban, South Africa.*

Requests for reprints should be sent to Clive Harber, Private Bag X10, School of Education, University of Natal, Durban, Dalbridge 4014, South Africa.

151

> The immediate case against compulsory school for adolescents is quite simply their barbarity: it is a triangle of hatred, humiliation and contempt. (Frank Musgrove)
>
> —from Meighan (1994, pp. 69, 84)

Many writers on education have commented on the dual and contradictory nature of formal education. On the one hand, schooling is often currently a vehicle for the perpetuation of violence both in terms of overt forms of physical violence and in terms of the psychological and structural violence of dehumanizing social relationships that harm the learners concerned. On the other hand, formal schooling is potentially a powerful vehicle for an education that is concerned with the peaceful resolution of conflicts through analyzing the causes of violence and teaching values and skills that are congruent with peaceful behavior. This second possible role for education is well captured by the Director General of UNESCO:

> Wars will not cease, either on the ground or in people's minds, unless each and every one of us resolutely embarks on the struggle against intolerance and violence by attacking the evil at its roots. Education offers us the means to do this. ... Education is what will enable us to move from a culture of war, which we unhappily know only too well, to a culture of peace. (cited in Tedesco, 1994, p. 1)

This article examines the violent context in which many schools in Africa have existed during the recent past in terms of war, violent military oppression, and resistance. It will also explore the context of structural violence—debt, economic decline, and poverty—and its effects on education. The article also argues that schools themselves have often been violent places both in terms of being sites of wider political or military conflicts and global inequalities and in terms of their own role as agents of structural violence through authoritarianism, physical punishment, and sexual harassment. Thus, although violence has, of course, by no means been a universal or consistent feature of African schools it has been a significant and worrying feature. However, the article ends on a more optimistic note by reviewing recent democratic political developments in Africa and notes that these are beginning to have positive effects on the nature of education in a number of countries. Namibia is examined in more detail as a case study of one country where attempts are being made to introduce a more peaceful culture of conflict resolution through more democratic forms of learning and decision making.

The Violent Context

O God! Save the continent from the wars, hunger, poverty and rebellions. War in Angola, Liberia, Sierra Leone, Sudan, Somalia etc. Please African leaders help alleviate the hunger, the wars and the poverty. Rebel leaders don't kill those you intend to rule. God, come down and help mama Africa!! (Musah Ahmed D. Bello of Ghana in special section on children in Africa in *Focus on Africa*, 1994, p. 28).

During the last 30 years, Africa has been plagued by war and violent conflict. It is not the purpose of this article to analyze the causes of these wars in detail but simply to outline the violent context in which many schools in Africa have had to operate. Most of these wars have had their origins in varying colonial situations and legacies. Some, such as those in Mozambique and Angola until the mid-1970s, have been wars of independence and liberation from a colonial power—in this case of these two countries, Portugal. In Eritrea, a 30-year war was fought against an African colonial power—Ethiopia. Elsewhere, as in Zimbabwe until 1980 and Namibia until 1990, wars have been fought by internal resistance movements against White settler regimes that excluded the majority of the population from participation. Elsewhere, such as in South Africa in the 1970s and 1980s and during the Mau Mau period in Kenya, though conflict never really reached the level of full scale war, there was marked violent resistance to the settler state. In both Mozambique and Angola, fighting was perpetuated after the anticolonial war had finished by a South African apartheid regime determined to destabilize its neighbors to demonstrate to its own majority that Black African rule had no future.

Ethnic conflict has been the cause of other wars and violence. However, such conflicts often have their origin in the colonial period during which both the nature and scale of *ethnicity*, or what constitutes the *tribe*, were determined as were the state structures and boundaries shaping the conflict. Perhaps the bloodiest of these conflicts have been the Nigerian civil war of 1967–1970 and, more recently, the turmoil in Rwanda Burundi. In Sudan the longstanding civil war has been less about ethnicity than religious identity with the Islamic north attempting to force its beliefs on an unwilling South where Christianity and traditional religions predominate. This war has also caused border tensions between Sudan and neighboring Uganda and Eritrea.

Another legacy of the weak state structures and lack of democratic preparation bequeathed by colonialism has been the widespread African phenomenon of dictatorial government, both military and civilian.

C. Harber

For, as Mazrui (1983) noted, "the African state is sometimes excessively authoritarian to disguise the fact that it is inadequately authoritative" (p. 293). Such dictators have carried out violence against their own people not only through murdering and imprisoning them, the two worst cases being Amin of Uganda and Bokassa of the Central African Republic, but also because their instruments of terror such as the army in Mobutu's Zaire or the Young Pioneers in Malawi have also carried out random violence of their own. Such regimes have also systematically abused and ignored human rights and freedoms. Indeed, in this latter category of the violation of human rights it would, until recently, be difficult to find an exception, though perhaps Botswana comes closest. The removal of such dictators has also often been violent and left a legacy of violence in its wake. Amin of Uganda was eventually overthrown as a result of a Tanzanian military invasion but there followed a cycle of revenge and repression until the eventual military success of the guerilla National Resistance Army in 1986. In Somalia the military dictator Siad Barre survived from 1969 by a divide and rule policy of encouraging clan factionalism. This eventually led to his downfall in 1991, leaving the warlords he had created to fight it out for themselves.

African people are also regularly on the receiving end of economic violence in that their lives are beset by poverty and economic insecurity. Although there are exceptions, the overall picture of economic development in Africa remains very bleak. At independence many African states inherited economic systems that had not evolved naturally but which had been artificially distorted by the needs of the colonial powers. The result was often a reliance on one or two primary products (copper, sisal, cocoa, etc.) for foreign export earnings. The rapid increase in the price of oil following the Arab–Israeli war of 1973 had a major impact on such economies. Surplus money from the Middle East was recycled into the banks of Western Europe and North America. The money was then recycled again in the form of loans to developing countries, including those in Africa. The recession or slowdown in the Western economies caused by the oil crisis (plus the increasing use of synthetic alternatives) led to a fall in demand for, and thus a reduction in the price of, the primary products that constitute the main exports of developing economies. This was coupled with an increase in the price of manufactured goods imported into the same countries.

This plus the strength of the dollar meant that debt repayment became crippling. Between 1970 and 1987 the public debt service as a percentage of exports in Africa rose from 3.5% to 14.7% (World Bank, 1989, Table 24). By 1991 debt in sub-Saharan Africa was 110% of gross national product ("A Continent Driven," 1994). By 1993 arrears of interest on long-term debt in Africa was 16 billion dollars (Brittain, 1996). World Bank "structural adjustment programmes" have cut back on state provision in welfare, health, and educational provision and have exacerbated inequality. Moreover, external economic problems have often been compounded by internal problems of war, drought, corruption, and mismanagement. Despite the phrase *developing countries*, many countries in Africa are actually de-developing.

The net result is that many Africans live in poverty. Of Africa's 500 million people, 300 million are living in absolute poverty and the situation is getting worse. Incomes dropped from $570 per capita in 1980 to $350 in 1992 (Brittain, 1994). Children are not immune from this as malnourishment is a serious problem. In Zambia, for example, 48% of children are recorded as malnourished—in Burkina Faso 40%, in Botswana and Kenya 32%, in Ethiopia and Senegal 30%, in Tanzania and Sierra Leone 27%, and in the Niger Republic 26% (Brittain, 1993).

Education and Violence

Children and education have been severely affected by the wars that have plagued Africa in recent times. Women and children account for 92% of Africa's war-related deaths. In Rwanda alone more than 200,000 children have been orphaned or separated from their families. In the early 1990s more children were dying in Mozambique every day than in all countries of the former Soviet Union (UNICEF, quoted in *Focus on Africa*, 1994). During the 1980s, the war in Mozambique caused the destruction or closure of 60% of the country's schools (World University Service, 1994). In Liberia, where there is a bloody civil war in process, 25 teachers have been murdered and, although 3,000 teachers are officially working, an estimated 5,000 teachers are in exile. Not surprisingly,

> the conditions of work are appalling in the aftermath of the war. Furniture and equipment has been stolen or broken leaving very little in the way of facilities. Children are obliged to sit on the concrete floors in dark classrooms and even if there was lighting, electricity is rarely available. Due to a number of school buildings having been totally destroyed in shelling, teachers can expect to face classes of up to 70 students. Due to the lack of material, children usually have to bring their own paper and pencils to school. (Danish Union of Teachers, 1994, pp. 2–3)

Schools have been sites of violence during these wars and even those young people that have not suffered physically have suffered severe psychological violence as a result of direct experience of war. Although the figures in the previous paragraph present something of the scale of this tragedy, personal accounts vividly bring home the absurd juxtaposition of war and education. During the war of resistance against South African occupation of Namibia, for example, South African soldiers carried guns while they taught in the schools. As one Namibian school student put it, "Imagine somebody teaching you, and if you make a mistake, or if he suspects you, he would just point his gun at you, telling you that he would shoot you or your mother" (Konig, 1983).

In what was then Rhodesia, the government security forces attempted to frighten school children into not supporting the liberation forces fighting for an independent Zimbabwe, but this tactic actually had the opposite effect:

Parading kids before corpses, or corpses before kids, was common practice. It happened in 1976 at Chikore mission school, 230 kilometres south of Umtali, when on three occasions pupils were shown bodies which the security forces had brought into the school and dumped into the parking lot—genitals exposed, fingers cut off from the knuckles, horrifying. Not surprisingly, 140 of the school's 380 pupils responded to this treatment by walking across the border into Mozambique in July 1976, whereupon the government closed the school and expelled five teachers. (Caute, 1983, p. 59)

Thomas Keneally spent a year traveling with the Eritrean Peoples' Liberation Front (EPLF) during the war with Ethiopia and wrote the novel *Towards Asmara* based on the experience. Here he captures the contradiction of both the seemingly hopeless context in which education in the EPLF bases took place and yet at the same time the great hope invested in education for future,

While we waited, pot bellied and shaven-headed children in dust-laden gowns straggled past us on their way to school in some cave. Their transience was just about palpable—you could taste it on the tongue, in this high, dry country, where a delay in rain or an upgrading of an Ethiopian offensive could cancel them. It was nearly beyond bearing to think of them learning their maths in holes in the ground or behind the negligible walls of scrub shelters. $\frac{7}{8} = \frac{3}{4}$, True or False? Training in a pocket of dust for the computer age. *This is the goat of Osman* changed through their schooling to *This is Osman's goat*. Language for a future of commerce with the West; the hard and fast curriculum of the Eritreans! Even the children with the swollen and mis-shapen skulls, even those who could not credibly expect to see twenty, even those whom one delay of rain or one small enteric fever could be expected to do for; even they were made to sit in a class. We watched the two village teachers, each with his assault rifle and his belt of grenades, boys of eighteen or twenty, saunter along chatting. (Keneally, 1989, pp. 206–207)

In South Africa the violent suppression of resistance to apartheid also took its toll. In the aftermath of the Soweto uprisings the police shot and killed some 1,000 students in 1976–1977, many more were injured and countless more arrested. In 1985 school and university students became increasingly militant and, with the South African army being used against its own people, they not only organized widespread boycotts, strikes, rallies, and pickets but also barricaded streets and waged street battles with the police and army. They burned property and attacked people they saw as collaborators. Their slogan became "Liberation Now, Education Later" (Christie, 1991, chap. 8).

The enormous economic problems confronting African countries outlined earlier have also had a violent impact on the provision and quality of education. The need to service debt, the decline in tax revenues due to static or negative growth, and the contents of structural adjustment programs have seriously affected the proportion of government resources devoted to education. In 1972, for example, Zaire allocated 15.2% of its total government budget to education. In 1986 this had been reduced to 0.8% (UNICEF, 1989). By 1983 expenditure per head on primary pupils in sub-Saharan Africa was 0.77 of what it had been in 1977—the figures for secondary and higher education were 0.16 and 0.54, respectively (World Bank, 1989). Cuts in expenditure seem to have hit the supply of classroom teaching materials such as textbooks, chalk, desks, and maps particularly hard (Heyneman, 1990). In the early 1980s 20% of schools in the Ed Duneim district in Sudan had no water and 57% had no latrines. In the Kilosa district of Tanzania, 42% of schools were without water and 10% without latrines. In Nigeria many schools in the north have no roofs, or collapsed walls. In some parts of the south, children can be seen carrying their own desks to school each day. A World Bank study of primary teachers' salaries in 18 countries of sub-Saharan Africa found that real salaries had declined in all but two between 1980 and 1985. In 11 countries, including Kenya,

Zambia, Zimbabwe, and Senegal, the falls were more than 10% (Graham-Brown, 1991, pp. 38–39). One Zambian writer described the situation as "wholesale systemic decay":

> Classrooms are overcrowded; teachers are overworked and underpaid, sometimes not paid at all for months on end; the books used in classrooms are often long out of date, and not enough to go round (it is not uncommon in rural African or Latin American schools to see a single textbook for a given subject shared by a whole class); and the school equipment and buildings are in such a state of neglect, due to lack of funds for maintenance and repair, that even the most basic functions, such as keeping out inclement weather, have been severely compromised. For long periods of time students and teachers have to go without the most rudimentary of classroom learning materials such as paper, pencils and chalk, let alone such equipment as stencil duplicating machines, and not to mention photocopiers and personal computers that have become part of the standard equipment for schools in the Western industrialised nations. Midday school meals for children is a luxury that is unheard of. Lack of housing for teachers in some of the more remote rural areas has at times meant that classrooms have had to be converted into living quarters. That any kind of learning is taking place in such circumstances is a miracle in itself. (Lulat, 1988, p. 316)

Not only is extreme global economic inequality a form of structural violence in itself, but the resulting lack of educational resources means that too many children in Africa are deprived of any education at all, and many schools cannot provide even a basic quality of education that could, for example, through the provision of literacy, numeracy, health education, and skills training, contribute toward at least ameliorating problems of hunger, disease, and poverty. Moreover, educational institutions themselves have also directly contributed to a culture of violence.

Schools and the Reproduction of Violence

African schools, along with the majority of schools elsewhere (Harber, 1991), have been essentially authoritarian institutions with power firmly in the hands of the headteacher and teachers and with little student participation in classrooms or school decision making. Classroom teaching is presently overwhelmingly teacher-centered with children sitting in rows and characterized by rote-learning, copying from the blackboard, and the recital of answers to teachers' questions. This description is of Botswana but has generally applicability to African classrooms:

> Students are preceived as passive recipients of vast amounts of information to be memorised and as apprentices in the aquisition of elementary skills required for the production of specific products. Learning is perceived to occur through repetition and drill, the effectiveness of which is assessed through the use of test questions requiring little more than simple recall. (Rowell & Prophet, 1990, p. 24)

This is a legacy of the authoritarian type of school organization and curriculum institutionalized during colonialism in the first part of the 20th century and which has come to be regarded as "normal" or the only model available (Harber, 1995b). Indigenous cultures have also often supported this authoritarian model of schooling (e.g., see Harber, 1989, chap. 5 on Nigeria; Tabulawa, 1995, on Botswana; and Nagel, 1992, on Zimbabwe). This authoritarian context does not produce teacher–student relationships based on trust and mutual respect. Schools in Zimbabwe, according to a study by Nagel, are "authoritarian and suppressive" with dehumanizing practices such as public ridiculing of students and a pronounced absence of free opinions and critical discourse (1992, pp. xv–xvii). At a recent conference on science and maths education held at the University of Natal, the conference brochure used a quote from a student to illustrate the general benefits of computers in South African schools, but the quote also has other implications:

> The computer never gets mad at me. I can make the same mistake ten times in a row and it doesn't tell me I am stupid or yell at me, or things like that. It just tells me I'm wrong, that I goofed, and asks me if I want to read that part again ... not like my teacher. (Centre for the Advancement of Maths and Science Education, 1995, p. 11)

One obvious, if unpleasant, indicator of the authoritarianism of schools is the widespread use corporal punishment. In colonial Mozambique, for example,

> Teachers mercilessly beat children, insulted them, made them work in their fields, compelled them to spend hours kneeling on brick

floors, pulled their ears, kicked them, and in some instances made them bleed. When one visited a Mozambican school in the 1960's one invariably found two devices of punishment: a stick or whip and a palmatoria—a wooden device shaped like an arm and a hand. The hand part had several holes so that when it struck the child's hand, it sucked some of the flesh, causing severe pain. (Alvedo, 1980)

This tradition has continued in postcolonial Africa. Davies (1993) discussed this form of institutional violence and gives the example of a university lecturer in Botswana who had gone to a school to give a careers talk. One female pupil asked him whether students at university got beaten for not knowing an answer. On being reassured not, she risked a further question: If students tried to give an answer and it was wrong, would they, as in her school, get beaten twice as hard as the beating for simply not knowing? Davies also records a newspaper headline in Zimbabwe saying "Son canned at St. John's College"—"My son was canned after four days at St. John's College for failing a French test ... five weeks later the bruises were still visible." The ensuing correspondence about the case was interesting in its greater concern about the spelling than about the corporal punishment itself: The latter was less unusual. Davies added,

> Interview data revealed that while teachers were not supposed to administer corporal punishment themselves, many did; and definitions of "beating" may vary anyway. I observed a teacher attempting to get children into line by fiercely kicking the shins of any stragglers; those bruises would probably be visible for five weeks as well, but parents would not complain. A letter from a pupil complaining that he was caned every morning for being late because of transport problems (in spite of getting up at 5 a.m.) resulted in the newspaper evoking a reply from the transport company rather than any discussion of the appropriateness of the punishment. (p. 167)

Even in Tanzania where education for self-reliance was supposed to usher in more democratic and egalitarian relationships, caning is still widespread (Harber, 1989, p. 67). Recently human rights lawyers in Kwa Zulu Natal, South Africa (where corporal punishment is theoretically forbidden) have threatened court action against some schools following incidents of indiscriminate beatings of pupils. One 18-year-old pupil said that he was whipped across the buttocks three times by a teacher who was passing his classroom and saw him talking to another pupil. Several children at the same school travel on the school bus and if this arrives late they are beaten as they alight from the bus and then again when they reach the classroom. A 15-year-old pupil from another school said that teachers at the school went from classroom to classroom and picked out children who were not in full uniform, who were then taken to the staffroom. Eight teachers were apparently standing in line with canes and the pupils had to walk past each teacher who hit them with the canes ("Lawyers to Investigate," 1995).

If schools in Africa have been predominantly authoritarian and hierarchical they have also been profoundly patriarchal with female students definitely at the bottom of the hierarchy. One disturbing feature of this is the widespread evidence of the sexual harassment of female students by both fellow male students and teachers. Sexual violence in schools in Africa hit the international headlines in July 1991 when 19 girls were killed and 71 raped by their male colleagues at St. Kizito mixed secondary school in Kenya. The incident led to an unprecedented level of national debate in Kenya about violence in schools. However, as Hallam (1994–1995) pointed out, except for its scale, it is unfortunately not an isolated event either in Kenya or elsewhere on the continent. She quoted a 1991 thesis that looked at the legal and medical aspects of rape in Senegal in which 62.71% of the rapes examined concerned schoolgirls and students. Hallam argued that sexual abuse by teachers, which exploits the trust of both students and teachers, is especially traumatic and is far more widespread than most institutions admit. Of 25 cases collected in 1992 from two education departments in the greater Durban area in South Africa, abuses by teachers ranged from sexual suggestions to intercourse with students between the ages of 11 to 13 years old. Some male teachers will use the promise of good marks, or the threat of failure, to pressure female students to have sexual relations with them. Hallam uses examples from Nigeria, Kenya, Zimbabwe, and Tanzania, though this example is from Somalia:

When male teachers made their intentions clear to female students and you refused, they had many ways of getting back at you. They would embarrass you in class, always pick on you to stand up and answer questions, to come to the blackboard and explain something to the whole class. Some teachers would banish you from their classes altogether and of course everyone would know the reason. Worse still, they would give you poor marks or fail you outright. I remember a girl in the final year of inter-immediate school. The history teacher pursued her relentlessly. She refused. He told her to choose between him and her final exams. She dropped out of school. (p. 18)

Finally, there are also regular accounts of violent riots and demonstrations by school students reported in the African press. Although I have discussed these in more detail elsewhere in relation to Kenya, Nigeria, Tanzania, and Ghana (Harber, 1989, pp. 124–126; 1993, pp. 298–299), it ought to be noted that the root cause of the problem is often the authoritarian nature of schools in which the students are socialized to depend on the authority structure of the school. However, at the same time students are very anxious about their success as families can have spent considerable amounts of money on their education and will have high expectations of them. Yet, because of resource problems, poor communications, and untrained staff, things often go wrong—food is in short supply, classes are left untaught, examination papers fail to appear on time. The system that the students are supposed to depend on and which is important to their future fails them. No explanation is forthcoming because there is no regular system of explanation and no expectation that the headteacher should explain what has happened. Indeed, complaints are often met with high-handed authoritarianism. This authoritarianism and lack of communication leads to misunderstanding and suspicion and resentment grows until a small incident can spark off serious and violent disturbances.

Education for Peace

Sniff no more
From the snuff-box of hate
But puff more tobacco
From the pipe of peace
—Jane Henrys, age 14, Oxford Junior Secondary School, Kumasi, Ghana (in special section on children in Africa in Focus on Africa, 1994)

In recent years, the political context in which African schools have operated has begun to change dramatically in the direction of greater democratization. One party and military government had clearly not delivered the social and economic development desired thereby creating internal opposition to dictatorial government. At the same time the collapse of communism in eastern Europe not only undermined the Marxist–Leninist model of development chosen by the rulers of countries such as Ethiopia, Mozambique, and Zimbabwe but also meant that American and European governments stopped seeing African governments in Cold War terms. The West was therefore less likely to support a dictatorial regime in Africa simply because it was anticommunist. Western aid and loan organizations have therefore begun to add political strings to economic packages—no multiparty democracy, no money. In addition, the collapse of apartheid and the introduction of democracy in South Africa has meant that it has become a supporter of peace in the region rather than a force for violent destabilization. Predictably, although there are still serious problems in countries such as Rwanda, Liberia, Sierra Leone, Sudan, and Nigeria, as the majority of governments in Africa have begun to move toward greater democracy, the incidents of the violent abuse of human rights by the state have also begun to decrease, though not disappear, and the relations between states, especially in southern Africa, have become more peaceful.

The debate in many African countries is now about the type of democracy that best suits the context and how it can be made sustainable in the long run. Education must play a part in this as the values and behaviors needed to support democratic political institutions are learned, they are not genetic. For example, Amelia Ward, the acting Minister of Planning in Liberia, considers that one of the reasons that the Liberian civil war was so violent and indiscriminate was a lack of education offered to the population through the public school system (Danish Union of Teachers, 1994). Indeed, in African countries where war and violence are still endemic, some novel first steps to peace education are being taken. In Liberia itself teenage militia are being offered education vouchers in exchange for guns by an organization known as Susukuu ("helping the poor to help themselves"). Most of the fighters in the Liberian civil war are of school age, some as young as 10, so the idea is to give them a reason to disarm and to encourage them to go to school to become responsible citizens ("Liberian Fighters," 1995). In Burundi UNICEF has used a puppet show based on stressing interdependence to try and encourage Hutu villagers to live peacefully with a neighboring Tutsi community. The puppet show is aimed in particular at one aspect of ethnic violence—neighbor killing neighbor. One UNICEF official said, "What makes peace education so difficult is that it is often a war of low-intensity murder by people who know each other. Most of the orphaned children say their parents were killed by someone they knew" ("Learning Not to Kill," 1995).

However, if schools in Africa in the future are going to educate for peace, democracy, and human rights and against prejudice, bias, hostility, and intolerance on a more systematic and permanent basis then both the curriculum and the organization of classrooms and schools must reflect this. Schools in Africa face enormous problems in developing more democratic and peaceful forms of education where they did not exist before. However, some states that have achieved their independence relatively recently such as Namibia (in 1990), Eritrea (in 1991), and South Africa (in 1994) have taken this challenge very seriously and have already begun the long-term process of educational reform. The remainder of this article will focus on educational reform in Namibia, which is the country that has had most time to develop policy in this regard.

At a conference on teacher education in Namibia held in Zambia in September 1989 Nahas Angula, soon to be Namibia's first Minister of Education and Culture, said,

> Education in independent Namibia will be both a challenge and an opportunity to all those who cherish the ideals of a truly free, democratic and just society. Education will be a challenge because it is expected to contribute to the integration and democratisation of society. It is equally expected to enhance equality, social justice, mutual understanding and national reconciliation. (United Nations Institute for Namibia, 1989, p. 15)

The gap between the desires of the new South West African Peoples Organization government and the reality on the ground was made clear at an important conference on basic education held in Etosha in April 1991. The President, Sam Nujoma, spoke of the need for learner-centered education to develop the skills necessary for responsible citizenship. He said,

> The special emphasis that I believe is guiding this conference is that education must be child or learner-centred. The Namibian basic education must support the actual processes of individual learning, rather than continue the colonial teacher-centered Bantu education with an emphasis on control, rigid discipline, parrot-like learning and negative assessment principles. (Snyder, 1991, p. 5)

Reports from inspectors and teachers drew attention to the obstacles facing such change noting that there was too much emphasis on passing traditional examinations based on memorization and that therefore rote learning was used as the mainstay in the majority of classes and subjects, that corporal punishment was still the order of the day in many schools, and that authoritarianism and dependency were the most common features of school organization and management (Ministry of Education and Culture, 1991b). Therefore, "a continuous, multi-dimensional process has been directed towards the transformation of Namibian primary and junior secondary education" (Ministry of Education and Culture, 1991a, p. 10). This transformation is directed at the creation of a democratic and egalitarian society and the philosophy behind it is summed up as "learner-centred education" that is aimed at encouraging openness, discussion, doubt, exploration, choice, trust, respect, participation, and problem-solving (Ministry of Education and Culture, 1993b).

Because learner-centered education emphasizes participation, enquiry, the application of knowledge to real life situations, and problem-solving, it has been necessary to move away from examinations based on memorization designed to fail a certain proportion of those taking them to assessment where students are rewarded for what they know, understand, and can achieve and which use a wide range of assessment techniques appropriate for different skills and attributes in different subjects. Teaching materials are also being produced that reflect the new philosophy. *Racing Ahead* (1994), for example, is a textbook for teaching English as a second language. This book has a Namibian and African focus and is balanced in terms of its portrayal of ethnic and gender groups. Throughout each chapter are tasks that encourage independent learning and that develop skills of comprehension, self-expression, communication, and cooperation. The publicity material for the book (correctly) states that two of the aims of the book are

> to encourage skills of critical thinking and argument. Learners need to be able to use the English language to express and support their opinions. But first they need to develop a critical attitude that will encourage critical awareness of contemporary issues such as gender, development, and the environment. (*Racing Ahead*, 1994, p. 3)

Reform of teacher education has also begun in order to make its processes and procedures more congruent with what is now desired in schools. If teachers are going to teach in a more active, participant, and democratic manner in schools then they must actually experience these learning methods on a regular basis in their own teacher education in college and methods of assessment in teacher education must match diversity required in schools. This philosophy is accepted by the Namibian government and clearly reflected, for example, in the new Basic Education Teacher Diploma, which is a course for those who will go on to teach in primary and junior secondary schools (Ministry of Education and Culture, 1993b, pp. 81–82).

The nature of school management will also be a crucial factor in introducing and facilitating learner-centered education. Buddy Wentworth, the Deputy Minister for Education and Culture, speaking to a course for school inspectors, described the system of educational administration in the former South West Africa as characterized by tight control and a rigid and inflexible dependence on top-down authority. He argued that it was a perfect system for exercising a negative and punishing type of authority and a perfect system for telling people exactly what to do to stay out of trouble, how to be passive, and avoid responsibility (Ministry of Education and Culture, 1992). Headteachers are seen as playing an important role in this. At a workshop for those who would go on to train primary school headteachers, for example, participants agreed that principals should not be unaccountable despots and that they should be aware of the desired hidden curriculum in a learner-centered school. The principal's responsibility was seen as being an example of well-mannered treatment of all persons without dominance or subservience, of setting an example of willingness to listen to others, to resolve differences of opinion amicably, to show fairness to all learners without favoritism, and to show proper professional conduct toward teachers and learners (Ministry of Education and Culture, 1993a, pp. 164–165).

The role of students in school management is described in the *User's Guide to the Education Code of Conduct* (1993), which has been agreed upon by both student and teacher organizations. At Grades 11 and 12 (sixth form level), students are directly represented through democratic election on School Boards along with parents and teachers. School Boards have responsibility for such important matters as discipline, budgets, appointing teachers, the use of school facilities, and school fees. At this level, therefore, students are fully involved in the democratic organization of the schools. Below this level, however, their role is better described as consultative rather than democratic. They have the right to have their opinions considered on matters regarding discipline, rules, and punishment but seem to have no formal role in actual decision making. Constructive student involvement in school decision making is, however, quite feasible at the pre-sixth form level (Harber, 1995a, chaps. 2 and 3) and is an area where democratic school organization could be further developed in Namibia in the future. Indeed, the evidence suggests that greater student involvement in school decision making in Africa can help to avoid some of the violent disturbances among students referred to earlier (Harber, 1993, pp. 298–299).

Finally, in April 1991, the Namibian Supreme Court ruled that corporal punishment was unconstitutional and since then the Namibian government has banned its use in schools and has published a booklet on alternatives called *Discipline From Within* (Ministry of Education and Culture, 1992). Corporal punishment is rightly seen as inconsistent with learner-centered education in that it humiliates learners, results in anger and resentment, removes cooperation, leads to an atmosphere of violence, and is of no long-term value (Ministry of Education and Culture, 1993b, pp. 132–133). Nevertheless, the Ministry has implemented this policy despite evidence that support for this form of punishment is still culturally ingrained. In one survey (Zimba, Auala, & Scott, 1994) more than 50% of students, 70% of parents. and 80% of teachers indicated that they supported the use of corporal punishment in schools.

Conclusion

If democracy and the peaceful settlement of political conflicts is to become sustainable and institutionalized in Africa then international agencies, donor countries, and African governments will have to pay attention to the role of education in the creation of a democratic political culture. This means ensuring better access to education on a continent where universal primary education has not been achieved and access to secondary and further education is highly restricted. It also means improving the quality of education where a significant proportion of teachers are often poorly trained or not trained at all and where, especially in the rural areas, there are shortages of all forms of teaching materials. Most of all it will mean altering the nature of schools and classrooms in a more democratic direction to provide experience of the values and skills of nonviolent conflict resolution and peaceful decision making. Although it is hoped that renewed economic growth in African countries will help pay for the required improvements in education, if the industrialized countries are serious about peace in Africa then they have a responsibility to contribute to the process of democratization. The majority of industrialized countries do not achieve the United Nations agreed-upon target for aid of 0.7% of the gross domestic product. Simply meeting this target would be a very useful start because, as the 1990 World Development Report put it, "effective action to help poor countries involves some costs for the non-poor in both developed and developing countries" (World Bank, 1990, p. 143).

C. Harber

References

Alvedo, M. (1980). A century of colonial education in Mozambique. In A. Mugomba & M. Nyaggah (Eds.), *Independence without freedom* (pp. 191–213). Santa Barbara, CA: ABCClio.

Brittain, V. (1993, February 13). Donors fail dark continent in decline. *The Guardian*, p. 33.

Brittain, V. (1994, March 14). Hope constantly deferred is Africa's lot under the West's economic reform. *The Guardian*, p. 11.

Caute, D. (1983). *Under the skin.* Harmondsworth, England: Penguin.

Centre for the Advancement of Maths and Science Education. (1995). *A profile.* Durban, South Africa: University of Natal.

Christie, P. (1991). *The right to learn.* Johannesburg, South Africa: SACHED/Ravan.

A continent driven to suicide. (1994, July 20). *The Guardian*, p. 12.

Danish Union of Teachers. (1994). Waiting for peace—Liberia's tragedy. *Education International, 1*(3), 2–3.

Davies, L. (1993). Teachers as implementers or subversives. *International Journal of Educational Development, 13*(2), 161–170.

Focus on Africa. (1994, October–December). *Children's special.* London: British Broadcasting Company.

Graham-Brown, S. (1991). *Education in the developing world: Conflict and crisis.* Harlow, United Kingdom: Longman.

Hallam, R. (1994–1995, June–February). Sexual harassment, sex education and teenage pregnancy. *African Woman,* pp. 15–20.

Harber, C. (1989). *Politics in African education.* London: Macmillan.

Harber, C. (1991). International contexts for political education. *Educational Review, 43,* 245–255.

Harber, C. (1993). Democratic management and school effectiveness in Africa: Learning from Tanzania. *Compare,* pp. 289–300.

Harber, C. (Ed.). (1995a). *Developing democratic education.* Ticknall, United Kingdom: Education Now.

Harber, C. (1995b, September). *The politics of school space in Africa.* Paper presented at the Conference on Learning Spaces Development in Southern Africa, University of Natal, Durban, South Africa.

Heyneman, S. (1990). Economic crisis and the quality of education. *International Journal of Educational Development, 10,* 115–130.

Keneally, T. (1989). *Towards Asmara.* London: Hodder & Stoughton.

Konig, B. (1983). *Namibia: The ravages of war.* London: International Defence and Aid Fund for Southern Africa.

Lawyers to investigate beating of pupils. (1995, August 6). *Sunday Tribune,* p. 7.

Learning not to kill your neighbor. (1995, March 18). *The Guardian,* p. 14.

Liberian fighters lured into school. (1995, April 17). *The Guardian,* p. 10.

Lulat, G. (1988). Education and national development: The continuing problem of misdiagnosis and irrelevant prescriptions. *International Journal of Educational Development, 8,* 315–328.

Mazrui, A. (1983). Political engineering in Africa. *International Social Science Journal, 25,* 279–294.

Meighan, R. (1994). *The freethinkers' guide to the educational universe.* Nottingham, England: Educational Heretics Press.

Ministry of Education and Culture. (1991a). *Annual report for the year ending 31 December 1991.* Windhoek, Namibia: Author.

Ministry of Education and Culture. (1991b). *Report on the monitoring of junior secondary curriculum reform, Grade 8.* Windhoek, Namibia: Author.

Ministry of Education and Culture. (1992). *A report on a course in educational management for inspectors of education.* Windhoek, Namibia: Author.

Ministry of Education and Culture. (1993a). *A report on the training of trainers.* Windhoek, Namibia: Author.

Ministry of Education and Culture. (1993b). *Toward education for all.* Windhoek, Namibia: Macmillan.

Nagel, T. (1992). *Quality between tradition and modernity: Patterns of communication and cognition in teacher education in Zimbabwe.* Oslo, Norway: University of Oslo, Pedagogisk Forskningsintitutt.

Racing ahead. (1994). Windhoek, Namibia: Macmillan.

Rowell, P., & Prophet, R. (1990) Curriculum-in-action: The practical dimension in Botswana classrooms. *International Journal of Educational Development, 10,* 17–26.

Snyder, W. (1991). *Consultation on change: Proceedings of the Etosha Conference.* Tallahassee: Florida State University.

Tabulawa, R. (1995). *Culture and classroom practice: A socio-cultural analysis of geography classrooms in Botswana secondary schools and implications for pedagogical change.* Unpublished doctoral dissertation, University of Birmingham, England.

Tedesco, J. (1994). Knowledge versus values. *Educational Innovation, 78,* 1–2.

UNICEF. (1989). *The state of the world's children.* New York: Author.

United Nations Institute for Namibia. (1989). *International Conference on Teacher Education for Namibia.* Lusaka, Zambia: Author.

User's guide to the education code of conduct. (1993). Windhoek, Namibia: Ministry of Education and Culture.

World Bank. (1989). *The world development report.* Washington, DC: Author.

World Bank. (1990). *Poverty: The world development report.* Oxford, England: Oxford University Press.

World University Service. (1994). *Education in Mozambique.* London: Author.

Zimba, R., Auala, R., & Scott, A. (1994, August). *Discipline problems in Namibian secondary schools.* Paper presented at the Workshop of the Namibia Educational Management and Administration Society, Windhoek, Namibia.

PEABODY JOURNAL OF EDUCATION, 71(3), 170–190

Peace Education in Postcolonial Africa

Birgit Brock-Utne

This article tries to illuminate the following central questions: Are the efforts of donor agencies and Third World governments toward achieving basic education for all likely to lead to a further development of peace education programs in Africa? Are the outcomes of the Education for All (EFA) conference in Jomtien, Thailand, March 5 to 9, 1990, likely to lead to positive peace[1]—that is, a situation where violence is not built into the structures, where equality of opportunity is strived for and self-fulfillment and self-worth enhanced? Is the new EFA strategy likely to lead to a self-reliant development for Third World countries? The expression *self-reliant development* is being used in the preamble of the World Declaration on Education for All (WDEFA, 1990, p. 3).

That expression was also being used to describe the aim of the educational system the first President of independent Tanzania, Julius Nyerere, wanted to build. In his well-known essay, "Education for

BIRGIT BROCK-UTNE *is Professor at the Institute for Educational Research, University of Oslo, Oslo, Norway.*

Requests for reprints should be sent to Birgit Brock-Utne, Institute for Educational Research, University of Oslo, P.B. 1092 Blindern, N–0317 Oslo, Norway. E-mail: birgit.brock-utne@ped.uio.no

[1]For a further discussion of the peace concept, see Brock-Utne (1989, pp. 39–68), with further references to Galtung (1969) and Wiberg (1981, 1990). For a discussion of the positive peace concept as it relates to education, see Brock-Utne (1995).

Self-Reliance," Nyerere (1967) saw education as the tool to combat oppression and further equity in the world. At the end of this article we shall also pose the questions: What are the special challenges to peace educators in the newly independent countries of Africa? What would an alternative to the current EFA strategy look like, a strategy that would lead to empowerment for the people in the South?

Successful Attempts at Changes Made in Jomtien
in the Draft Declaration

Some 1,500 participants met at the EFA conference in Jomtien, Thailand. There were delegates from 155 governments, 20 intergovernmental bodies, and 150 nongovernmental organizations. Forty-eight roundtables were arranged along with some 70 exhibits. There were cross-regional caucuses amongst nongovernmental organizations (NGOs), donor agencies, and national delegations. There was South–South caucusing, as well as North–South. Delegations were actually encouraged to propose changes in the Draft C of the WDEFA and the Framework for action that were circulated before the meeting. But what came out of this last round of consultation and lobbying? What major changes were proposed and accommodated in the final version?

Norrag News (King, 1990) documented that significant changes were made in the document during the conference. For instance, the disabled were accepted as important beneficiaries of education for all, and stronger emphasis was put on education for girls and women. Here a whole new section was adopted to emphasize the need for the programming of aid to be much more gender-conscious. This section now constitutes Point 45e of the Framework for Action (1990) that now reads:

> *Education programmes for women and girls.* These programmes should be designed to eliminate the social and cultural barriers that have discouraged or even excluded women and girls from benefits of regular education programmes, as well as to promote equal opportunities in all aspects of their lives. (p. 18)

An aspect of positive peace, that of promoting equal opportunities for women, has here come into the official Framework for action. The problem remains: What are the possibilities of following up this point in actual practice?

Groups coming from the countries in the South, especially from Latin America and the Caribbean, but also from Africa and Asia together with signatories from Europe and the International Development Research Center (IDRC), were successfully lobbying for more explicit safeguards for higher education. IDRC was also instrumental in introducing into the final text an emphasis on traditional knowledge and indigenous cultural heritage. We shall return to these last two points.

The Reluctance to Deal With the Effects of the Debt Servicing and the Structural Adjustment Policies on the Education Sector—An Unsuccessful Attempt at Change

By far the most contentious issue at the Jomtien conference was related to the trade-off between the debt burden and the search to extend education to all. No fewer than 13 Latin American countries along with France and the Ivory Coast were signatories to a recommendation that targeted debt as the main problem, presenting debt servicing or attending to basic needs, especially those of education as alternatives, and placing responsibilities on the North to take the initiative. A different version of this dilemma about debt versus education for all was prepared by World University Service, and the International Coalition for Development Action, along with 20 other NGOs. In a proposal for the preamble, they argued the need for rethinking debt in the context of macroeconomic relations, maintaining that

> a resolution of the economic crisis associated with debt and North–South economic relations is a necessary precondition for the achievement of Education for All. Resources currently flowing from South to North in debt service, if reoriented to the service of education and development, could provide the debtor countries with an enhanced capacity to ensure the survival of children to school age, and release families, communities and nations from the poverty which prevents universal participation in pre-school, school and adult education. (King, 1990, p. 7)

Even stronger than this was the set of proposals from the African Association for Literacy and Adult Education (AALAE) and the association for Participatory Research in Asia (PRIA), supported by several other NGOs. These too set the responsibility solidly in the North for the conditions that constrained the South. We quote an excerpt of the proposal by AALAE here (taken from King, 1990):

We call on all governments of the North and all international financial institutions to cancel all existing debts as these are an intolerable
burden on the people, make it impossible for them to mobilise the
resources necessary for basic education, and ferment revolt and
strife. It is necessary further to put an end to structural adjustment
programs and attendant conditionalities that have caused so much
suffering to the people and undermined their capacity to mobilise
resources for their basic needs.

AALAE also suggested that a special development fund be set up into
which all cancelled debts would be deposited in local currencies and to
which they would make additional contributions to finance development activities in the South, including basic education.

When we now read what the final text says about the debt burden,
we are safe in concluding that the African and Asian countries behind
the proposal quoted previously were not paid much attention to. The
development fund is not mentioned anywhere, and neither is the responsibility of the North for the sad state of the social sectors in the
South. In the final text it is no longer only the North that has to act and
it is no longer a straightforward trade-off between debt service and
educational development. This is how the debt problem is treated in
the WDEFA:

Creditors and debtors must seek innovative and equitable formulae
to resolve these burdens (heavy debt burdens), because the capacity
of many developing countries to respond effectively to education
and other basic needs will be greatly helped by finding solutions to
the debt problem. (WDEFA, Article 10, last part of Point 2, p. 9)

AALAE held a workshop in Mauritius from October 28 to November
10 1990 to assess the outcomes of the EFA conference. After the workshop, the Second General Assembly of AALAE adopted a declaration
giving their views on EFA. Here it says in the Preamble: "Though the
Declaration on 'Education for All' is positive in its aims, its broad and
universal framework fails to take specific account of the prevailing
socioeconomic conditions in the different parts of the world, Africa in
particular" (AALAE, 1990). One of Thailand's leading papers, the *Nation*, ran a special supplement each day of the EFA conference called the
"Jomtien Journal." The editorial of the "Jomtien Journal" of March 10
was called: "After the World Conference on Education, What Next?"
This editorial raised some very critical comments about the way the

conference had been organized and its failure to sufficiently address the question of debt.

In particular, the editorial reported on the intervention of Errol Miller of Jamaica on the tendency of the Conference to lean too much toward Northern research findings, and Northern advice about the means of reaching EFA. Applications of many suggestions made by Northern experts made his country's situation worse, not better, he maintained.

The editorial holds that all delegates agreed that the debt crisis has had a major impact on the quality and quantity of education in the South. But banks and aid agencies maintained that structural adjustment was for the large part not responsible for the general deterioration of the education sector in most of the South over the 1980s, arguing that Southern delegates were "confused" about the cause of their problem. Structural adjustment is the medicine, not the cause of the disease, and Africa's economy will improve during this decade as a result of it they said. African and Latin American delegates, however, repeatedly expressed doubts about these sorts of predictions. They complained that charging school fees caused parents to pull their children out of school—bringing down the enrollment rate— and that increasing class size and introducing double shifts in rural areas affected the quality of teaching, causing the literacy rate to drop.

It is easy to understand that the WDEFA could not contain an appeal to the North to cancel the debts in the South or to abandon the structural adjustment program. The representatives from the North meeting at Jomtien had no mandate from their governments to alter the macroeconomic policies even though those policies, and here I agree with my African colleagues, are of the highest importance for the education sector in the developing countries. We shall here give an example of how the liberalization of the economy and the so-called structural adjustment policy meted out for a poor country like Tanzania means a threat to the prospects of obtaining positive peace, and how the reintroduction of school fees, so-called cost-sharing policies along with privatization means building up structures to the benefit of the children of the affluent and to the detriment of children of the poor.

Effects of the Structural Adjustment Policies on the Education Sector in a Country Like Tanzania

Debt Servicing

The structural adjustment policies with the liberalization of the economy, building down of the public sector, and increased privatization is the special medicine meted out by the International Monetary Fund/World Bank and now also supported by bilateral donors. They seem to believe that the application of this medicine will increase the likelihood that poor countries will be able to repay their debts to the North. Some main items on the national budgets of Tanzania for two different years are given in Table 1.

The situation in Tanzania comes easily to mind when we read the warning words from the Economic Commission of Africa:

Reductions in budget deficits must not be accomplished at the expense of expenditures on the social sector, i.e. education, health, and other social infrastructure ... efforts must be made to ensure that the annual average of at least 30 percent of total government outlays is devoted to the social sector and that in any case, the annual rate of growth of social investment is significantly higher than the population growth rate. (African Alternatives to Structural Adjustment Programmes, 1989, p. 3)

One can easily see that the suggestion from AALAE at the Jomtien conference of cancellation of debt and the creation of a special development fund into which all cancelled debts would be deposited to finance starved sectors like education would mean a New Deal for Tanzania, a chance to follow her original policy of self-reliance (*kujitegemea*) and her special type of African socialism (*ujamaa*).

The Reintroduction of School Fees

During the colonial period, the issue of school fees was one of the issues around which mass discontent was mobilized against the colonial authorities. Soon after Tanzania got her independence, school fees

Table 1. Percentages of Expenditures for Main Items in the National Budget

Budget Item	1966–1967	1987–1988
Education	14.2	5.3
Health	4.9	3.9
Cultivation	10.4	7.3
Transport	12.1	6.0
Debt servicing	8.0	33.2

Note. Data from Economic Survey 1970–1971 and Hali ya Uchumi wa Taifa katika miaka 1983–1988.

for all educational levels were abolished as one of the measures to ensure the legitimacy of the postcolonial state. Through the Arusha Declaration and the policy of Education for Self-Reliance the whole country was mobilized to eradicate illiteracy, to provide universal primary education, and to change the content of the inherited educational system. After 26 years of independence, Tanzania—with a population of 25 million—could boast of 3,500,000 children in more than 10,000 primary schools, with at least one primary school in every village (Roy-Campbell, 1992, p. 147). The achievement of universal primary education, where all Tanzanian children have access to a basic education, was commendable for one of the poorest countries in the world. As a result of its vibrant Adult Education Program and because Tanzania had succeeded in having its own national language, Kiswahili, as the language of instruction both in primary school and in adult education, Tanzania had achieved a literacy rate of 90% in 1984 (vs. 33.3% in 1970), the highest in Africa. However, with the liberalization of the Tanzanian economy in the 1980s, culminating in the signing of the IMF agreement in 1986, the very essence of Education for Self-Reliance is being threatened. The illiteracy rate, which was only 10% by 1984, had gradually risen to 20% and then to 30% by 1992 (Tanzania Education System for the 21st Century, 1993, p. 6). Universal access to education is being undermined by the reintroduction of school fees. This policy has been advocated both by the World Bank and the IMF as part of the structural adjustment program.

According to the newest report on Tanzania's educational system, Universal Primary Education was supposedly attained in 1981 with a gross enrollment ratio of about 98%. However, primary school gross enrollment ratio has gradually declined to 70% in 1992 (Tanzania Education System for the 21st Century, 1993, p. 6).

The reintroduction of school fees in Tanzania has been received as an extremely unpopular measure by the Tanzanian population. The heated debates in Parliament and discontent of parents and students at the recent raising of the secondary school fees is an indication of such discontent.

Difficulty in payment of school fees is a class issue as well as a gender issue. An African research group that has been concerned about this issue is the group Women, Education, Development (WED) at the University of Dar es Salaam. (For more information about the group see Brock-Utne, 1991.) The WED researchers Sumra and Katunzi (1991) found that the reintroduction of school fees in secondary schools affected girls more than boys and girls from the middle and lower classes much more than girls from the upper classes. Their sample consisted of 235 girls and 84 boys drawn from three locations, one in Dar es Salaam, one in Kilimanjaro, and one in Handeni. Sumra and Katunzi found that the reintroduction of school fees was of no consequence for the relatively few children of well-to-do parents. The results for children coming from less well-to-do homes are found in Table 2. If students come to school without fees, they are sent home. In Handeni Secondary School, of the students not reporting during the first week, 68% were girls and of those who were sent away, 80% were girls (Sumra & Katunzi, 1991, p. 27). As one girl stated:

> I have been sent home three times, twice this year. Last year I was sent away once. This year when I went to collect money, my father informed me that the money was spent to pay my mother's hospital bill. My brother was given the fees first and I was asked to wait till my father could sell his coffee again. (p. 27)

While students are looking for school fees, the lessons continue at school:

> I remain behind my colleagues because I waste a lot of time going back home to collect school fees. Teachers are unwilling to offer compensatory classes. I copy notes from my friends without understanding what they mean. (Sumra & Katunzi, 1991, p. 27)

The nice words in the WDEFA about "promoting equal opportunities in all aspects of the lives" of girls and women (here especially pertaining to education) are of little value if the reintroduction of school fees forces parents to choose whether the little money available will be used for educating a boy or a girl.

Control of the Publishing Industry

The rapid development of communications both for travelling, listening, and keeping in contact that has been going on in the last part of

Table 2. Difficulties in Paying School Fees

Students	Percentage	
	Girls	Boys
Middle-class families	20.6	12.1
Lower class families	53.0	30.3

177

this millennium has made other parts of the globe accessible to us in an historically unparalleled way. Within some hours we can physically visit any place on the globe—provided of course that we have money to travel. If we don't, we can at least meet people from other parts of the planet indirectly but in our living rooms daily through television. If they and we are linked to the Internet, we can communicate cheaply and swiftly.

But those who say that the rapid development of communications has made us all into a global family often forget to add that this is a capitalist and patriarchal family where the power is very unevenly distributed. The power to define the news and our images lies with a small group of White people, mostly men in the affluent countries of the North. The market economic principles this group adheres to and has forced the whole world to adopt make the rich richer and the poor poorer. See Table 3, taken from the United Nations Development Program (UNDP) Human Development Report of 1994, which reports the distribution of income for the years 1960 and 1991. Most of the affluent who are becoming even richer live in the northern hemisphere, in the industrialized west. They are the creators of the news, which others just receive. Some people in this world have ample publishing opportunities, others have hardly any. Books originating in the developing countries, especially in Africa, are highly underrepresented in the world today. According to the 1988 United Nations Educational, Social and Cultural Organization (UNESCO) Statistical Yearbook, Norway (with 4 million inhabitants) produced 3,031 new titles in the years 1984 to 1986, which was greater than the number of book titles produced in Nigeria (1260), Tanzania (166), Zimbabwe (157), Mozambique (66), Ethiopia (227), Angola (14), Mali (160), Madagascar (321), Gambia (72), and Malawi (75) combined for the same years.

The writing, publishing, and distribution of textbooks is of vital importance for the educational and cultural survival of a nation. About 50% of the total turnover of the publishing industry in developed countries is derived from educational publishing. In poor countries the percentage of educational publishing is upwards of 90% of publisher's

Table 3. Distribution of Income for 1960 and 1991

	1960	1991
Income of the 20% richest people in the world as percentage of total income	70.0	85.0
Income of the 20% poorest people in the world as percentage of total income	2.3	1.4

turnover (World Bank/ODA, 1988). It is from the profits made in educational publishing that investments can be made to publish other categories of books—fiction, biographies, poetry, plays, and so on. Therefore, when textbook publishing suffers for one reason or another, all publishing suffers.

In their guidelines for a popular alternative to the "Education for All" strategy from Jomtien, the AALAE warned against "the use of imported technologies which in the majority of cases are inappropriate and reinforce foreign domination" (paragraph 31) and "aid packages which include foreign personnel" (paragraph 33) and recommend that "loans, grants and donations should be accepted only when it is clear that they have no disadvantageous strings attached and that they will be for the benefit to the receiving organization and country" (paragraph 42). We shall now take a look at what is happening in the schoolbook sector in Tanzania and relate those events to AALAE warnings and recommendations. The events are in line with the World Bank policies and the structural adjustment program but threaten the very concept of positive peace because they reduce the chances of self-reliance and self-fulfillment for the people in the South. They also go counter to the emphasis on traditional knowledge and indigenous cultural heritage that the IDRC was instrumental in introducing into the final text of the WDEFA.

During the paper crisis in Tanzania in the early 1980s, for example, printers in Tanzania were forbidden from printing magazines and other light reading matter to conserve all paper for textbook printing. (Bgoya, 1990, p. 6)

There was no model of publishing left in Tanzania at the time of independence to be perpetuated or improved upon. The publishing model that a number of African countries adopted—the early joint ventures with Macmillan in Tanzania, Ghana, and Zambia—was the first "state" model which, ironically, was the one that a private transnational company was proposing. As long as the partnership venture benefited the foreign transnational publisher, there was no criticism of the state publishing model where books were written by a state institution (Institute of Curriculum Development), published by a state publishing house (Tanzania Publishing House), and distributed by a state-owned company (Tanzania Elimu Supplies). Walter Bgoya (1990), the former Director of Tanzania Publishing House, told how this model had fallen out of favor, even though it could have been made to work. In fact, it worked well for a number of years and Bgoya holds that when it is questioned today, it is because it does not favor the transnationals.

The contribution of Nordic countries had a critical input in the formal education sector as well as in the literacy campaign that was launched in 1970. Swedish International Development Agency (SIDA) support was given in the form of paper and other inputs for the printing industry, relieving the foreign exchange shortage that printers faced. Bgoya (1990) claimed:

> One of the unfortunate outcomes of that support, however, was that in time the Ministry of Education and other institutions involved in formal and informal education developed such dependence on SIDA that other efforts to find a solution seemed unnecessary and even undesirable. As it was, support was given to the Government through the Ministry of Education. In turn, the Ministry gave the paper and other inputs to the parastatal printing firms; and publishers, parastatal and private alike were by-passed because, it was argued, they were unnecessary middle men. (p. 9)

At the moment there is a desperate need for textbooks in Tanzania. There are hardly any books in the schools. According to a World Bank (1988) book sector study, a survey made in 1987 suggested an average textbook availability of 1 book per 13 students.

When I, in the spring of 1992, was doing my interviewing of Tanzanian officials responsible for the education sector the people at the Institute for Curriculum Development (ICD) told me about the first o-level examinations being made in Tanzania in 1971. They had helped with the examinations and saw that they were based on a Cambridge curriculum:

> We could not use the curriculum from the UK. That curriculum did not promote the socialist values we want to promote. The books came from Britain. Nyerere talked about us becoming self-reliant, using our own curricula, our own books. We got the ICD Act.13. 1975 where it said in point 4 what the functions of the Institute should be. Point 4a) says that the Institute shall assume the responsibility for the development of educational programmes within the United Republic having regard to objectives specified by the Government. IDC shall further undertake the evaluation of courses of study and practices on the basis of such objectives.

In a discussion with Adama Ouane at the UNESCO Institute in Hamburg, Germany he told me that the exact same process of undermining local curriculum development and the local textbook industry is going on at the same time in Mali. Since its independence, Mali has for many years had indigenous publishing of schoolbooks. As a result of educational reforms in 1962 the content of the textbooks was completely revised. A National Pedagogical Institute (IPN) was established to develop curricula and teaching material of relevance for Mali. Before this period the books had been written in France and were highly irrelevant for the context of Mali. In the late 1980s, while implementing its fourth educational project, financed by the World Bank and conceived within the Structural Adjustment Policy, it was decided that local development and production of school textbooks by the IPN was too expensive. The responsibility of IPN was restricted to small-scale experimental work, and the textbooks are now being developed by Editions Classique d'Expression Française (EDICEF) in France or Tunisia and later sent to Mali.

The former Director of Tanzania Publishing House, Walter Bgoya, with whom I had several talks about the book sector in Tanzania, shared the same fears that the staff at ICD had—namely that, unless special provisions were made to support publishing in Tanzania by Tanzanians, liberalization of the textbook industry would only mean that the profit would go to foreign multinationals. He reminded me of what happened to textbook publishing under the English Language Support.

The objective of that particular project, which was introduced in Tanzania in 1987 through British development aid (£1.46 million), was to increase the competence of English-language teachers and to provide books for that purpose. Nine specialists from the United Kingdom were brought to Tanzania to implement the project. In the early days of the project it was realized that there was a great need for relevant books in English, preferably written by Tanzanians in place of books written primarily for English students. Such books had already been given away for free in large quantities to many secondary schools.

Through the English Language Teaching Support Project (see Brock-Utne, 1993), it was proposed that Tanzanians be invited to write books or, where such books already existed with publishers in manuscript form, that they should be submitted to the project for approval, editing, and eventual publication. Bgoya (1992) states that a number of Tanzanian publishers thought the Tanzanian publishing industry might benefit from the project, which would buy no less than 20,000 copies of the English supplementary readers if published under the project. They had books in manuscript form in which they had already invested a lot of time and work but had not been able to publish because of lack of funds. But the Tanzanian publishers were not helped to survive through the project. On the contrary:

As it turned out, the agreement stipulated that the first edition of all books published under the project had to be published in the UK and by either Longman, Macmillan, Oxford University Press or Evans. Only a reprint could be published in Tanzania under a copublication arrangement between the UK publisher and a local one. But even this was revised, and no book was published in Tanzania. British publishers, it is said, insisted that they should publish the books in the UK even if the manuscripts originated in Tanzania. English-language teaching is also good business for publishers in the UK. (Bgoya, 1992, p. 179)

In a Promemoria written in SIDA about Swedish support for school book provision in Tanzania, the role of the ICD seems to be nonexistent. In the same Promemoria, the Swedes also admit that "the proposed new policy represents a 180 degree turn in emphasis away from a government led system towards a market oriented approach" (Wickmann, 1993, p. 3). It would be interesting to know how many of the degrees of the turn have been made under the pressure of not getting support if the turn is not being made.

In all fairness, it has to be mentioned that whereas the World Bank is only concerned about African schoolchildren getting schoolbooks wherever they are being developed and published, the Swedes have been concerned with helping Tanzania develop their own publishing industry. However, this concern does not seem to be followed up with the necessary rigor. In the aforementioned Promemoria from the Education Office of SIDA the following questions are raised:

Is it desirable that school book publishers are indigenous local firms? What bearing could that possibly have on developing local authors of fiction? What bearing on the production of post literacy reading material? Or could all these aspects as well be taken care of by foreign publishing houses? (Wickmann, 1993, p. 3)

Indigenous publication of schoolbooks is important not only because the content of the schoolbooks should be locally conceptualized and developed but also because developing a local schoolbook industry will help the publication of other books, for instance books within African peace education. Certainly the school book publishing should not be taken care of by foreign publishing companies. Even the posing of the question by the Swedes seems disconcerting.

If the aim of indigenization of the school book industry is to have any chance of being fulfilled, however, regulations have to be passed allowing the Government to regulate the importation of schoolbooks to Tanzania in order to protect a very fragile publishing industry, be it private or parastatal. Foreign interests in private Tanzanian publishing industry should also be severely limited to, say, 20% to 30%. According to the liberalization policy that forms part of the Structural Adjustment Program, such protective measures seem not be allowed.

May we end here by lending our ear once more to one of the recipients of aid to the education sector, the former director of Tanzania Publishing House:

> One cannot emphasise enough that what is at stake is institution building and that African publishing will not develop unless publishing houses, both private or parastatal, are able to command adequate resources to finance, train staff and equip them so that they may be able, in the next ten to fifteen years, to produce books that meet their countries' needs.
>
> Unless this is done, what is likely to happen given that book production is being managed from Ministries of Education, is that when loans such as the one Tanzania has just signed with the World Bank are finished, there will be no publishing industries left in place and countries will go back to importing books. (Bgoya, 1990, p. 12)

Effects on Higher Education of a Concentration of Resources on Basic Education

A Tanzanian colleague wrote to me recently:

> My own view is that education for all is fine as a goal. Who is against education for all? All wish to achieve that. But the problem is *how* to achieve it? What is the opportunity cost of achieving it? Reduced expenditure on higher education?

My colleague voices the opinion that was held by most African statesmen and educationists before the Jomtien conference. They were afraid that the cry for basic education would not mean that more money would be coming to the education sector (e.g., through a transfer from military to educational expenditure as suggested in Article 9 of the WDEFA), but would rather mean that scarce resources would now be shifted from higher education to basic education.

Knowing the attitude of the World Bank to higher education in Africa, there is certainly reason to fear that the renewed emphasis on basic education will indeed lead to a further starvation of higher education and intellectual life in Africa. This also means a starvation of the possibilities of developing an African peace education system based on an African understanding of the reasons for the conflicts raging within Africa and research into traditional African ways of problem solving. At a meeting with African vice-chancellors in Harare in 1986, the World Bank argued that higher education in Africa was a luxury—most African countries were better off closing universities at home and training graduates overseas. Recognizing that its call for a closure of universities was politically unsustainable, the World Bank subsequently modified its agenda, calling for universities in Africa to be trimmed and restructured to produce only those skills that the market demands. Such was its agenda for university restructuring, for instance, in Nigeria in the late 1980s (Mamdani, 1993).

At the Jomtien conference, a whole series of countries were lobbying for more explicit safeguards for higher education, research, and access to high technology. The thrust of this concern was from Latin America with other signatories coming from Africa and Asia, the Caribbean, and Europe. *Norrag News* (King, 1990, p. 6) claimed that IDRC was also instrumental in successfully inserting a parallel recommendation arguing that "sound basic education is fundamental to the strengthening of higher levels of education and of scientific and technological literacy and capacity and thus to self-reliant development" (WDEFA, 1990, preamble, p. 3). Once the spirit of the Latin American resolution had also been accepted, a dual justification of the need for higher education in relation to basic education was secured:

> Societies should also insure a strong intellectual and scientific environment for basic education. This implies improving higher education and developing scientific research. Close contact with contemporary technological and scientific knowledge should be possible at every level of education. (WDEFA, 1990, Article 8, Point 2, p. 8)

In an evaluation of the outcomes of the EFA conference from an African perspective, Aimé Damiba (1991), the program specialist in education and planning in UNESCO's regional office in Dakar, Senegal, concluded:

> We must avoid the danger of limiting ourselves to basic education and neglecting high level manpower training and research. It is not possible to solve the problems of Education for All without a na-

tional pool of expertise and without an indigenous capacity for research. (p. 11)

However, Third World countries seem to interpret the results from the Jomtien conference as a wish from the donor community to limit their renewed effort within the education sector to basic education and tell developing countries to do the same.

When I interviewed Tanzanian educators and officials in the educational task force that had been set up after the Jomtien conference in the spring of 1992, one of them told me:

Instead of limiting ourselves to basic education, which was a wish from the Jomtien conference, we in Tanzania wanted to look at the whole educational sector. Each country after the Bangkok conference was to set up a committee to work with the implementations of the conference. We made this modification that we included other levels than basic education.

African universities and institutes of higher learning are of the greatest importance if Africa is to develop its own counter-expertise capable of evaluating and criticizing aid packages being offered and capable of building their own science and technology using local sources and based on local traditions. Research going on in the institutions of higher learning should also be of an empowering kind, concentrating on the rewriting of history from an African perspective and building on indigenous knowledge.

The Universality of Values

As peace educators, we shall have to be beware of the tendency of the West to claim universality for values that are particular to Western history and culture. Yash Tandon (1995), former minister in Uganda, now living in Zimbabwe, criticized the way the concept of human rights has come to mean civil rights embedded in Western liberal and individual expression in a recent article. To create intercultural awareness, we need to acknowledge that the universality of values should not be taken for granted. Tandon writes about the tendency of the West to claim a universality for their definition of human rights and worse, applying them as conditionalities for aid. In doing so, "the West commits the classic error of transposing its values on weaker populations who pretend to share those values for the sake of aid or development assistance" (p. 11). It is not so easy for us who live in the affluent West to start questioning our own values and behaviors, and to approach the culture of other people with an open mind and a willingness to learn from them. How much are men willing to listen to and learn from women? How much are we in the West willing to listen to the indigenous peoples of this world?

African Methods of Conflict Resolution

It is important that African peace educators do not derive their theories mostly from Western peace educators but search in their own heritage for an African way to deal with conflicts. The AALAE, which is a pan-African association, has outlined a 3-year research project in peace education. Among the main objectives we find the following:

- To research the African concepts and terms of conflict, as well as African methods, techniques, and processes of conflict prevention, management, and resolution.
- To establish and articulate a philosophy, principles, and world outlook that underline African concepts of conflict, conflict prevention, management, and resolution.
- To promote and generate public interest in African concepts of conflict as well as methods, techniques, and processes of conflict prevention, management, and resolution as a resource for managing and solving contemporary conflicts. (AALAE, 1994, p. 19)

The action component of intercultural awareness would be a method of training in listening to and learning from people from other cultures.

Education for Empowerment and Self-Reliance as an Alternative to the EFA Strategy

The AALAE is critical to the WDEFA partly on the grounds that the initiative to the EFA conference was spearheaded by the World Bank, which

has repudiated education as a public responsibility through its "Structural Adjustment Programmes" forced on most African countries. Indeed there is every reason to believe that this broad framework is intended to give the World Bank and its allies a free hand to determine the detailed, specific education agenda on a country-by-country basis, and in particular apply the Bank's "Structural Adjustment Programmes" on the education sector. ... Even the participation of UNESCO and the African governments would seem to have been used merely to give legitimacy to positions already taken by the Bank. (AALAE, 1990, preamble, p. 1)

I am afraid AALAE's skepticism is warranted. There is all reason to monitor the implementation of the WDEFA and the Framework for Action.

After having analyzed the current foreign aid patterns and policies on education in developing countries in some Western bilateral aid agencies, the Danish historian Lene Buchert (1993) concluded that the Jomtien emphasis on cost, efficiency, and effectiveness is likely to reemphasize a Western curriculum rather than a locally adapted curriculum based on indigenous knowledge systems, socialization methods, and locally identified needs for specific skills and, thereby, impede locally designed innovative experiments in recipient countries.

AALAE (1990) claims:

There is a need to articulate and elaborate practical alternative strategies to develop policies and carry out educational programmes based on the basic needs of the African peoples and to identify and propose the areas and strategies through which we can act at the regional, sub-regional, national and local levels to achieve our ideal of basic education for empowerment and self-reliance. (p. 4)

This ideal is built on positive peace, on the absence of oppression and structural violence, and on a high degree of equality and self-fulfillment. Building peace systems in Africa depends on a quality in education, a quality that comes from commitment to the peoples of the South, respect for indigenous culture, and the building up of sustainable education that does not rely on external sources. The following example is a recent example of quality education in Zimbabwe:

In a remote school in Matabeleland there was a young student teacher whose working conditions and social background were just as poor as that of any other student teacher and as that of the fifth grade children he was teaching. The children were busy doing different things. They seemed interested in what they were doing and smiled friendly to us, the intruders. Often children in these remote areas used to stare at foreigners with a frightened look. They would hardly understand what you asked them, let alone try to answer. Not so with these children.

In one corner of the class-room there was a book-shelf made of old bricks and planks wrapped up in newspaper. There were a few booklets and some magazines that the teacher had collected together with the children. In the windows, some with broken panes, big seeds had been threaded on strings and were waving happily as decoration in the light breeze from the broken windows. In one corner the organization of SADCC was illustrated by means of empty coke-tins and stones. Newspaper pictures were glued to the boxes, symbolizing different SADCC departments.

On the floor maps of different countries were shaped with pebbles. There was hardly an empty space on the mud-floor. But children stepped carefully around the creations not to destroy them. In another corner was a "spelling tree"—just a few branches with cards hanging on strings like a Christmas tree. Children worked in pairs, asking each other to spell the difficult words. In another group some children were playing with a set of home-made math cards.

To honour the guests, the children picked their self-made costumes from the hooks on the wall, one drummed and the others performed a joyful and very rhythmic dance. To teach children about traditional handicraft techniques, like how to build a proper hut or how to make a hob-kerry, elderly people from the village were invited to the school to share their wisdom and knowledge with the children.

This wizard of a young teacher had also taught the children, boys and girls, how to knit and had just started to teach them sewing, but this was a problem because material was scarce. His wisdom lay in seeing the future for these children, how hard it would be for them to get a job, like any of the other 200,000 pupils leaving school every year. Therefore he wanted to teach them useful things which they could make and which they would need, for their own use, hopefully for sale as well as for consumption. (Nagel, 1992, p. xviii)

References

African Alternatives to Structural Adjustment Programmes (AA–SAP): A framework for transformation and recovery. (1989, April). *United Nations Economic Commission for Africa* (E/ECA/CM.15/6/REV.2). Presented at the Conference of Ministers Responsible for Economic Planning and Development, Addis Ababa, Ethiopia.

African Association for Literacy and Adult Education (AALAE). (1990, November). *Education for all: Issues and guidelines for a popular alternative.* Adopted by the Second General Assembly of the AALAE, Mauritius.

African Association for Literacy and Adult Education (AALAE). (1994). *The third three-year programme 1995–97.* Nairobi, Kenya: Author.

Bgoya, W. (1990, October). *Economics of publishing in Africa.* Paper presented at the 1990 Oslo Book Fair, Oslo, Norway.

Bgoya, W. (1992). The challenge of publishing in Tanzania. In P. Altbach (Ed.), *Publishing and development in the Third World* (pp. 169–190). London: Hans Zell.

Brock-Utne, B. (1989). *Feminist perspectives on peace and peace education.* New York: Pergamon.

Brock-Utne, B. (1991). Women and education in Tanzania: Report from a new African research group and a seminar. *Women's Studies International Forum, 14*(1–2) in Feminist Forum section, III–IV.

Brock-Utne, B. (1993). Language of instruction in African schools—A socio-cultural perspective. *Nordisk Pedagogik, 4,* 225–247.

Brock-Utne, B. (1995). Educating all for positive peace. *Internatonal Journal of Educational Development, 15,* 321–333.

Buchert, L. (1993, September). *Current foreign aid patterns and policies on education in developing countries. The case of DANIDA, SIDA and DGIS.* Paper presented at the Oxford Conference on the Changing Role of the State in Educational Development, Oxford, England.

Damiba, A. (1991, March). The World Conference on Education for All and Africa's expectations. *UNESCO AFRICA,* pp. 8–11.

Framework for Action. (1990). In *World declaration on education for all and framework for action to meet basic learning needs.* New York: UNICEF House.

Galtung, J. (1969). Violence, peace and peace research. *Journal of Peace Research, 6*(3), 167–191.

King, K. (Ed.). (1990, June). What happened at Jontien and the beginnings of a follow-up. *Norrag News,* p. 8.

Mamdani, M. (1993). University crisis and reform: A reflection on the African experience. *Review of African Political Economy, 58,* 7–19.

Nagel, T. (1992). *Quality between tradition and modernity, patterns of communication and cognition in teacher training in Zimbabwe.* Unpublished doctoral dissertation, University of Oslo, Oslo, Norway.

Nyerere, J. (1967). *Education for self-reliance.* Dar es Salaam, Tanzania: Government Printer.

Roy-Campbell, M. (1992). The politics of education in Tanzania: From colonialism to liberalization. In H. Campell & H. Stein (Eds.), *Tanzania and the IMF. The dynamics of liberalization* (pp. 147–169). Boulder, CO: Westview.

Sumra, S., & Katunzi, N. (1991). *The struggle for education: School fees and girls' education in Tanzania* (WED Report No. 5). Dar es Salaam, Tanzania: WED Faculty of Education, UDSM.

Tandon, Y. (1995). Norwegian south policy for a changing world. *Development Today, 5*(5), 10–11.

Tanzania Education System for the 21st Century. (1993). *Report of the Task Force.* Dar es Salaam: United Republic of Tanzania, Ministry of Education and Culture & Ministry of Science, Technology and Higher Education. (Printed by the print service—A division of University of Leeds Media Services)

B. Brock-Utne

Wiberg, H. (1981). *Journal of Peace Research* 1964–1980: What have we learnt about peace? *Journal of Peace Research, 18*(2), 11–148.
Wiberg, H. (1990). *Konfliktteori och Fredsforskning* [Theory of conflict and peace research]. Stockholm: Esselte Studium.
Wickmann, K. (1993). Swedish support to school book provision in Tanzania. *Promemoria, 29*(12). Stockholm: SIDA, Undervisningsbyrån.
World Bank/ODA. (1988). *Book sector study*. Washington, DC: Author.
World declaration on education for all and framework for action to meet basic learning needs. (1990). New York: UNICEF House.

For Product Safety Concerns and Information please contact our EU
representative GPSR@taylorandfrancis.com
Taylor & Francis Verlag GmbH, Kaufingerstraße 24, 80331 München, Germany

9 781138 866874